CATALOGUE

OF THE

PUBLIC LIBRARY

OF THE

CITY OF BOSTON.

BOSTON:
PRINTED BY JOHN WILSON & SON,
22, School Street.
1854.

NOTICE.

The following Catalogue lays no claim to bibliographical merit of any sort. It is merely a condensed Index to the contents of the Public Library, giving the title of each book only once, and having no object but to render all the books useful. The collection is still small, and in every department imperfect. It consists almost exclusively of works in the English language, and chiefly of such as will be most widely interesting and instructive. But it is fast increasing, especially in the divisions devoted to the mechanic arts and to practical science; and, in time, we doubt not that it will become, through the munificence of its patrons, not less than from the resources of the city, such a library in all languages and in all departments of human knowledge as the inhabitants of Boston ought to have. And we venture to predict, that they will so use it as to increase the respectability, the prosperity, and the moral and religious worth, of a community that rests to a remarkable degree for its best distinctions on its free schools and the general education of its people.

Meantime the condition of the Institution justifies its Trustees in asking suggestions on the subject of such books as are most pressingly wanted, since they are anxious to select for early acquisition those that will be read first, oftenest, and with the most permanent satisfaction and benefit. Occasionally — perhaps frequently — books that should certainly be in the Library will not be found on the Catalogue. On inquiry, it may be learned that many of them have been ordered, and are not yet received; but it may be hoped that this circumstance will not prevent any person who may happen urgently to need one, from giving notice that it is wanted. Indeed, it is probable that many desirable works have been overlooked, and it is certain that many have been omitted, from the want of means as yet to purchase all that the Library should possess, with as little delay as possible.

Many deficiencies will, we feel sure, be supplied by gifts of books that will thus be known to be wanting. This, in fact, has been the case already. For not a few persons among us have works on their shelves which are no longer interesting to them, and yet which are important to many others. Contributions, therefore, — some of them of great value, and all welcome, — have frequently been sent to the Public Library. If those who have works that have ceased to be of consequence to them will continue to remember that a book is never so much in the way of its duty as it is when it is in use, they may, with little or no sacrifice to themselves, easily become efficient benefactors to the public, by sending these unused books to the Public Library, where they will be accessible to many who are little likely to get them in any other way. Indeed, as we suppose that nobody ever heard it suggested that a public library anywhere had done any thing but good, so those who contribute to increase and build up such an institution will necessarily be counted among the truest and surest friends of progress in whatever is deemed, by a community like ours, most worthy to be sought.

It will be noticed that duplicates of the same work are rare in the present Catalogue; and, where they occur, one copy has often been presented to the Library. But their number will be largely increased, as experience may indicate what books are oftenest asked for.

The books marked with an asterisk are reserved for reference and use in the Reading Room, and are not open to general circulation; but such of them as relate to the science of medicine may be taken out by persons who professionally study or practise the healing art, and were, in fact, most of them, given expressly for this purpose.

The whole number of volumes in the Library somewhat exceeds twelve thousand.

Public Library, Mason-street,
April, 1854.

ALPHABETICAL CATALOGUE.

A star (*) prefixed to a title denotes that the book is not for general circulation. — The letters n. d. following a title indicate that no date is printed with the volume.

A.

Shelf.	No.	
95	20	Abbot (A.) Letters written in Cuba. 8vo. 1829.
178	9	——— Sermons, with Memoir. 12mo. 1831.
539	8	Abbott (J.) Philip Musgrave. 16mo. 1846.
177	5	——— Corner Stone. 12mo. 1852.
81	6	——— Rollo on the Atlantic. 16mo. 1853.
96	13	——— Summer in Scotland. 12mo. 1848.
187	10	——— Teacher. 12mo. 1844.
177	4	——— Way to do Good. 12mo. 1852.
177	2	——— Young Christian. 12mo. 1851.
60	4	——— History of Alexander the Great. 16mo. n. d.
60	11	——— History of Alfred the Great. 16mo. n. d.
60	15	——— History of Charles the First. 16mo. n. d.
60	16	——— History of Charles the Second. 16mo. 1852.
60	6	——— History of Cleopatra. 16mo. n. d.
60	2	——— History of Cyrus the Great. 16mo. 1852.
60	3	——— History of Darius the Great. 16mo. n. d.
60	7	——— History of Hannibal. 16mo. n. d.
60	8	——— History of Julius Cæsar. 16mo. 1852.
60	17	——— History of Maria Antoinette. 16mo. n. d.
60	13	——— History of Mary, Queen of Scots. 16mo. n. d.
60	10	——— History of Nero. 16mo. 1853.
60	14	——— History of Queen Elizabeth. 16mo. n. d.
60	1	——— History of Romulus. 16mo. 1852.
60	12	——— History of William the Conqueror. 16mo.
60	5	——— History of Xerxes. 16mo. 1852.
60	18	Abbott (J. S. C.) History of Madame Roland. 16mo. 1853.
60	19	——— History of Josephine. 16mo. 1852.
437	6	Abdy (E. S.) Tour in the United States. 3 vols. 8vo. 1835.

Shelf.	No.	
89	6	ABERCROMBIE (J.) on the Intellectual Powers. 18mo. n. d.
509	21	——— on the Intellectual Powers. 18mo. 1833.
89	18	——— Philosophy of the Moral Feelings. 18mo. 1848.
*544	2	——— on the Diseases of the Stomach. 8vo. 1845.
*544	3	——— on the Brain. 8vo. 1843.
626	10	ABERNETHY (J.) Surgical Works. 2 vols. 8vo. 1825.
*469	13	ABINGDON (Earl) on the Letter of E. Burke to Sheriffs of Bristol. 8vo. 1777.
*412	1	ACADEMY (American), Memoirs of. 4 vols. 4to. 1785, 1818.
*412	2	——— (American), Memoirs of. New series. 5 vols. 4to. 1833–53.
*412	3	——— Proceedings. vols. 8vo. 1846–52.
*470	3	ACADIA, French Memorials concerning. 8vo. 1756.
498	11	ACCUM (F.) Chemical Tests. 12mo. 1820.
539	7	ACLAND (T.) Manners and Customs of India. 16mo. 1847.
*594	5	ACTON (W.) Urinary and Generative Organs. 8vo. 1852.
*472	9	ADAIR (J.) History of American Indians. 4to. 1775.
484	3	ADAM (A.) Latin Grammar. 8vo. 1822.
26	3	——— Roman Antiquities. 8vo. 1833.
32	1	——— Roman Antiquities. 8vo. 1836.
25	4	ADAM (W.) Slavery in British India. 12mo. 1840.
8	12	ADAMS (Miss A.) Journal and Correspondence. 12mo. 1841.
8	13	——— Journal and Correspondence. Vol. 2. 12mo. 1842.
479	4	ADAMS (Mrs. A.) Letters. 16mo. 1848.
197	1	ADAMS (H.) Compendium of Sects. 8vo. 1784.
198	2	——— View of All Religions. 8vo. n. d.
*454	6	——— History of New England. 8vo. 1799.
69	16	——— Memoir of. 12mo. 1832.
75	5	——— Memoir of. 12mo. 1832.
25	2	——— History of the Jews. 2 vols. 12mo. 1812.
187	6	——— On the Christian Religion. 12mo. 1804.
1	1	ADAMS (J.) Works. Vols. 2–8. 7 vols. 8vo. 1850–53.

Vol. 2. Diary, with Autobiography.
3. Autobiography; Essays; and Controversial Papers of the Revolution.
4. Controversial Papers of the Revolution; Works on Government.
5. Works on Government.
6. On Government.
7. Official Letters, Messages and Papers.
8. Official Letters, Messages and Papers.

Shelf.	No.	
5	9	——— Correspondence with Wm. Cunningham. 8vo. 1823.
*175	21	——— Discourses on Davila. 8vo. 1805.
479	3	——— Letters. 16mo. 1841.
16	2	——— Novanglus, &c. 8vo. 1819.
35	4	ADAMS (Rev. J.) History of Rome. 2 vols. 8vo. 1792.
*4	5	ADAMS (J. Q.) Duplicate Letters, the Fisheries, &c. 8vo. 1822.
154	4	——— Dermot MacMorrogh. 8vo. 1832.
26	5	——— Letters on the Masonic Institution. 8vo. 1847.
180	29	——— Letters to his Son. 32mo. 1850.

Shelf.	No.	
69	10	ADAMS (J. Q.) Lives of Madison and Munroe. 12mo. 1850.
484	9	——— On Oratory and Rhetoric. 2 vols. 8vo. 1810.
477	15	ADAMS (N.) Annals of Portsmouth. 8vo. 1825.
537	4	ADDISON (J.) Works. Vols. 1, 2, 3. 3 vols. 12mo. 1853.
		Vol. 1. Life; Translations; Poems. 2. Dialogues on Medals; Travels; Essay on Virgil's Georgics; Discourse on Ancient and Modern Learning; of the Christian Religion; Letters; Political Writings. 3. Freeholder; Plebeian; the Old Whig; Tatler; Guardian; Lover.
189	5	——— Evidences of the Christian Religion. 12mo. 1795.
159	2	——— Poetical Works. 18mo. n. d.
524	6	——— Spectator. 8vo. 1827.
526	1	——— Spectator. 4 vols. 12mo. 1851.
*432	8	——— Works. 4 vols. 4to. 1721.
		Vol. 1. Poems on Several Occasions; Cato; Poemata; Diologues on Ancient Medals. 2. Remarks on Italy; Tatler; Spectator. 3. Spectator. 4. Spectator; Guardian; Present State of the War; Tryal of Count Tariff; Whig Examiner; Freeholder; of the Christian Religion.
110	7	——— Selections from the Spectator. 2 vols. 18mo. n. d.
33	1	ADOLPHUS (J.) History of France. 3 vols. 8vo. 1803.
457	2	——— History of England. 7 vols. 8vo. 1840–45.
172	16	ADSHEAD (J.) Prisons and Prisoners. 8vo. 1845.
110	1	ADVENTURE by Land and Sea. 2 vols. 18mo. 1847.
486	18	ÆLFRIC'S Anglo-Saxon Homily. 12mo. 1849.
485	4	ÆSCHYLUS. Tragedies. 8vo. 1840.
120	7	——— Tragedies. 18mo. 1852.
408	14	——— Tragedies, translated by Buckley. Post 8vo. 1849.
102	9	AGASSIZ (L.) & CABOT (J. E.) Lake Superior. 8vo. 1850.
418	5	AGASSIZ & GOULD. Comparative Physiology. Post 8vo. 1851.
499	3	——— Comparative Physiology. 12mo. 1853.
506	23	——— Comparative Physiology. 12mo. 1851.
125	12	AGUILAR (G.) Days of Bruce. 2 vols. 12mo. 1852.
125	9	——— Mother's Recompense. 12mo. 1853.
125	11	——— Vale of Cedars. 12mo. 1852.
124	12	——— Woman's Friendship. 12mo. 1853.
124	18	——— Woman's Friendship. 12mo. 1850.
125	18	——— Women of Israel. 2 vols. 12mo. 1852.
152	6	AIKIN (J.) British Poets: Jonson to Beattie. 8vo. 1850.
129	5	AIKIN (J.) & BARBAULD (A. L.) Evenings at Home. 16mo. n. d.
118	10	——— Evenings at Home. 16mo. 1851.
129	12	——— Juvenile Budget Opened. 18mo. 1840.
129	13	——— Juvenile Budget Re-opened. 18mo. n. d.
55	6	AIKIN (L.) Memoir of John Aikin. 8vo. 1824.
45	9	——— Court of King Charles the First. 2 vols. 1833.
67	14	——— Life of Joseph Addison. 16mo. 1846.

Shelf.	No.	
*663	2	Ainsworth (R.) English and Latin Dictionary abridged. 8vo. 1831.
153	7	Akenside (M.) Pleasures of the Imagination. 8vo. 1788.
150	2	——— Poetical Works. 32mo. 1806.
148	7	——— Poetical Works. 12mo. 1845.
158	3	Album, British. 2 vols. 18mo. 1792.
*401	2	Alcedo (A. de) Dictionary of America and West Indies. 5 vols. 4to. 1812–15.
487	10	Alembert (M. J. le R. d') Eulogies of Members of French Academy. 2 vols. 12mo. 1799.
437	7	Alexander (J. E.) Explorations in British America. 2 vols. 12mo. 1849.
*563	2	Alexander (J. H.) Dictionary of Weights and Measures. 8vo. 1850.
75	11	Alfieri (V.) Autobiography. 12mo. 1845.
166	15	Alford (H.) Poetical Works. 16mo. 1853.
108	16	Ali Bey. Travels: Boston and Vicinity. 12mo. 1818.
486	14	Alison (A.) Essays on Taste. 12mo. 1850.
47	7	Alison (A.) Epitome of History of Europe. 12mo. 1852.
42	2	——— History of Europe. 4 vols. 8vo. 1850.
8	15	Allen (E.) Captivity of. 16mo. 1846.
*475	11	Allen (I.) Capture of the Olive Branch. 8vo. 1805.
417	1	Allen (J.) Battles of the British Navy. 2 vols. post 8vo. 1852.
51	6	Allen (W.) Memoir of John Codman. 8vo. 1853.
*391	1	——— American Biographical Dictionary. 8vo. 1832.
498	21	Allen (J. F.) On Grape Vine. 12mo. 1853.
483	11	Allen (Z.) Philosophy of Mechanics. 8vo. 1852.
126	8	Allen Prescott. 2 vols. 12mo. 1834.
525	11	Allston (W.) Lectures on Art, and Poems. 12mo. 1850.
*670	1	Almanac, American. 1830–54. 25 vols. 12mo. 1830–54.
670	2	——— American. 12mo. 1835.
*660	14	Almanach de Gotha. 32mo. 1838.
*663	6	——— Royal. 8vo. 1826.
*663	8	——— Imperial. 8vo. 1812.
137	7	Almacks Revisited. 2 vols. 12mo. 1828.
121	8	——— Revisited. 3 vols. post 8vo. 1828.
*470	15	America. Controversy between Great Britain and her Colonies. 8vo. 1769.
*469	5	American Congress. Answer to the Declaration of. 8vo. 1776.
*469	33	——— Envoys, Correspondence with Tallyrand. 12mo. 1798.
*337	1	——— State Papers. 1789–1818. 11 vols. 8vo.
*327	3	——— State Papers. Supplem. to Monthly Anthology. 8vo.
*444	1	Ames (F.) Works, with Life. 8vo. 1809.
483	12	——— Works, with Life. 8vo. 1809.
170	17	Anacreon. 18mo. 1852.
164	11	——— Translated by Thomas Moore. 12mo. 1804.
140	7	Andersen (H. C.) Story Book. 16mo. 1852.
117	21	——— Wonderful Tales. 16mo. 1852.

Shelf.	No.	
123	1	ANDERSEN (H. C.) Only a Fiddler! and O. T. 3 vols. post 8vo. 1845.
121	1	——— Two Baronesses. 2 vols. post 8vo. 1848.
27	7	ANDERSON. History of Commerce. 6 vols. 8vo. 1790.
506	26	ANDERSON (J.) Course of Creation. 12mo. 1851.
63	11	ANDERSON (R.) Life of Smollett. 8vo. 1806.
186	17	ANDERSON (W.) Mercantile Correspondence. 12mo. 1851.
*584	11	ANDRAL (G.) Medical Clinic. 3 vols. 8vo. 1843.
		Vol. 1. Abdomen. 2. Chest. 3. Encephalon.
*476	4	ANDREWS (J.) War with America, &c. 4 vols. 8vo. 1785.
*262	10	ANDREWS (J. P.) History of Great Britain. 4to. 1794.
*448	8	ANDRY (F.) Diseases of the Heart. 12mo. 1846.
508	20	ANGLER's Guide, American. 16mo. 1849.
		ANNUAL Register. 94 vols. 8vo. 1758–1852.
*545	1	Vols. 1–20.
*555	1	,, 21–37.
*565	1	,, 38–50.
*575	1	,, 51–64.
*585	1	,, 65–78.
*595	1	,, 79–92.
*605	1	,, 93, 94, and Index up to 1819.
*553	2	ANNUAL Biography and Obituary. 21 vols. 8vo. 1817–37.
*443	2	ANSPACH, Margravine of. Memoirs. 2 vols. 8vo. 1826.
497	4	ANSTED (D. T.) Ancient World. 12mo. 1847.
169	5	ANSTER Fair. 18mo. 1815.
126	15	ANTAR. 4 vols. 12mo. 1819–20.
123	2	ANTENORS Modernes, ou Voyages en France. 3 vols. 8vo. 1806.
*327	2	ANTHOLOGY, Monthly. 10 vols. 8vo. 1804–11.
499	1	ANTHON (C.) Manual of Greek Literature. 8vo. 1853.
96	7	ANTHON (C. E.) Pilgrimage to Treves. 12mo. 1845.
344	5	ANTHON (J.) Law Student. 8vo. 1850.
*395	1	ANTIQUARISK Tidsskrift. 1846–48. 8vo.
171	13	ANTI-SLAVERY. Boston Female Society of. 12mo. 1836.
*478	5	ANTIQUARIAN Society. Archæologia Americana. 8vo. 1820.
*478	6	——— Archæologia Americana. 8vo. 1836.
*633	11	ANTISELL (T.) Hand-book of Useful Arts. 12mo. 1852.
*393	4	APPLETON's Dictionary of Mechanics. 2 vols. 8vo. 1851–52.
*394	4	——— Library Manual. 8vo. 1852.
*325	6	APOLLO, American. 8vo. 1792.
112	9	ARABIAN NIGHTS. 8vo. 1852.
72	7	ARDECHE (L. de l'.) History of Napoleon. 8vo. n. d.
153	3	ARIOSTO (L.) Orlando Furioso. By Hoole. 5 vols. 8vo. 1785.
408	15	ARISTOTLE's Rhetoric. By Buckley. Post 8vo. 1851.
408	16	——— Ethics, translated by Browne. Post 8vo. 1853.
409	1	——— Logic, translated by Owen. 2 vols. post 8vo. 1853.
409	2	——— Politics and Economics. By Walford. Post 8vo. 1853.

Shelf.	No.	
6	6	ARMITAGE (J.) History of Brazil. 2 vols. 8vo. 1836.
8	10	ARMSTRONG (J.) War of 1812. 2 vols. 12mo. 1840.
27	3	——— (L.) History of the Temperance Reformation. 12mo. 1852.
*583	1	ARNAULT (A. V.) Biographie Nouvelle. 20 vols. 8vo. 1820–25.
38	12	ARNOLD (T.) Lectures on Modern History. 12mo. 1852.
32	5	——— History of Later Roman Commonwealth. 8vo. 1846.
200	12	——— Rugby School Sermons. 16mo. 1846.
52	2	——— Life and Correspondence. 8vo. 1846.
52	16	——— Life and Correspondence. 8vo. 1846.
512	11	——— Miscellaneous Works. 8vo. 1845.
*392	12	ARNOT (D. H.) Gothic Architecture. 4to. 1851.
179	10	ARNOT (W.) Race for Riches. 12mo. 1853.
492	11	ARNOTT (N.) Elements of Physics. 8vo. 1848.
*554	3	ASHWELL (S.) Diseases of Females. 8vo. 1848.
504	7	ARTS, Papers on Polite and Fine. 1 vol. 8vo. 1810–43.
131	3	ARVINE (K.) Anecdotes of Literature and the Fine Arts. 8vo. 1853.
623	1	——— Religious Anecdotes. 8vo. 1852.
45	2	ASHBURNHAM (J.) Attendance on Charles the First. 2 vols. 8vo. 1830.
*448	17	ASHE (T.) Travels in America. 12mo. 1808.
75	1	ASHMUN (J.) Memoir of Rev. S. Bacon. 8vo. 1822.
*271	11	ATLAS, American, Historical, Chronological and Geographical, folio. 1827.
23	5	AUBIGNÉ (J. H. Merle d'.) History of Reformation. 8vo. 1843.
24	5	——— History of Reformation. 3 vols. 12mo. 1852–53.
83	13	AULDJO (J.) Visit to Constantinople. 8vo. 1835.
135	22	AUSTEN (J.) Emma. 16mo. 1851.
136	17	——— Mansfield Park. 16mo. 1847.
135	16	——— Northanger Abbey—Persuasion. 16mo. 1851.
136	16	——— Pride and Prejudice. 16mo. 1853.
135	15	——— Sense and Sensibility. 16mo. 1846.
*445	6	AUSTIN (J. T.) Life of Elbridge Gerry. 2 vols. 8vo. 1828–9.
51	20	——— Life of Elbridge Gerry. 2 vols. 8vo. 1828–29.
527	3	AUSTIN (S.) Characteristics of Goethe. 3 vols. 12mo. 1833.
184	19	AUSTIN (W.) Character of Christ. 8vo. 1807.
94	12	——— Letters from London. 8vo. 1804.
80	5	AYDER ALI KHAN. History of. 12mo. 1774.
160	7	AYTOUN (W. E.) Life and Times of Richard I. 18mo. 1840.

B.

Shelf.	No.	
187	11	BABINGTON (T.) Christian Education. 12mo. 1818.
185	1	BACHE (A. D.) Education in Europe. 8vo. 1839.
*436	6	BACK (G.) Arctic Expedition, 1833–35. 8vo. 1836.
509	18	BACKWOODS of Canada. 18mo. 1846.
512	3	BACON (F.) Works. 3 vols. 8vo. 1842.
		Vol. 1. Life; Essays; Appendix to Essays; Meditationes Sacræ; of the Colours of Good and Evil; Tracts upon Human Philosophy; Apophthegms; Ornamenta Rationalia; Advancement of Learning; New Atlantis; Wisdom of the Ancients; Civil History; Biography; Miscellaneous Tracts.
		2. Sylva Sylvarum; Tracts relating to Scotland, Ireland, Spain, and England; Speeches; Charges; Papers relating to the Earl of Essex; Theological, Miscellaneous, and Judicial Tracts.
		3. Letters; Law Tracts; Novum Organum; Translations; Index.
486	26	——— Essays. 16mo. 1845.
100	8	——— Essays. 18mo. n. d.
398	8	——— Moral and Historical Works. Post 8vo. 1852.
419	8	——— Physical and Metaphysical Works. 8vo. 1853.
63	16	BACON (J.) Life and Times of Francis I. 2 vols. 8vo. 1830.
92	11	BACON (J. F.) Six Years in Biscay. 8vo. 1838.
175	18	BACON (L.) Essays on Slavery. 12mo. 1846.
156	11	BAILEY (P. J.) Festus. 12mo. 1851.
190	4	BAILEY (S.) Essays on Opinions. 12mo. 1831.
530	11	——— Essays on Truth. 12mo. 1831.
155	15	BAILLIE (J.) Dramatic and Poetical Works. 8vo. 1851.
494	13	BAINES (E., Jr.) Cotton Manufacture in G. Britain. 8vo. n.d.
95	10	BAIRD (R.) West Indies and N. America. 12mo. 1850.
184	4	——— Religion in America. 8vo. 1844.
199	12	——— Protestantism in Italy. 12mo. 1845.
498	18	BAIRD (R. H.) American Cotton Spinner. 16mo. 1852.
*252	6	BAKER (R.) Chronicle of Kings of England. Folio. 1674.
493	12	BAKEWELL (R.) Introduction to Geology. 8vo. 1839.
78	12	BALBOA, Cortez, and Pizarro, Lives of. 18mo. n. d.
*643	3	BALDWIN (T.) Complete Gazetteer of the U. S. 8vo. 1854.
*660	4	BALDWIN (T.) Pronouncing Gazetteer. 12mo. 1847.
181	16	BALFOUR (W.) Inquiry. 8vo. 1824.
504	1	BALL (S.) Cultivation and Manufacture of Tea in China. 8vo. 1848.
*433	4	BALLANTYNE'S Novelist's Library. By Scott. 10 vols. 8vo. 1821–24.
		Vol. 1. Fielding.
		2. Smollett.
		3. Smollett.
		4. Le Sage and Johnstone.
		5. Sterne; Goldsmith; Johnson; Mackenzie; Walpole; Reeve.
		6, 7, 8, Richardson.
		9. Swift, Bage, and Cumberland.
		10. Radcliffe.
614	11	BALLARD (E.) On the Abdomen. 12mo. 1852.

Shelf.	No.	
25	3	Ballou (H.) Ancient History of Universalism. 12mo. 1842.
67	3	Ballou (M. M.) Biography of Rev. Hosea Ballou. 12mo. 1852.
181	3	Balmes (J.) Protestantism and Catholicity Compared. 8vo. 1851.
*201	1	Baltard. Paris et ses Monumens. Folio. 1803.
539	22	Baltic, Letters from the Shores of the. 12mo. 1844.
*340	1	Baltimore, Ordinances of. 8vo. 1801.
*339	20	——— Ordinances of. 8vo. 1816.
79	8	Bancroft (A.) Life of Washington. 2 vols. 18mo. 1839.
3	1	Bancroft (G.) History of United States. 5 vols. 8vo. 1852–53.
*453	1	——— History of United States. 5 vols. 8vo. 1852–53.
3	2	——— History of United States. 5 vols. 8vo. 1852–53.
3	3	——— History of United States. 5 vols. 8vo. 1852.
4	3	——— History of United States. 5 vols. 8vo. 1838–52.
*470	10	Bancroft (E.) Natural History of Guiana. 8vo. 1769.
510	5	Banfield (T. C.) Industry of the Rhine. 2 vols. 18mo. 1848.
*433	5	Bankes (H.) Constitutional History of Rome. 2 vols. 8vo. 1818.
*348	2	Bangor City Ordinances. 8vo. 1851.
25	5	Bangs (N.) History of the Methodist E. Church. 16mo. 1845.
176	9	Banker's Commonplace Book. 16mo. 1850.
27	1	Banks, History of. 12mo. 1837.
80	16	Banvard (J.) Life of Webster. 16mo. 1853.
192	5	Baptist Library. 3 vols. 8vo. 1843.
526	4	Barbauld (A. L.) Works. 2 vols. 12mo. 1826.
526	5	——— Legacy for Young Ladies. 12mo. 1826.
14	5	Barber (J. W.) Historical Collections of Massachusetts. 8vo. 1848.
7	2	——— History and Antiquities of Northern States. 8vo. 1847.
103	15	Barca (Mad. C. de la). Life in Mexico. 8vo. 1843.
117	16	Barham (R. H.) Ingoldsby Legends. 16mo. 1852.
514	6	Barker (W. B.) Lares and Penates. 8vo. 1853.
180	21	Barlow (J.) Political Writings. 12mo. 1796.
153	1	——— Vision of Columbus. 8vo. 1787.
503	20	Barnard (H.) School Architecture. 8vo. 1848.
504	6	——— School Architecture. 8vo. 1848.
171	37	Barnes (A.) Notes on the Gospels. 2 vols. 12mo. 1852.
171	38	——— Notes on Acts. 12mo. 1852.
171	39	——— Notes on Romans. 12mo. 1852.
171	40	——— Notes on 1 Corinthians. 12mo. 1849.
171	41	——— Notes on 2 Corinthians. 12mo. 1851.
171	42	——— Notes on Ephesians, &c. 12mo. 1852.

Shelf.	No.	
171	43	Barnes (A.) Notes on Thessalonians. 12mo. 1853.
171	44	——— Notes on Hebrews. 12mo. 1852.
171	45	——— Notes on James, Peter, &c. 12mo. 1852.
171	46	——— Notes on Revelation. 12mo. 1852.
181	15	——— Notes on Job. 2 vols. 12mo. 1845.
184	12	——— Notes on Isaiah. 2 vols. 12mo. 1853.
52	11	Barney (Com. J.), Memoir of. 8vo. 1832.
63	1	Baron (J.) Life of Edward Jenner. 2 vols. 8vo. 1838.
39	13	Barrington (Sir J.) Rise and Fall of the Irish Nation. 12mo. n. d.
109	12	Barrow (Sir J.) History of Voyages to Arctic Regions. 16mo. 1846.
104	11	——— History of Voyages to Arctic Regions. 8vo. 1818.
98	7	Barrow (J.) Life of Peter the Great. 18mo. 1848.
445	3	——— Life of Sir William Sidney Smith. 2 vols. 8vo. 1848.
539	9	——— Life of Sir F. Drake. 16mo. 1844.
122	9	——— Sketches of his own Times. 12mo. 1853.
82	11	——— Travels in Southern Africa. 2 vols. 4to. 1806.
395	7	Barrow (J. jun.) Excursions in the North of Europe. 12mo. 1834.
109	16	——— Tour round Ireland. 12mo. 1836.
36	6	Barruel (Abbé). Histoire du Jacobinism. 4 vols. 8vo. 1797–98.
*477	4	Barry (J. S.) History of Hanover, Mass. 8vo. 1853.
*477	6	Barry (W.) History of Framingham, Mass. 8vo. 1847.
418	6	Barry, Opie, and Fuseli. Lectures on Painting. Post 8vo. 1848.
*477	10	Barstow (G.) History of New Hampshire. 8vo. 1842.
636	13	Barth (M.) and Roger (H.) on Auscultation. 8vo. 1847.
435	5	Barthélémy (J. J.) Travels of Anacharsis. 6 vols. 8vo. 1817.
*544	12	Bartlett (E.) Fevers of the United States. 8vo. 1852.
*604	20	——— Philosophy of Medical Science. 8vo. 1844.
*633	3	Bartlett (J. R.) Dictionary of Americanisms. 8vo. 1848.
492	10	Bartlett (W. H. C.) Mechanics. 8vo. 1850.
82	10	Bartlett (W. H.) Nile Boat. 8vo. 1851.
*403	3	——— Pilgrim Fathers of New England. 8vo. 1853.
51	2	Bartlett (W. S.) Frontier Missionary. 8vo. 1853.
494	8	Bartol (B. H.) Marine Boilers of United States. 8vo. 1851.
525	14	Barton (B.) Memoir, Letters, and Poems. 12mo. 1850.
73	5	Barton (W.) Life of David Rittenhouse. 8vo. 1813.
106	12	Bartram (W.) Travels through North and South Carolina, Georgia, &c. 8vo. 1791.
*447	6	——— Travels. 8vo. 1792.
55	9	Bausset (L. F. J. de). Court of Napoleon. 8vo. 1828.
*448	18	Baxter (B.) Posing Question. 8vo. 1661.
177	9	Baxter (R.) Call to the Unconverted. 12mo. 1851.
		——— Practical Works. 23 vols. 8vo. 1830.

Shelf.	No.	
566	3	BAXTER (R.) Practical Works. Vols. 1–15. 8vo. 1830.
576	1	——— Practical Works. Vols. 16–23. 8vo. 1830.

Vol. 1. Life.
2, 3. Christian Ethics.
4. Economics.
5. Ecclesiastics.
6. Politics.
7. On Conversion; Call to the Unconverted.
8. On Conversion.
9–20. Miscellaneous.
21. Reasons of the Christian Religion.
22, 23. Saints' Rest; and Index.

Shelf.	No.	
183	11	——— Select Writings. 2 vols. 8vo. 1831.
14	8	BAYLIES (F.) Colony of N. Plymouth. 3 vols. 8vo. 1830.
148	1	BEATTIE (J.) Poetical Works. 16mo. 1831.
51	8	BEAUCHESNE (A. de). Louis the Seventeenth, Life of, &c. 2 vols. 12mo. 1853.
*425	2	BEAUMONT (F.) & FLETCHER (J.) Works, with Notes and Memoir by A. Dyce. 11 vols. 8vo. 1843–46.

Vol. 1. Memoir; Commendatory Poems; Woman Hater; Thierry and Theodoret; Philaster; Maid's Tragedy.
2. Faithful Shepherdess; Knight of the Burning Pestle; King and no King; Cupid's Revenge; the Masque; Four Plays in one.
3. Scornful Lady; Coxcomb; Captain; Honest Man's Fortune; Little French Lawyer.
4. Wit at Several Weapons; Wit without Money; Faithful Friends; the Widow; Custom of the Country.
5. Bonduca; Knight of Malta; Valentinian; Laws of Candy; Queen of Corinth.
6. Loyal Subject; Mad Lover; False One; Double Marriage; Humorous Lieutenant.
7. Women Pleased; Woman's Prize; the Chances; Monsieur Thomas; Island Princess.
8. Pilgrim; Wild-Goose Chase; Prophetess; Sea Voyage; Spanish Curate.
9. Beggars' Bush; Love's Cure; Maid in the Mill; Wife for a Month; Rule a Wife and Have a Wife.
10. Fair Maid of the Inn; Noble Gentleman; Elder Brother; Nice Valour; Bloody Brother.
11. Lover's Progress; Night Walker; Love's Pilgrimage; Two Noble Kinsmen; Poems by Beaumont; Poems by Fletcher; Index to the Notes.

Shelf.	No.	
154	1	BEAUMONT & FLETCHER. 10 vols. 8vo. 1750.

Vol. 1. Maid's Tragedy; Philaster; King and No King; Scornful Lady.
2. Custom of the Country; Elder Brother; Spanish Curate; Wit without Money; Beggar's Bush.
3. Humorous Lieutenant; Faithful Shepherdess; Mad Lover; Loyal Subject; Rule a Wife and Have a Wife.
4. Laws of Candy; False One; Little French Lawyer; Valentinian; and Monsieur Thomas.
5. Chances; Bloody Brother; Wild-Goose Chase; Wife for a Month; Lover's Progress; Pilgrim.
6. Captain; Prophetess; Queen of Corinth; Bonduca; Knight of the Burning Pestle.
7. Love's Pilgrimage; Double Marriage; Maid in the Mill; Knight of Malta; Love's Cure.
8. Women Pleas'd; Night Walker; Woman's Prize; Island Princess; Noble Gentleman.
9. Coronation; Sea Voyage; Coxcomb; Wit at Several Weapons; Fair Maid of the Inn; Cupid's Revenge.
10. Two Noble Kinsmen; Thierry and Theodoret; Woman Hater; Nice Valour; Honest Man's Fortune; Masque; Four Plays.

Shelf.	No.	
*448	11	Beaumont (J.) Treatise on Apparitions, &c. 8vo. 1750.
74	15	Beard (Rev. J. R.) Life of Toussaint l'Ouverture. 16mo. 1853.
*614	1	Beasley (H.) Pocket Formulary. 12mo. 1852.
172	10	Beccaria. Crimes and Punishments. 8vo. 1804.
417	2	Bechstein (J. M.) Cage and Chamber Birds. 8vo. 1853.
496	8	Beck (L. C.) Botany of U. S. North of Virginia. 8vo. 1848.
110	13	Beckford (W.) Italy, with Sketches of Spain and Portugal. 2 vols. 12mo. 1834.
85	6	——— Italy, Spain, and Portugal. 12mo. 1845.
139	10	——— Vathek. 18mo. 1834.
397	2	Beckmann (J.) History of Inventions, &c. 2 vols. post 8vo. 1846.
407	6	Bede (Venerable). Ecclesiastical History of England. 8vo. 1849.
*546	1	——— Works. 12 vols. 8vo. 1843.

Vol. 1. Life; Poems; Letters.
2. Ecclesiastical History.
3. Ecclesiastical History and Index.
4. Historical Tracts.
5. Homilies.
6. Scientific Tracts and Appendix.
7–9. Commentaries on the Old Testament.
10–12. Commentaries on the New Testament.

Shelf.	No.	
171	23	Beecher (C.) Review of the Spiritual Manifestations. 12mo. 1853.
507	12	Beecher (C. E.) On Domestic Economy. 12mo. 1849.
507	13	——— Domestic Receipt Book. 12mo. 1852.
519	2	——— Remedy for the Wrongs of Woman. 12mo. 1851.
171	30	Beecher (E.) Conflict of Ages. 12mo. 1853.
171	33	Beecher (L.) Works. 3 vols. 12mo. 1853.

Vol. 1. Lectures on Atheism and Intemperance.
2. Sermons.
3. Views of Theology.

Shelf.	No.	
*436	1	Belcher (E.) Voyage round the World. 2 vols. 8vo. 1843.
*445	11	Belknap (J.) American Biography. 2 vols. 8vo. 1794–98.
100	1	——— American Biography. 3 vols. 18mo. 1851.
*454	3	——— History of New Hampshire. 3 vols. 8vo. 1813.
*454	2	——— History of New Hampshire. 8vo. 1831.
77	14	——— Life. 16mo. 1847.
77	15	——— Life. 16mo. 1847.
*654	4	Bell (Benj.) Surgery. 7 vols. 8vo. 1801.
*654	10	——— On Ulcers. 1 vol. 8vo. 1791.
*654	11	——— On the Venereal. 2 vols. 8vo. 1797.
497	10	Bell (Sir C.) On the Hand. 12mo. 1835.
*433	3	——— Anatomy of Expression. 4to. 1847.
*564	2	——— On the Arteries. 8vo. 1833.
*584	3	——— Operative Surgery. 2 vols. 8vo. 1807–09.
*671	8	——— On the Spine. 4to. 1824.

Shelf.	No.	
88	14	Bell (H. G.) Life of Mary, Queen of Scots. 2 vols. 18mo. 1846.
169	11	Bell. Classical Arrangement of Fugitive Poetry. 15 vols. 16mo. 1790–2.
86	9	Bell (J.) Observations on Italy. 12mo. 1826.
*564	7	Bell (J. & Ch.) Surgery. 4 vols. 8vo. 1826.
506	21	Bell (J.) On Regimen and Longevity. 12mo. 1842.
70	15	Bell (R.) Life of George Canning. 16mo. 1846.
*443	10	——— Life of George Canning. 8vo. 1846.
50	10	——— Lives of Literary and Scientific Men of Great Britain. 2 vols. 12mo. 1839.
30	13	——— History of Russia. 3 vols. 18mo. n. d.
556	3	Beloe (W.) Anecdotes. 6 vols. 8vo. 1807–12.
556	2	——— Sexagenarian. 2 vols. 8vo. 1817.
200	10	Belsham (T.) Importance of the Christian Revelation. 12mo. 1808.
95	13	Beltrami (J. C.) Pilgrimage in Europe and America. 2 vols. 8vo. 1828.
*437	4	Belzoni (G.) Discoveries in Egypt. 2 vols. 8vo. 1822.
*344	3	Bemis (G.) Report of the Case of John W. Webster. 8vo. 1850.
23	2	Benedict (D.) History of Baptists. 8vo. 1813.
74	14	Benger (E. L.) Anne Boleyn. 12mo. 1851.
63	10	——— Anne Boleyn. 8vo. 1822.
74	13	——— Mary, Queen of Scots. 2 vols. 12mo. 1851.
446	3	——— Memoir of Elizabeth Hamilton. 2 vols. 8vo. 1818.
502	5	Benjamin (A.) Architect and Carpenter. 4to. 1851.
*604	10	Bennet (J. H.) Inflammation of the Uterus. 8vo. 1853.
498	19	Bennett (J. C.) Poultry Book. 12mo. 1852.
*646	9	Bennett (J. H.) On Cancerous and Cancroid Growths. 8vo. 1849.
*402	2	Bentivoglio (Cardinal). History of the Wars of Flanders. Folio. 1678.
38	10	Berington (J.) Literary History of Middle Ages. 12mo. 1846.
*576	3	Berkeley (G.) Works. 3 vols. 8vo. 1820.
508	22	Bernan (W.) On Warming and Ventilating. 2 vols. 16mo. 1845.
129	9	Berquin's Children's Friend. 2 vols. 16mo. 1846.
179	3	Bethune (G. W.) Orations and Discourses. 12mo. 1850.
188	9	Beveridge (W.) Sermons on Ordinances of the Church of England. 12mo. 1845.
183	7	Bible (The). Genesis, with English Translation. 8vo. 1844.
171	21	——— Hebrew Prophets, translated by G. R. Noyes. 3 vols. 12mo. 1833–37.
180	6	——— Psalms, translated by G. R. Noyes. 12mo. 1846.
179	20	——— Job, translated by G. R. Noyes. 12mo. 1838.

Shelf.	No.	
179	16	Bible (The). Proverbs, translated by G. R. Noyes. 12mo. 1846.
189	11	—— Isaiah, translated by Robert Lowth. 16mo. 1794.
194	6	—— New Testament, Murdock's Translation from Syriac. 8vo. 1852.
178	6	—— Novum Testamentum Græce ex Recensione Jo. Jac. Griesbachii. 8vo. 1809.
179	14	Biblical Trinity. 12mo. 1830.
*404	14	Bibliotheca Americana. 4to. 1789.
484	12	Bielfeld (J. F.) Elements of Universal Erudition. 3 vols. 8vo. 1770.
92	15	Bigelow (A.) Travels in Malta and Sicily. 8vo. 1831.
85	5	—— Rambles in N. Britain and Ireland. 12mo. 1821.
*339	3	Bigelow (G. T.) Report of Trial of Abner Rogers. 8vo. 1844.
*666	16	Bigelow (H. J.) Ether and Chloroform. 8vo. 1848.
*666	17	—— Fragments of Medical Science and Art. 8vo. 1846.
*666	18	—— Iron Bar through the Head. 8vo. 1850.
*666	19	—— Introductory Surgical Lecture. 8vo. 1850.
*666	20	—— Orthopedic Surgery. 8vo. 1845.
*666	21	—— Strictures of the Urethra. 8vo. 1849–51.
507	10	Bigelow (J.) On the Useful Arts. 2 vols. 12mo. n. d.
497	5	—— On the Useful Arts. 12mo. 1851.
497	19	—— On the Useful Arts. 2 vols. 12mo. 1851.
503	9	—— Plants of Boston. 8vo. 1814.
503	11	—— Plants of Boston. 8vo. 1824.
*336	6	Bigelow (L.) Digest. 8vo. 1825.
*336	7	—— Supplement to. 8vo. 1830.
*554	4	Billard (C. M.) Diseases of Infants. 8vo. 1839.
*604	4	Billing (A.) Principles of Medicine. 8vo. 1851.
*646	19	—— On the Lungs and Heart. 8vo. 1852.
82	12	Billings (Com. J.) Expedition to North of Russia. 4to. 1802.
34	5	Bingham (H.) Sandwich Islands. 8vo. 1847.
*546	2	Bingham (J.) Origines Ecclesiasticæ. 9 vols. 8vo. 1840.
75	17	Binney (T.) Sir T. F. Buxton. The Wife. 8vo. 1853.
*593	1	Biographie des Hommes Vivants. 5 vols. 8vo. 1816–19.
56	8	—— de tous les Ministres. 8vo. 1825.
*614	5	Bird (G.) Urinary Deposits. 12mo. 1851.
98	17	Birds, Natural History of. 18mo. 1850.
108	7	Birkbeck (M.) Letters from Illinois. 12mo. 1818.
95	15	—— Journey in America. 8vo. 1818.
*646	20	Birkett (J.) Diseases of the Breast. 8vo. 1850.
*448	14	Bitaubé (M.) Joseph. 12mo. 1767.
*432	12	Blackmore (R.) Prince Arthur. Folio. 1695.
*422	2	—— Paraphrase on Job. Folio. 1700.
337	4	Blackstone (W.) Commentaries on the Laws of England. 4 vols. 8vo. 1807.

Shelf.	No.	
*329	1	Blackwood's Edinburgh Magazine. Vols. 1–17. 8vo. 1817–25.
*330	1	——— Edinburgh Magazine. Vols. 18–31. 1825–32.
117	11	——— Stories from. 16mo. 1852.
*391	6	Blake (J. L.) Biographical Dictionary. 8vo. 1850.
37	2	——— Manners and Customs of all Nations. 12mo. 1853.
184	13	Blair (H.) Sermons. 2 vols. 8vo. 1814.
*221	5	Blair (J.) Maps of Ancient Geography. Folio. 1768.
*221	4	——— Chronology and History of the World. 1754.
*		Blair & Rives. Congressional Globe. 26 vols. 4to. 1833–53.
*301	1	From 1833 to 1844.
*311	1	From 1844 to 1851.
*321	1	From 1851 to 1853.
*321	3	Vol. 12 (duplicate).
*321	5	Vol. 16 (duplicate).
*321	4	Appendix to vol. 16.
*321	6	Vol. 19 (duplicate).
*321	7	Vol. 20 (duplicate).
*321	8	Vol. 26 (duplicate).
*321	2	Appendix to vol. 26.
*321	9	Appendix to vol. 26.
43	3	Blanc (L.) History of the Ten Years, 1830–40. 2 vols. 8vo. 1844.
519	5	Blanchard (L.) Sketches from Life. 12mo. 1848.
45	7	Blaquiere (E.) Spanish Revolution. 8vo. 1822.
83	6	——— Second Visit to Greece. 8vo. 1825.
44	9	——— French Revolution. 8vo. 1825.
117	6	Blessington (Lady). Confessions of an Elderly Lady and Gentleman. 2 vols. 12mo. 1838.
*5	3	Bliss (L. jun.) History of Rehoboth. 8vo. 1836.
*613	5	Blunt (J.) Shipmasters' Assistant. 8vo. 1848.
394	13	——— Shipmasters' Assistant. 8vo. 1851.
170	13	Blunt (I. J.) Reformation in England. 18mo. 1840.
53	4	Boaden (J.) Memoirs of Mrs. Siddons. 2 vols. 8vo. 1831.
179	4	Boardman (H. A.) Bible in the Counting House. 12mo. 1853.
140	16	Boccaccio (G.) Decameron. 2 vols. 18mo. 1822.
*433	10	Boeckh (A.) Public Economy of Athens. 2 vols. 8vo. 1825.
*394	5	Bohn (H. G.) Catalogue of Books. Vol. 1. 8vo. 1847.
418	7	——— Hand Book of Games. Post 8vo. 1850.
515	2	Boileau (N.) Œuvres Complètes. 3 vols. 8vo. 1824.
26	12	Boismont (A. B. de). Hallucinations. 8vo. 1853.
514	8	Bolingbroke (Henry St. John). Works. 4 vols. 8vo. 1841.

Vol. 1. Life; Letter to Sir W. Windham; Reflections upon Exile; Occasional Writer; Vision of Camilick; Answer to London Journal; Answer to Defence of the Enquiry into the Reasons of the Conduct of Great Britain; on the History of England.

2. Dissertation upon Parties; on Study of History.

3. On Archbishop Tillotson's Sermon; Essays addressed to Pope.

4. Essays continued; Index.

Shelf.	No.	
58	8	Bombet (L. A. C.) Lives of Haydn and Mozart. 16mo. 1839.
131	15	Bondman (The). 12mo. 1833.
23	6	Bonnechose (E. de). Reformers before the Reformation. 8vo. 1844.
188	18	Bonnet (C.) On Christianity. 12mo. 1803.
*395	8	Bonnycastle (R. H.) Newfoundland in 1842. 2 vols. 12mo. 1842.
514	3	Bonomi (J.) Nineveh and its Palaces. 8vo. 1853.
*479	5	Book (The). Conduct of Princess of Wales. 8vo. 1813.
*422	5	Book of Sports, British and Foreign. 4to. 1843.
*666	8	Boot (F.) Life of John Armstrong, and Marsh Fever. 2 vols. 8vo. 1833.
140	2	Borrow (G.) Lavengro. 16mo. 1851.
195	6	——— Bible in Spain, and Gipsies of Spain. 8vo. 1851.
539	13	——— Bible in Spain. 16mo. 1843.
539	6	——— Zincali. 16mo. 1846.
167	2	Boscawen (W.) Poems. 16mo. 1801.
*604	18	Bostock (J.) Physiology. 8vo. 1844.
189	20	Boston (T.) Fourfold State. 18mo. 1853.
189	21	——— Crook in the Lot. 18mo. 1852.
526	10	——— Book. 12mo. 1850.
597	1	——— Auditors' Annual Reports. Nos. 20 to 29. 8vo. 1831–41.
*597	2	——— Auditors' Annual Reports. Nos. 20 to 38. 8vo. 1831–50.
*480	6	——— By-Laws and Orders of. 12mo. 1818.
*		——— City Documents.
*597	3	——— 1834.
*597	4	——— 1835.
*597	5	——— 1836.
*597	6	——— 1837.
*597	7	——— 1842.
*597	8	——— 1846.
*597	9	——— 1847.
*507	10	——— 1849.
*597	11	——— 1850.
*597	12	——— 1851. Vol. 1.
*607	1	——— 1851. ,, 2.
*607	2	——— 1852. ,, 1.
*607	3	——— 1852. ,, 2.
*339	17	——— Charter and Ordinances. 8vo. 1827.
*339	15	——— Charter and Ordinances. 8vo. 1834.
339	16	——— Charter and Ordinances. 8vo. 1834.
*		——— Directory.
*580	12	——— 1810, 1818. 16mo.
*580	12	——— 1820–36. 16mo.
*590	1	——— 1837–46. 16mo.
*590	2	——— 1825. 16mo.

Shelf.	No.	
*590	3	Boston Directory. 1826. 16mo.
*590	4	——— 1826. 16mo.
*590	5	——— 1828. 16mo.
*590	6	——— 1829. 16mo.
*590	7	——— 1830. 16mo.
*590	8	——— 1833. 16mo.
*590	9	——— 1834. 16mo.
*590	10	——— 1834. 16mo.
*590	11	——— 1836. 16mo.
*590	12	——— 1837. 16mo.
*590	13	——— 1837. 16mo.
*590	14	——— 1839. 16mo.
*590	15	——— 1841. 16mo.
*600	1	——— 1842. 16mo.
*600	2	——— 1842. 16mo.
*600	3	——— 1843. 16mo.
*600	4	——— 1844. 16mo.
*600	5	——— 1844. 16mo.
*666	11	——— Medical Police. 8vo. 1852.
*338	5	——— Ordinances. 8vo. 1850.
171	6	——— Report on the Harbor. 1852. 8vo. 1853.
*271	7	——— Intelligencer. Folio. 1816–17.
*271	6	——— Patriot. 4 vols. folio. 1809–11.
*271	5	——— Weekly Messenger. Folio. 1813–15.
*394	10	——— Library Catalogue. 8vo. 1844.
*83	2	Boswell (J.) Tour to the Hebrides. 12mo. 1810.
538	12	——— Tour to the Hebrides. Post 8vo. 1852.
538	18	——— Life of Dr. Johnson. 4 vols. 12mo. n. d.
62	5	——— Life of Dr. Johnson. 2 vols. 8vo. 1850.
*538	19	——— Life of Dr. Johnson. 4 vols. 12mo. 1851–52.
*38	15	——— Account of Corsica, with Memoir of Paoli. 8vo. 1769.
*633	5	Bosworth (Rev. J.) Anglo-Saxon Dictionary. 8vo. 1849.
7	16	Bosworth (N.) Hochelaga Depicta. 12mo. 1839.
*475	6	Botta (C.) War of American Independence. 2 vols. 8vo. 1847.
14	11	——— War of American Independence. 2 vols. 8vo. 1838.
28	5	——— Histoire des Peuples d'Italie. 3 vols. 16mo. 1825.
*623	9	Bottin (S.) Almanach du Commerce de Paris. 8vo. 1826.
*465	1	Bouchette (J.) Lower Canada. 8vo. 1815.
170	6	Bounty, The Mutiny of. 18mo. 1839.
93	3	Bourgoanne (Chev. de). Travels in Spain. 3 vols. 8vo. 1789.
108	14	Bourne (B. F.) Captive in Patagonia. 12mo. 1853.
508	25	Bourne (J.) Catechism of the Steam Engine. 16mo. 1851.
502	4	——— Treatise on the Steam Engine. 4to. 1851.
72	12	Bourrienne (M. D.) Life of Napoleon. 8vo. 1832.

Shelf.	No	
39	8	Bouterwek (F.) History of Spanish Literature. 12mo. 1847.
508	13	Bowditch (H. I.) Young Stethoscopist. 16mo. 1846.
*594	17	——— Young Stethoscopist. 12mo. 1848.
529	8	Bowdler. Poems and Essays. 12mo. 1827.
181	2	Bowen (F.) Lowell Lectures. 8vo. 1849.
*614	9	Bowman (J. E.) Medical Chemistry. 12mo. 1850.
150	11	Bowring (J.) Matins and Vespers. 16mo. 1827.
155	16	——— Poetry of the Magyars. 12mo. 1830.
166	13	——— Specimens of the Russian Poets. 12mo. 1822.
429	3	——— Ancient Poetry of Spain. 12mo. 1824.
129	2	Boyardo (M. M.) Roland l'Amoureux. 2 vols. 12mo. 1783.
*411	5	Boyer (A.) Dictionary, French and English. 4to. 1759.
*402	11	——— French Dictionary. 4to. 1792.
70	22	Boyhood of Great Men. 16mo. 1853.
86	1	Boyle (J.) Letters from Italy. 12mo. 1773.
80	8	——— Life and Writings of Jonathan Swift. 12mo. 1752.
*332	1	Boyle (R.) Works. 6 vols. 4to. 1772.
96	2	Brace (C. L.) Hungary in 1851. 12mo. 1852.
94	7	——— Home Life in Germany. 12mo. 1853.
118	6	Brackenridge (H. H.) Modern Chivalry. 2 vols. 12mo. 1819.
7	17	Brackenridge (H. M.) History of the War of 1812. 12mo. 1839.
8	20	——— Recollections of Persons and Places in the West. 12mo. n. d.
52	3	Bradford (A.) Life of Mayhew. 8vo. 1838.
18	2	——— History of Massachusetts, 1620–1820. 8vo. 1835.
*463	2	——— History of Massachusetts, 1620–1820. 8vo. 1835.
479	6	——— History of Massachusetts, 1620–1820. 8vo. 1835.
463	4	——— History of Massachusetts, 1764–1820. 3 vols. 8vo. 1822–29.
14	4	Bradford (A. W.) Antiquities of America. 8vo. 1841.
671	9	Bradford (D.) Wonders of the Heavens. 4to. 1837.
165	6	Brainard (J. G. C.) Literary Remains. 12mo. n. d.
*470	9	Brainerd (D.) Mission to the Indians. 8vo. 1746.
*462	7	Brand (J.) on Popular Antiquities. 2 vols. 4to. 1813.
407	7	——— on Popular Antiquities. 3 vols. post 8vo. 1848–49.
*613	1	Brande (W. T.) Dictionary of Science, Literature, and Art. 8vo. 1851.
419	10	Bremer (F.) Diary. H—— Family, &c. Post 8vo. 1853.
122	10	——— Home. 12mo. 1850.
398	3	——— Home. Post 8vo. 1853.
126	7	——— Neighbors. 12mo. 1850.
121	9	——— Neighbors. 2 vols. post 8vo. 1842.
398	2	——— Neighbors. Post 8vo. 1852.
134	2	——— President's Daughters. 3 vols. post 8vo. 1843.
398	4	——— President's Daughters. Post 8vo. 1852.
89	12	Brewster (Sir D.) Natural Magic. 18mo. n. d.
88	18	——— Life of Sir Isaac Newton. 18mo. n. d.

Shelf.	No.	
160	25	BREWSTER (Sir D.) Life of Sir Isaac Newton. 18mo. 1831.
90	10	——— Martyrs of Science. 18mo. 1847.
170	9	——— Natural Magic. 18mo. 1834.
49	4	——— On Optics. 18mo. 1851.
*454	11	BRICKELL (J.) Natural History of North Carolina. 8vo. 1737.
477	18	BRIDGMAN (T.) Epitaphs from Copp's Hill Burial Ground. 12mo. 1851.
*479	10	——— Epitaphs from Copp's Hill Burial Ground. 12mo. 1851.
480	15	——— Epitaphs, Northampton. 12mo. 1850.
*477	17	BRIEF Narrative of the Indian Charity School. 8vo. n. d.
*656	8	BRIGHT (J.) Diseases of the Chest. 12mo. 1850.
109	1	BRISSOT DE WARVILLE (J. P.) Travels in United States. 12mo. 1797.
*104	3	——— Travels in United States. 2 vols. 8vo. 1794.
96	1	BRISTED (C. A.) Five Years in an English University. 12mo. 1852.
*543	1	BRITISH Association Reports, 1831–51. 21 vols. 8vo. 1833–52.
*553	1	——— Association Reports, 1852. 8vo. 1853.
97	10	BROCKEDEN (W.) Excursions in the Alps. 12mo. 1845.
498	29	BROCKLESBY (J.) Elements of Meteorology. 12mo. 1849.
12	15	BRODHEAD (J. R.) History of State of New York. 8vo. 1853.
*604	9	BRODIE (B. C.) Diseases of the Joints. 8vo. 1847.
436	7	BRODIE (G.) History of the British Empire. 4 vols. 8vo. 1822.
166	14	BROOKS (C. T.) German Lyrics. 16mo. 1853.
516	6	——— Songs and Ballads, translated from Uhland and others. 12mo. 1842.
522	8	BROOKS (E.) Answer to J. A. Lowell. 8vo. 1851.
103	16	BROOKS (J. T.) Four Months among the Gold-finders. 8vo. 1849.
137	4	BROTHERS (The). 2 vols. 12mo. 1835.
490	10	BROUGHAM (Lord). Dialogues on Instinct. 18mo. 1844.
508	31	——— Dialogues on Instinct. 18mo. 1845.
487	5	——— Letters and Speeches. 2 vols. 12mo. 1840.
72	13	——— Men of Letters, Time of George III. 8vo. 1845.
199	5	——— On Natural Theology. 12mo. 1835.
199	6	——— On Natural Theology. 12mo. 1835.
176	10	——— Opinions. 2 vols. 12mo. 1839.
510	4	——— Pleasures of Science. 18mo. 1846.
566	1	——— Political Philosophy. 3 vols. 8vo. 1853.
530	10	——— Sketches of Public Characters. 2 vols. 16mo. 1839.
482	2	——— Speeches. 4 vols. 8vo. 1838.
484	1	——— Speeches. 2 vols. 8vo. 1841.
500	8	——— Statesmen, Time of George III. 6 vols. 18mo. 1845.
110	5	——— Uses of Science and Literature. 18mo. n. d.
*654	9	BROUSSAIS (F. G. V.) Physiology. 8vo. 1826.
*654	8	——— Pathology. 8vo. 1832.
*654	7	——— Chronic Phlegmasiæ. 2 vols. 8vo. 1831.

Shelf.	No.	
*623	5	Brown (J.) Dictionary of the Bible. 8vo. 1848.
*623	7	——— Dictionary of the Bible. 2 vols. 8vo. 1811.
*391	7	Brown (J. N.) Encyclopedia of Religious Knowledge. 8vo. 1850.
*448	12	Brown (T.) Complete Works. 8vo. 1710.
508	21	Brown (Capt. T.) Conchologist's Text Book. 16mo. 1836.
498	3	Browne (D. J.) American Bird Fancier. 12mo. 1850.
498	2	——— American Bird Fancier. 12mo. n. d.
497	8	——— American Poultry-yard. 12mo. 1850.
492	14	——— Trees of America. 8vo. 1851.
485	11	Browne (R. W.) History of Classical Literature. 8vo. 1852.
407	8	Browne (T.) Works. 3 vols. 8vo. 1852.
*394	3	Brown University Library, Catalogue of. 8vo. 1843.
165	9	Browning (E. B.) Poems. 2 vols. 16mo. 1850.
164	3	Browning (R.) Poems. 2 vols. 16mo. 1850.
177	1	Brownson (O. A.) Essays and Reviews. 12mo. 1852.
*436	8	Bruce (J.) Travels, 1768–73. 7 vols. 8vo. 1804.
*432	4	——— Travels, Atlas to. 4to. 1813.
158	6	Bruce (M.) Poems. 16mo. 1782.
97	16	Bruen (M.) Essays on Scenes in Italy, Switzerland, and France. 12mo. 1823.
135	21	Brunton (M.) Discipline. 16mo. 1849.
*393	3	Bryan (M.) Dictionary of Painters and Engravers. 8vo. 1853.
108	18	Bryant (W. C.) Letters of a Traveller. 12mo. 1850.
155	12	——— Poems. 12mo. 1851.
98	20	——— Selections from American Poets. 18mo. n. d.
*566	2	Brydges (E.) Restituta; Titles, &c., of Old Books Revived. 4 vols. 8vo. 1814–16.
86	8	Brydone (P.) Sicily and Malta. 12mo. 1813.
*447	2	——— Sicily and Malta. 2 vols. 8vo. 1775.
13	1	Buccaneers of America. 8vo. 1853.
*432	3	Buchanan (F.) Journey from Madras to Mysore, &c. 3 vols. 4to. 1807.
69	4	Bucke (C.) Life of Akenside. 16mo. 1832.
89	1	——— Beauties of Nature. 18mo. 1846.
170	12	——— Ruins of Ancient Cities. 2 vols. 18mo. 1840.
90	13	——— Ruins of Ancient Cities. 2 vols. 18mo. 1848.
170	14	——— Life of John, Duke of Marlborough. 18mo. 1839.
*584	14	Budd (G.) On the Liver. 8vo. 1853.
104	12	Buckingham (J. S.) America, Historical, Statistic, and Descriptive. 2 vols. 8vo. 1841.
6	15	Buckingham (J. T.) Annals of the Massachusetts Charitable Mechanic Association. 8vo. 1853.
520	15	——— Miscellanies. 12mo. 1822.
*271	9	——— New England Galaxy. Folio. 1817–18.
305	2	——— New England Magazine. 1831 to 1834. 7 vols. 8vo.

Shelf.	No.	
67	21	Buckingham (J. T.) Personal Memoirs and Recollections. 2 vols. 16mo. 1852.
520	5	——— Specimens of Newspaper Literature. 2 vols. 12mo. 1852.
178	17	Buckminster (J. S.) Works, with Memoir. 2 vols. 12mo. 1839.
*469	3	——— Phi Beta Kappa Discourse. 8vo. 1809.
509	8	Buel (J.) Farmers' Instructor. 2 vols. 18mo. 1847.
498	20	——— Farmers' Companion. 12mo. 1847.
104	8	Buenos Ayres and Chili. Letters from. 8vo. 1819.
495	3	Buffon. Œuvres Complètes. Vols. 1–19. 8vo. 1819–21.
496	1	——— Œuvres Complètes. Vols. 20–25. 8vo. 1821–22.
107	23	Buffum (E. G.) Six Months in the Gold Mines. 12mo. 1850.
498	26	Buist (R.) Kitchen Gardener. 12mo. 1850.
		Bulletin de la Société d'Encouragement pour l'Industrie Nationale. 44 vols. 4to. 1844.
*661	6	——— 1802–20.
*671	16	——— 1821–33.
*681	16	——— 1834–44 and 1848.
*681	17	——— Table Analytique et Raisonnée de 1802–37 compris.
*596	3	——— de la Société pour l'Instruction Élémentaire. 5 vols. 8vo. 1837–41.
498	23	Bullock (J.) History and Rudiments of Architecture. 12mo. 1853.
81	3	Bullock (W.) Six Months in Mexico. 8vo. 1824.
39	9	Bulwer (E. L.) Athens; its Rise and Fall. 2 vols. 12mo. 1852.
126	12	——— Disowned. 4 vols. post 8vo. 1829.
520	10	——— England and the English. 2 vols. 12mo. 1833.
135	11	——— Eugene Aram. 2 vols. 12mo. 1832.
167	17	——— Lady of Lyons. 16mo. 1838.
118	9	——— Pelham. 2 vols. 16mo. 1835.
122	14	Bungener (L.) Preacher and King. 12mo. 1853.
29	10	——— Priest and Huguenot. 2 vols. 12mo. 1854.
*475	3	Bunker Hill Monument, view from. 8vo. 1848.
81	4	Bunn (A.) Old and New England. 12mo. 1853.
110	2	Bunner (E.) History of Louisiana. 18mo. n. d.
188	4	Bunyan (J.) Pilgrim's Progress, with Life. 12mo. 1847.
188	24	——— Pilgrim's Progress, Scott's Notes. 18mo. 1840.
188	23	——— Pilgrim's Progress, Scott's Notes. 18mo. 1841.
538	14	——— Pilgrim's Progress. Post 8vo. 1853.
192	1	——— Works of. 8vo. 1853.
*449	3	Burgess (R.) Circus on the Via Appia. 12mo. 1828.
443	9	Burgon (J. W.) Life of Sir Thomas Gresham. 2 vols. 8vo.
*475	13	Burke (E.) European Settlements in America. 2 vols. 8vo. 1760.
486	12	——— On the Sublime and Beautiful. 12mo. 1846.

Shelf.	No.	
487	12	BURKE (E.) On the Sublime and Beautiful. 12mo. 1806.
*173	14	——— Reflections on the Revolution in France. 8vo. 1791.
*469	4	——— Speech on American Taxation, April 19, 1774. 8vo. 1775.
488	2	——— Works and Correspondence. 8 vols. 8vo. 1852.

Vol. 1. Correspondence, 1744–91.
2. Correspondence, 1791–97; Vindication of Natural Society; on the Sublime and Beautiful.
3. Short Account of a Late Short Administration; Observations on the Present State of the Nation; Thoughts on the Cause of the Present Discontents; Speech on American Taxation; Speeches at Bristol, 1774; Speech on Conciliation with the Colonies; Letter on American Affairs; Two Letters on Trade of Ireland; Speech on the Independence of Parliament; Speeches at Bristol, 1780; Speech on Fox's East India Bill; Representation to his Majesty.
4. Speech on the Nabob of Arcot's Debts; Speech on the Army Estimates; Reflections on the French Revolution; Letter to a Member of the National Assembly; Appeal from the New to the Old Whigs; Letters on the Penal Laws against Irish Catholics; Hints for a Memorial to Monsieur de M. M.; Thoughts on French Affairs.
5. Considerations on the Present State of Affairs; on the Policy of the Allies; on the Conduct of the Minority; Preface to M. Brissot's Address; Letter to W. E. Elliot, Esq.; Thoughts on Scarcity; Letter to a Noble Lord; Four Letters on Peace; a Regicide; Letter to the Empress of Russia; Letter to Sir C. Bingham; Letter to C. J. Fox; Letter to Marquis of Rockingham; Address to the King; Address to the British Colonists in North America; Letters to Pery, Burgh, and Merlott; Letters, with Reflections, on the Execution of the Rioters in 1780; Letter to Dundas, with the Sketch of a Negro Code; Letter on the Duration of Parliaments.
6. On the Laws against Popery in Ireland; Letters to W. Smith; Langrishe; R. Burke; on the Affairs of Ireland; Fragments and Notes of Speeches; Hints for an Essay on the Drama; Essay towards an Abridgment of the English History; Ninth and Eleventh Reports from the Committee of the House of Commons, on the Affairs of the East India Company; Articles of Charge against Warren Hastings.
7. Articles (continued); Speeches on the Impeachment of Warren Hastings.
8. Speeches on Impeachment (continued); Report from Committee relating to Warren Hastings' Trial; General Index.

Shelf.	No.	
*393	1	BURKE (J. & J. B.) Royal Families of Great Britain. 2 vols. 8vo. 1848.
*393	5	BURKE (J. B.) Peerage and Baronetage of Great Britain. 8vo. 1853.
78	4	BURKE (J. W.) Life of Emmett. 12mo. 1852.
173	15	BURLAMAQUI (J. J.) Principles of Natural and Political Law. 2 vols. 8vo. 1807.
*395	2	BURMEISTER (H.) Manual of Entomology. 8vo. 1836.
*433	11	BURN (J. H.) Catalogue of London Traders, &c. 8vo. 1853.
*462	9	BURNABY (A.) Travels through North America. 4to. 1775.
*435	10	BURNES (A.) Travels in Bokhara. 3 vols. 8vo. 1834.
195	3	BURNET (G.) Exposition of the 39 Articles. 8vo. 1852.
*252	3	——— History of Reformation. 3 vols. folio. 1681, 1753.
13	6	BURNET (J.) Notes on North-west Territory. 8vo. 1847.

Shelf.	No.	
503	3	Burnett (G. T.) Outlines of Botany. 8vo. 1835.
524	10	Burney (C.) Life of Metastasio. 3 vols. 8vo. 1796.
*402	7	——— History of Music. 4 vols. 4to. 1789.
103	1	Burney (J.) North-eastern Voyages of Discovery. 8vo. 1819.
*462	1	——— Chronological History of Voyages in South Seas. 2 vols. 4to. 1803.
58	9	Burns (J.) Mothers of the Wise and Good. 12mo. 1850.
148	12	Burns (R.) Poetical Works. Aldine Poets. 3 vols. 16mo. 1839.
*426	4	——— Works and Life, by Dr. J. Currie. 5 vols. 8vo. 1820.
162	6	——— Works and Life, by Cunningham. 8vo. 1845.
165	10	——— Works and Life, by R. Chambers. 4 vols. 12mo. 1852.
153	11	——— Poetical Works. 8vo. 1826.
54	9	Burr (A.) Private Journal. 2 vols. 8vo. 1838.
*428	5	Burrell (Lady). Poems. 2 vols. 8vo. 1793.
524	3	Burton (R.) Anatomy of Melancholy. 8vo. 1840.
512	10	——— Anatomy of Melancholy. 8vo. 1853.
*458	2	Burton (T.) Diary of Parliament. 4 vols. 8vo. 1828.
187	3	Burton (W.) District School as it Was. 12mo. 1852.
490	18	Bury (B.) Racine and the French Classical Drama. 18mo. 1845.
74	11	Bush (Mrs. F.) The Queens of France. 2 vols. 12mo. 1851.
88	7	Bush (G.) Life of Mohammed. 18mo. 1847.
*656	10	Bushe (G.) On the Rectum. 8vo. 1837.
*671	10	——— On the Rectum. Plates. 4to. 1837.
*449	9	Bushnan (J. S.) On Fishes, with Memoir of Salviani. 16mo. 1840.
62	10	Butler (A.) Fathers and Martyrs. 4 vols. 8vo. 1844–45.
*477	5	Butler (C.) History of Groton, Pepperell, Shirley. 8vo. 1848.
530	1	Butler (C.) Reminiscences. 12mo. 1825.
108	8	Butler (F. K.) Journal. 2 vols. 12mo. 1835.
85	18	——— Year of Consolation. 12mo. 1847.
189	1	Butler (J.) Analogy of Religion. 12mo. 1822.
399	9	——— Analogy of Religion. Post 8vo. 1852.
196	10	——— Works. 2 vols. 8vo. 1804.
		Vol. 1. Life, by Kippis; Preface, by Halifax; Analogy. 2. On Personal Identity; Charge to the Clergy of Durham; Sermons; Correspondence.
154	3	Butler (S.) Hudibras. 3 vols. 8vo. 1819.
149	6	——— Works. 2 vols. 16mo. 1835.
78	1	Buxton (Sir T. F.) Memoirs. 12mo. 1850.
539	12	——— Memoirs. 16mo. 1849.
58	11	Byron (Lord). Life and Letters, by Moore. Index at the end of vol. 6. 6 vols. 8vo. 1851.

Shelf.	No.	
162	9	Byron (Lord). Poetical Works. 8vo. 1851.
168	8	——— Poetical Works. 10 vols. 16mo. 1851.

Vol. 1. Hours of Idleness; Occasional Pieces; English Bards and Scotch Reviewers.
2. Childe Harold.
3. Occasional Pieces; Hints from Horace; Curse of Minerva; the Waltz; the Giaour; the Bride of Abydos; the Corsair; Appendix; Remarks on Romaic Language.
4. Ode to Napoleon; Lara; Hebrew Melodies; Siege of Corinth; Domestic Pieces, 1816; Monody on the Death of Sheridan; Prisoner of Chillon; the Dream; Occasional Pieces, 1814–16.
5. Manfred; Lament of Tasso; Beppo; Mazeppa; Ode on Venice; Morgante Maggiore of Pulci, Canto 1; Prophecy of Dante; Occasional Pieces.
6. Francesca of Rimini; Stanzas to the Po; Stanzas; the Blues; Marino Faliero; Vision of Judgment; Occasional Pieces.
7. Heaven and Earth; Sardanapalus; Two Foscari; the Deformed Transformed.
8. Cain; Werner; Age of Bronze; The Island; Stanzas; Lines on Thirty-sixth Birthday.
9. Don Juan, Cantos 1–6.
10. Don Juan, Cantos 7–16; Index.

C.

515	3	Cabinet of Curiosities. 8vo. n. d.
79	3	——— British, in 1853. 16mo. 1853.
73	12	Cabot (Sebastian), Memoir of. 8vo. 1832.
120	4	Cæsar (C. J.) Commentaries. 2 vols. 18mo. 1852.
409	4	——— Commentaries. Post 8vo. 1851.
*435	9	Caillié (R.) Travels to Timbuctoo. 2 vols. 8vo. 1830.
*469	29	Calamy (E.) Ejected Ministers. 2 vols. 8vo. 1727.
62	1	Caldwell (C.) Genius and Character of Rev. H. Holley. 8vo. 1828.
73	11	——— Genius and Character of Rev. H. Holley. 8vo. 1828.
62	4	Calhoun (J. C.) Life and Select Speeches. 8vo. 1843.
488	1	——— Works of. 4 vols. 8vo. 1853–54.

Vol. 1. Disquisition on Government; on the Constitution and Government of the United States.
2. Speeches.
3. Speeches.
4. Speeches.

*463	5	Callender (J.) History of Rhode Island. 8vo. 1843.
29	9	Callery & Yvan. Insurrection in China. 12mo. 1853.
*411	2	Calmet (A.) Dictionary of the Bible. 4 vols. 4to. 1800–3.

Vol. 1. A—J.
2. K—Z.
3, 4. Fragments.

187	2	——— Phantom World. 12mo. 1850.
85	8	Calvert (G. H.) Scenes in Europe. 12mo. 1852.
85	21	——— Scenes in Europe. Second Series. 12mo. 1852.

Shelf.	No.	
194	11	CALVIN (J.) Institutes. 2 vols. 8vo. 1838.
90	15	CAMP (G. S.) Democracy. 18mo. 1845.
74	12	CAMPAN (Mad.) Marie Antoinette. 2 vols. 12mo. 1851.
193	6	CAMPBELL (G.) On Theology and Pulpit Eloquence. 8vo. 1810.
197	3	—— Translation of the Four Gospels. 4 vols. 8vo. 1811.
65	3	CAMPBELL (J. Lord). Chief Justices of England. 2 vols. 8vo. 1851.
		Vol. 1. From Norman Conquest to the Resignation of Sir M. Hale. 2. From the Resignation of Sir M. Hale to the Death of Lord Mansfield.
64	3	—— Lord Chancellors of England. 7 vols. 8vo. 1851.
		Vol. 1. 605—1547. 2. 1547—1645. 3. 1646—1685. 4. 1687—1733. Vol. 5. 1737—1793. 6. 1793—1801. 7. 1801—1820.
68	1	CAMPBELL (T.) Life and Letters. 2 vols. 12mo. 1850.
68	2	—— Life and Letters. 2 vols. 12mo. 1850.
*446	4	—— Life and Letters. 2 vols. 12mo. 1850.
55	4	—— Life and Times of Petrarch. 2 vols. 8vo. 1843.
150	10	—— Works. 16mo. 1821.
167	22	—— Works. Sargent's Edition. 12mo. 1854.
*427	4	—— Specimens of the British Poets. 7 vols. 8vo. 1819.
152	1	—— Specimens of the British Poets. 8vo. 1853.
156	7	—— Complete Works. 16mo. 1852.
95	2	—— Letters from the South. 12mo. 1836.
539	11	—— Essay on English Poetry, and Notices of English Poets. 16mo. 1848.
169	8	—— Essay on English Poetry. 18mo. 1819.
69	5	CAMPBELL (W. W.) Robin Hood and Captain Kidd. 12mo. 1853.
76	14	—— Life of De Witt Clinton. 12mo. 1849.
8	2	—— Border Warfare of New York. 12mo. 1849.
*404	1	CANADA. Tables of Trade and Navigation of Canada, 1850. 8vo. 1851.
44	4	CANCELLIERI (F.) Dissertazioni sopra Christoforo Colombo. 8vo. 1809.
483	8	CANNING (G.) Speeches and Memoirs. 8vo. 1850.
*479	9	CAPE COD Centennial Celebration at Barnstable. 8vo. 1840.
65	13	CAPPE (C.) Life. 8vo. 1824.
184	14	CAPPE (N.) Discourses. 8vo. 1818.
505	10	CAREY (G. G.) Astronomy. 8vo. n. d.
175	14	CAREY (H. C.) Slave Trade. 12mo. 1853.
176	12	—— Slave Trade. 12mo. 1853.
175	1	—— Past, Present, and Future. 8vo. 1848.
173	9	CAREY (M.) New Olive Branch. 8vo. 1820.
175	3	—— Political Economy. 8vo. 1822.
121	16	CARLEN (E.) Rose of Tistelön. 2 vols. 8vo. 1844.

Shelf.	No.	
63	17	CARLETON (Capt. G.) Memoirs of, with Anecdotes of the War in Spain. 8vo. 1808.
8	26	CARLETON (J. H.) Battle of Buena Vista. 16mo. 1848.
*402	4	CARLISLE (A.) Hunterian Oration. 4to. 1820.
37	12	CARLYLE (T.) History of French Revolution. 2 vols. 12mo. 1838.
37	6	——— History of French Revolution. 2 vols. 16mo. 1847.
529	5	——— Latter-day Pamphlets. 12mo. 1850.
139	4	——— Sartor Resartus, and Past and Present. 12mo. 1844.
517	9	——— Sartor Resartus. 12mo. 1846.
69	14	——— Life of Schiller. 12mo. 1846.
66	13	——— Life of John Stirling. 12mo. 1852.
539	10	CARNARVON (Earl). Portugal and Galicia. 16mo. 1848.
*437	5	CARNE (J.) Travels in the East. 8vo. 1830.
97	7	CARNES (J. A.) Voyage to West Coast of Africa. 12mo. 1852.
*646	1	CARNOCHAN (J. M.) Congenital Dislocations. 8vo. 1850.
506	11	CARPENTER (W. B.) On Alcoholic Liquors. 12mo. 1851.
*574	10	——— Principles of Human Physiology. 8vo. 1853.
8	24	CARPENTER (W. H.) History of Massachusetts. 12mo. 1853.
10	9	——— History of Vermont. 12mo. 1853.
106	6	CARPENTER (W. W.) Travels in Mexico. 12mo. 1851.
*469	22	CARRANZA (D. G.) Coasts, Harbors, and Seaports of Spanish West Indies. 8vo. 1740.
47	9	CARREL (A.) Counter Revolution in England. 12mo. 1846.
*443	8	CARTWRIGHT (J.) Life and Correspondence. 2 vols. 8vo. 1826.
*86	2	CARVER (J.) Travels in North America. 12mo. 1813.
*430	5	CASCALES (F. de). Cartas Philologicas. 8vo. 1779.
93	10	CARUS (C. G.) King of Saxony's Journey. 8vo. 1846.
68	4	CARY (H.) Memoirs of Rev. H. F. Cary. 2 vols. 8vo. 1847.
55	7	CARY (R.), Memoirs of. 8vo. 1808.
188	5	CARY (S.) Review of "Grounds of Christianity." 12mo. 1813.
186	4	CASS (L.) France: its King and Government. 8vo. 1848.
77	12	CATLANE (Miss), Life of. 12mo. 1788.
*463	1	CATLIN (G.) North American Indians. 2 vols. 8vo. 1848.
*211	8	CATS (J.) Alle de Werken so ouden, als nieuven. Folio. 1658.
487	23	CATULLUS (C. V.) Catulli, &c. Opera. 18mo. 1749.
*484	2	CAVENDISH (Sir H.) Debates on the Quebec Bill, 1774. 8vo. 1839.
*432	13	CAWTHORN (J.) Poems. 4to. 1771.
138	10	CAYLUS (Madame de). Souvenirs. 12mo. 1823.
*656	11	CAZENAVE (P. L. A.) Traité des Syphilides. 8vo. 1843.
211	7	——— Traité des Syphilides Atlas. Folio. 1843.

Shelf.	No.	
177	13	CECIL (R.) Works. 3 vols. 12mo. 1850.
		Vol. 1. Sermons. 2. Remains; Miscellanies. 3. Original Thoughts on Scripture.
400	10	CELLINI (B.) Memoirs of Himself. Post 8vo. 1850.
75	18	——— Memoirs of Himself. 2 vols. 16mo. 1845.
*432	1	CEPHALOPODA. Monograph of the Eocene Mollusca. 4to. 1849.
140	14	CERVANTES SAAVEDRA (M. de). Don Quixote. 4 vols. 18mo. n. d.
495	1	CHABERT, FLANDRIN, &c. Instructions et Observations sur les Maladies des Animaux Domestiques. 6 vols. 8vo. 1806–13.
63	14	CHABOULON (M. F. de). Napoleon. 2 vols. 8vo. 1820.
		CHALMERS (A.) Biographical Dictionary. 32 vols. 8vo. 1812–17.
*563	4	Vol. 1. Aa—All. 2. All—Arn. 3. Arn—Bar. 4. Bar—Ben. 5. Ben—Boh. 6. Boh—Bri. 7. Bri—Bzo. 8. Caa—Cay. 9. Ceb—Cok. 10. Cok—Cre. 11. Cri—Des. 12. Des—Dye. 13. Eac—Eze. 14. Fab—Fou. 15. Fou—Gio. 16. Gio—Gyl. 17. Haa—Hoa.
*573	1	Vol. 18. Hoa—Jen. 19. Jep—Lan. 20. Lan—Lut. 21. Lux—Med. 22. Med—Mye. 23. Næv—Oze. 24. Pas—Pit. 25. Pit—Ral. 26. Ram—Rym. 27. Saa—Sil. 28. Sim—Stu. 29. Sua—Toz. 30. Tra—Wal. 31. Wal—Whi. 32. Whi—Zui.
		——— English Poets. 21 vols. 8vo. 1810.
*423	1	Vols. 1–17.
*424	1	„ 18–21.

Vol. 1. Chaucer.
2. Gower, Skelton, Surrey, Wyat, Gascoigne, Tubervile.
3. Spenser, Daniel.
4. Drayton, Warner.
5. Shakspeare, Davies, Donne, Hall, Stirling, Jonson, Corbet, Carew, Drummond.
6. Sir J. Beaumont & G. & P. Fletcher, F. Beaumont, Browne, Davenant, Habington, Suckling, Cartwright, Crashaw, Sherburne, Brome, C. Cotton.
7. Cowley, Denham, Milton.
8. Waller, Butler, Rochester, Roscommon, Otway, Pomfret, Dorset, Stepney, J. Philips, Walsh, Dryden.
9. Dryden, Smith, Duke, King, Sprat, Halifax, Parnell, Garth, Rowe, Addison.
10. Hughes, Sheffield, Prior, Congreve, Blackmore, Fenton, Gay.
11. Lansdowne, Yalden, Tickell, Hammond, Somervile, Savage, Swift.
12. Broome, Pope, Pitt, Thomson.
13. Watts, A. Philips, West, Collins, Dyer, Shenstone, Young.
14. Mallet, Akenside, Gray, Lyttelton, Moore, Cawthorne, Churchill, Falconer, Cunningham, Grainger, Boyse.
15. W. Thompson, Blair, Lloyd, Green, Byrom, Dodsley, Chatterton, Cooper, Smollett, Hamilton.

Shelf.	No.	
		CHALMERS (A.) English Poets, *continued.*
		16. Smart, Wilkie, P. Whitehead, Fawkes, Lovibond, Harte, Langhorne, Goldsmith, Armstrong, Johnson.
		17. Glover, W. Whitehead, Jago, Brooke, J. Scott, Mickle, Jenyns.
		18. Dr. Cotton, Logan, T. Warton, J. Warton, Blacklock, Cambridge, Mason, Jones, Beattie, Cowper.
		19. Translations: Pope's Homer, Dryden's Virgil and Juvenal, Pitt's Virgil's Æneid, and Vida's Art of Poetry, Francis's Horace.
		20. Rowe's Lucan, Grainger's Tibullus, Fawkes's Theocritus, Apollonius Rhodius, Coluthus, Anacreon, Sappho, Bion, Moschus, and Musæus, Garth's Ovid, Lewis's Statius, Cooke's Hesiod.
		21. Hoole's Ariosto and Tasso, Mickle's Lusiad.
*475	4	CHALMERS (G.) Revolt of the American Colonies. 2 vols. 8vo. 1845.
*472	14	——— Annals of the American Colonies. 4to. 1780.
178	7	CHALMERS (T.) Astronomical Discourses. 8vo. 1818.
184	17	——— Astronomical Discourses. 8vo. 1818.
418	8	——— Bridgewater Treatise. 8vo. 1853.
188	11	——— Commercial Discourses. 12mo. 1821.
176	6	——— Political Economy. 12mo. 1833.
197	5	——— Posthumous Works. 9 vols. 12mo. 1848–51.
		Vol. 1, 2, 3. Daily Scripture Readings.
		4, 5. Sabbath Scripture Readings.
		6. Sermons.
		7, 8. Institutes of Theology.
		9. Prelections on Butler's Analogy and Paley's Evidences.
179	19	——— Selection from Correspondence. 12mo. 1853.
487	11	CHAMBAUD (L.) French Exercises. 12mo. 1801.
391	4	——— Cyclopædia of English Literature. 2 vols. 8vo. 1851.
		Vol. 1. Earliest Times to 1727.
		2. 1727 to Present Time [1843].
*603	1	——— Cyclopædia of English Literature. 2 vols. 8vo. 1844.
527	2	CHAMBERS (R.) Papers for the People. 6 vols. 12mo. 1850–51.
518	10	——— Papers for the People. 12 vols. 12mo. 1850–51.
537	3	——— Pocket Miscellany. 6 vols. 18mo. 1852–53.
519	3	——— Select Writings. 4 vols. 12mo. 1847.
		Vol. 1, 2. Essays Familiar and Humorous.
		3. Essays Moral and Economic.
		4. Essays Philosophical, Sentimental; Historical Sketches.
340	4	CHAMBERS (T.) & TATTERSALL (G.) Laws relating to Buildings. 12mo. 1845.
537	1	CHAMBERS (W.) Miscellany. 10 vols. 16mo. n. d.
537	2	——— Miscellany. 10 vols. 16mo. n. d.
512	4	CHAMBERS (W. & R.) Information for the People. 2 vols. 8vo. 1851.
138	1	CHAMIER (Capt.) Life of a Sailor. 2 vols. 12mo. 1833.

Shelf.	No.	
*344	12	CHANCERY Jurisdiction in Massachusetts. 8vo. n. d.
470	13	CHANDLER (P. W.) American Criminal Trials. 2 vols. 12mo. 1841–44.
*442	6	CHANDLER (R.) Life of Waynflete. 8vo. 1811.
*435	8	——— Travels in Asia, &c. 8vo. 1825.
177	15	CHANNING (W. E.) Discourses. 12mo. 1832.
198	4	——— Works. 6 vols. 12mo. 1849.
197	4	——— Works. 6 vols. 12mo. 1843.

Vol. 1. Remarks on Milton; Napoleon; Fenelon; Argument against Calvinism; Remarks on National Literature; on Associations; the Union; Remarks on Education.
2. Slavery; Abolitionists; Annexation of Texas to the United States; on Catholicism; Creeds; Temperance; Self-Culture.
3. Discourses; Duties of Children; Honor Due to All Men; Evidences of Christianity.
4. Character of Christ; Christianity; Spiritual Freedom; Self-Denial; Imitableness of Christ's Character; Evil of Sin; Immortality; Love to Christ; Future Life; War; Discourses.
5. On the Slavery Question; on War; Elevation of the Laboring Portion of Community; on the Death of Dr. Follen; Charges; Miscellanies; Appendix.
6. Emancipation; Life of Rev. J. Tuckerman; Present Age; the Church; Duty of the Free States; Address at Lenox, 1842.

Shelf.	No.	
69	1	CHANNING (W. H.) Memoir of W. E. Channing. 3 vols. 12mo. 1851.
160	16	CHARLES I., and some of the Regicides, Trials of. 18mo. 1838.
*670	3	CHARLESTON, S. C. Census for 1848. 8vo. 1849.
448	9	CHARRON (S. de). Of Wisdom. 2 vols. 8vo. 1707.
110	15	CHASLES (P.) Notabilities in France and England. 12mo. 1853.
527	1	——— Anglo-American Literature. 12mo. 1852.
106	7	CHASTELLUX (M. de). Travels in North America. 2 vols. 8vo. 1787.
169	9	CHATEAUBRIAND (F. A. de). Portrait of Bonaparte. 18mo. 1814.
83	8	——— Travels in Greece, Palestine, &c. 8vo. 1814.
69	6	CHATTERTON (T.) Works, with Life. 2 vols. 12mo. 1842.
*428	1	——— Works, with Life. 3 vols. 8vo. 1803.
164	5	CHAUCER (G.) Select Poetical Works. 12mo. 1847.
147	4	——— Poetical Works, with Memoir. 6 vols. 16mo. 1845.
*196	14	CHAUNCY (C.) On Episcopacy. 8vo. 1771.
184	2	CHEEVER (G. B.) On Pilgrim's Progress. 8vo. 1844.
96	16	——— Wanderings of a Pilgrim. 16mo. 1848.
85	11	CHEEVER (H. T.) Sandwich Islands. 12mo. 1851.
109	5	——— Whale and his Captors. 12mo. 1850.
106	8	——— Islands of the Pacific. 12mo. 1851.
*554	8	CHELIUS (J. M.) System of Surgery. 3 vols. 8vo. 1847.
503	18	CHEMISTRY and Mineralogy. 8vo. 1810–43.
*448	7	CHESELDEN (W.) Anatomy. 8vo. 1726.

Shelf.	No.	
508	28	CHESS, Stratagems of. 18mo. 1817.
512	12	CHESTERFIELD (Earl). Works. 8vo. 1853.
*447	3	——— Letters to his Son. 4 vols. 8vo. 1774.
530	23	——— Letters to his Son. 3 vols. 18mo. 1813.
102	8	CHEVALIER (M.) Society, &c., in United States. 8vo. 1839.
123	15	CHILD (L. M.) Fact and Fiction. 12mo. 1849.
140	9	——— Flowers for Children. 16mo. 1852.
78	3	——— Good Wives. 12mo. 1850.
80	4	——— Isaac T. Hopper. 12mo. 1853.
519	21	——— Letters from New York. 12mo. 1852.
519	22	——— Letters from New York. Second Series. 12mo. 1852.
528	13	——— Mother's Book. 12mo. 1849.
180	24	——— Oasis. 16mo. 1834.
125	5	——— Philothea. 12mo. 1836.
417	3	CHINA, Pictorial and Historical. Post 8vo. 1853.
440	2	CHIPMAN (D.) Memoir of Colonel S. Warner. 16mo. 1848.
78	18	CHIVALRY and Charity. Du Guesclin and Howard. 18mo. 1840.
70	3	CHORLEY (H. F.) Memorials of Mrs. Hemans. 2 vols. 12mo. 1836.
*306	1	CHRISTIAN Disciple. 1813–18. 3 vols. 8vo. 1813–18.
*306	2	——— New Series. 5 vols. 8vo. 1819–23.
*306	3	CHRISTIAN Examiner. Vols. 1–15. 8vo. 1824–34.
*307	2	——— Vol. 16. 8vo. 1834.
*574	1	CHRISTISON (R.) & Griffith's Dispensatory. 8vo. 1848.
*574	4	——— On Poisons. 8vo. 1845.
*626	5	——— On the Kidneys. 8vo. 1841.
*328	1	CHRONICLE, Monthly. 3 vols. 8vo. 1840–42.
407	9	CHRONICLES of the Crusades. Post 8vo. 1848.
*271	12	CHRONOLOGICAL Tables of Ancient History. Folio. 1835.
148	4	CHURCHILL (C.) Poetical Works. 3 vols. 16mo. 1844.
*426	2	——— Poems. 2 vols. 8vo. 1769.
*594	8	CHURCHILL (F.) Diseases of Women. 8vo. 1852.
41	13	CHURCHILL (J.) Duke of Marlborough, Letters and Dispatches. 5 vols. 8vo. 1845.
158	15	CIBBER (C.) Dramatic Works. 4 vols. 12mo. 1760. Vol. 1. Love's Last Shift; Woman's Wit; Love Makes a Man; She Would and She Would Not. 2. Careless Husband; Rival Fools; Lady's Last Stake; Richard III. 3. Double Gallant; Ximena; Comical Lovers; Non-Juror. 4. Refusal; Provoked Husband; Love in a Riddle; Papal Tyranny.
409	5	CICERO (M. T.) Academic Questions, De Finibus, &c. by Yonge. Post 8vo. 1853.
52	15	——— Life and Letters, by Middleton. 8vo. 1848.
409	7	——— Offices, Old Age, Friendship, by Edmonds. Post 8vo. 1853.

Shelf.	No.	
119	17	CICERO (M. T.) On the Orator, by Guthrie. 18mo. n. d.
485	14	——— Orationes Selectæ. 8vo. 1770.
120	5	——— Orations, Offices, Cato, and Lælius. 3 vols. 18mo. 1852. Vol. 1, 2. Orations by Duncan. 3. Offices, by Cockman; Cato and Lælius, by Melmoth.
409	6	——— Orations, translated by Yonge. 4 vols. post 8vo. 1851–52.
487	4	——— Tusculan Questions, translated by G. A. Otis. 12mo. 1839.
*338	6	CINCINNATI. Charter, Amendments, &c. 8vo. 1850.
136	7	CLAN-ALBIN. 4 vols. 12mo. 1815.
10	8	CLAPP (W. W.) Record of the Boston Stage. 12mo. 1853.
83	14	CLAPPERTON (H.) Second Expedition to Africa. 8vo. 1829.
445	8	CLARENDON (E.) Earl of. Life. 3 vols. 8vo. 1759.
*221	3	——— State Papers. 3 vols. folio. 1767–73.
179	18	CLARK (D. W.) Methodist Episcopal Church. 12mo. 1850.
*594	14	CLARK (J.) On Climate. 8vo. 1841.
67	6	CLARKE (A.) Memoirs of the Wesley Family. 12mo. 1851.
*391	2	CLARKE (B.) British Gazetteer. 3 vols. 8vo. 1852.
81	2	CLARKE (E. D.) Travels in Europe, Asia, and Africa. 11 vols. 8vo. 1816.
104	7	——— Travels in Europe, Asia, and Africa. 8vo. 1813.
171	27	CLARKE (J.) Letters to a Student. 18mo. 1796.
200	15	——— Discourses to Young Persons. 12mo. 1804.
*393	2	CLARKE (M. C.) Concordance to Shakspeare. 8vo. 1852.
165	7	CLARKE (S. J.) Grace Greenwood's Poems. 12mo. 1851.
550	2	CLARKE (W.) Pompeii. 2 vols. 12mo. n. d.
25	1	CLARKSON (T.) Abolition of the Slave Trade. 3 vols. 12mo. 1836.
77	11	——— Life of Penn. 2 vols. 12mo. 1813.
180	20	——— On Slavery. 12mo. 1804.
55	3	——— On the Life of Wilberforce. 8vo. 1838.
198	3	——— Portraiture of Quakerism. 3 vols. 8vo. 1806.
6	4	CLAVIGERO (F. S.) History of Mexico. 3 vols. 8vo. 1817.
*18	8	——— History of Mexico. 3 vols. 8vo. 1817.
172	9	CLAY (C. M.) Writings. 8vo. 1848.
486	6	CLEVELAND (C. D.) Compendium of English Literature. 12mo. 1851.
487	2	——— English Literature of 19th Century. 12mo. 1851.
97	9	CLEVELAND (R. J.) Voyages. 12mo. 1850.
*462	10	CLINTON (H. F.) Fasti Hellenici. 4to. 1830.
*514	10	CLUB-ROOM. Nos. 1–4. 8vo. 1820.
507	29	CLUTTON (J.) Ward's Pill and Drops. 12mo. 1736.
*428	10	COBB (S.) Poems. 12mo. 1707.
437	2	COBBETT (W.) Porcupine's Works. 12 vols. 8vo. 1801. See vol. 1, for General Contents. See vol. 12, for General Index.

Shelf.	No.	
110	12	Cobbett (W.) Year in the United States. 12mo. 1818.
92	4	Cochrane (J. D.) Pedestrian Tour through Russia, &c. 8vo. 1824.
65	8	Cockburn (Lord). Life of Lord Jeffrey. 2 vols. 8vo. 1852.
77	7	Cockburn (Sir G.) Buonaparte's Voyage to St. Helena. 12mo. 1833.
*477	2	Coffin (J.) History of Newbury. 8vo. 1845.
29	4	Coke (T.) History of the West Indies. 3 vols. 8vo. 1808–11.
*614	12	Colbatch (J.) Medical Tracts. 8vo. 1704.
77	8	Colburn (Z.) Memoir by himself. 12mo. 1833.
52	17	Colden (C. D.) Life of Fulton. 8vo. 1817.
520	14	Coleridge (H.) Essays and Marginalia. 2 vols. 16mo. 1851.
77	10	——— Lives of Northern Worthies. 3 vols. 16mo. 1852.
486	1	Coleridge (H. N.) Introduction to the Study of Greek Classics. 12mo. 1842.
160	13	——— Six Months in the West Indies. 18mo. 1832.
520	7	Coleridge (S. T.) Aids to Reflection. 12mo. 1825.
169	13	——— Works. 3 vols. 16mo. 1835. Vol. 1. Juvenile Poems; Sibylline Leaves. 2. Ancient Mariner; Christabel; Miscellaneous Poems; Remorse; Zapolya; Fall of Robespierre. 3. Piccolomini; Death of Wallenstein.
525	7	——— Works. 7 vols. 12mo. 1853. Vol. 1. Aids to Reflection; Statesman's Manual. 2. The Friend. 3. Biographia Literaria. 4. Lectures upon Shakespeare and other Dramatists. 5. Literary Remains. 6. Church and State; Table Talk. 7. Juvenile Poems; Sibylline Leaves; Ancient Mariner; Christabel; Miscellaneous Poems; Remorse; Zapolya; Piccolomini; Death of Wallenstein.
523	4	Collegian. 8vo. 1830.
166	16	Collier (J. P.) Notes and Emendations to Shakespeare. 12mo. 1853.
*596	1	Collins's Peerage of England. 9 vols. 8vo. 1812.
148	5	Collins (W.) Poetical Works. 16mo. 1830.
*428	12	——— Poetical Works. 12mo. 1798.
502	16	Colman (H.) European Agriculture. 2 vols. 8vo. 1844–49.
503	6	——— Reports on Agriculture of Massachusetts. 8vo. 1838–40.
502	17	——— Reports on Agriculture of Massachusetts. 8vo. 1841.
*469	15	Colonies (British). Considerations on Imposing Taxes. 8vo. 1766.
199	10	Colossians, Lectures on. 12mo. 1846.
51	16	Colton (C.) Life of Henry Clay. 2 vols. 8vo. 1846.
108	11	Colton (W.) Three Years in California. 12mo. 1851.
96	4	——— Ship and Shore. 12mo. 1851.
*443	6	Columbus, Memorials of. 8vo. 1823.
66	4	——— Memorial of. 8vo. 1823.

Shelf.	No.	
103	3	Columbus's Personal Narrative. 8vo. 1827.
86	11	Colvocoresses (G. M.) Exploring Expedition. 12mo. 1852.
509	2	Combe (A.) On Digestion. 18mo. n. d.
509	4	——— On Infancy. 18mo. 1846.
98	9	——— Principles of Physiology. 18mo. 1851.
505	11	Combe (G.) Constitution of Man. 12mo. 1848.
506	7	——— Constitution of Man. 12mo. 1848.
75	12	——— Life of A. Combe. 12mo. 1850.
509	3	——— Moral Philosophy. 18mo. n. d.
95	4	——— Notes on the United States. 2 vols. 12mo. 1841.
498	1	——— System of Phrenology. 12mo. 1849.
492	9	——— System of Phrenology. 8vo. 1851.
*430	6	Comedias Nuevas. 4to. 1651.
529	2	Companions to my Solitude. 12mo. 1852.
529	3	——— to my Solitude. 12mo. 1852.
507	19	Comstock (J. L.) Natural Philosophy. 12mo. 1846.
507	3	——— Chemistry. 12mo. 1840.
*594	3	Condie (D. F.) Diseases of Children. 8vo. 1853.
79	4	Condorcet (Marquis de). Life of Voltaire. 12mo. 1792.
78	8	Congar (Capt. O.) Autobiography. 18mo. 1851.
*469	16	Congress (American Continental). Extracts from Proceedings. 8vo. 1774.
4	1	——— History of, from 1789–93. 8vo. 1834.
*426	7	Congreve (W.) Mourning Bride, &c. 8vo. 1761.
70	17	Conkling (M. C.) Memoirs of Mother and Wife of Washington. 12mo. 1853.
*272	12	Connecticut Common School Journal. 8vo. 1838–39.
136	9	Conscience (H.) Flemish Tales. 12mo. 1849.
105	8	Constitutions of the Holy Apostles. Edited by Irah Chase. 8vo. 1848.
12	14	Constitutions (The) of the several States and United States. 8vo. 1853.
128	6	Contrast. 3 vols. post 8vo. 1832.
77	20	Cooke (W.) Memoirs of Foote. 2 vols. 12mo. 1806.
171	12	Cooke (W.) Medical and Moral Life. 12mo. 1853.
*653	3	Cooley (A. J.) Encyclopædia of Six Thousand Receipts. 8vo. 1851.
49	5	Cooley. History of Maritime and Inland Discovery. 3 vols. 18mo. 1830.
*584	5	Cooper (A.) Dislocations and Fractures. 8vo. 1851.
*413	2	——— On Hernia. 8vo. 1844.
*636	3	——— Surgery. 3 vols. 8vo. 1836–43.
132	8	Cooper (J. F.) Afloat and Ashore. 12mo. 1852.
133	9	——— Bravo. 12mo. 1852.
133	11	——— Chainbearer. 12mo. 1852.
133	3	——— Crater. 12mo. 1852.
132	13	——— Deerslayer. 12mo. 1852.
87	11	——— Gleanings in Europe. England. 2 vols. 12mo. 1837.

Shelf.	No.	
95	7	COOPER (J. F.) Gleanings in Europe. France. 2 vols. 12mo. 1837.
97	20	——— Gleanings in Europe. Italy. 2 vols. 12mo. 1838.
133	14	——— Headsman. 12mo. 1852.
127	3	——— Headsman. 3 vols. post 8vo. 1833.
133	13	——— Heidenmauer. 12mo. 1852.
14	6	——— History of United States Navy. 8vo. 1848.
133	4	——— Home as Found. 12mo. 1852.
133	5	——— Homeward Bound. 12mo. 1852.
132	14	——— Jack Tier. 12mo. 1852.
132	7	——— Last of the Mohicans. 12mo. 1852.
133	16	——— Lionel Lincoln. 12mo. 1852.
58	7	——— Lives of American Naval Officers. 12mo. 1846.
60	20	——— Lives of American Naval Officers. 12mo. 1846.
65	1	——— Memorial. 8vo. 1852.
133	18	——— Mercedes of Castile. 12mo. 1852.
132	9	——— Miles Wallingford. 12mo. 1852.
133	17	——— Monikins. 12mo. 1852.
133	1	——— Ned Myers. 12mo. 1852.
133	2	——— Oak Openings. 12mo. 1852.
132	10	——— Pathfinder. 12mo. 1852.
132	16	——— Pilot. 12mo. 1852.
132	15	——— Pioneers. 12mo. 1852.
132	11	——— Prairie. 12mo. 1852.
132	4	——— Precaution. 12mo. 1852.
132	6	——— Red Rover. 12mo. 1852.
133	10	——— Red Skins. 12mo. 1852.
121	7	——— Residence in France. 2 vols. post 8vo. 1836.
133	12	——— Satanstoe. 12mo. 1852.
133	19	——— Sea Lions. 12mo. 1852.
94	9	——— Sketches of England. 8vo. 1837.
86	18	——— Sketches of Switzerland. 2 vols. 12mo. 1836.
86	19	——— Sketches of Switzerland. Second part. 2 vols. 12mo. 1836.
133	15	——— Spy. 12mo. 1852.
133	6	——— Travelling Bachelor. 12mo. 1852.
109	10	——— Travelling Bachelor. 2 vols. 12mo. 1828.
132	5	——— Two Admirals. 12mo. 1852.
132	17	——— Water-Witch. 12mo. 1852.
133	8	——— Wept of Wish-ton-Wish. 12mo. 1852.
132	12	——— Wing-and-Wing. 12mo. 1852.
133	7	——— Wyandotte. 12mo. 1852.
127	2	——— Wyandotte. 3 vols. post 8vo. 1843.
*564	5	COOPER (S.) Surgical Dictionary. 8vo. 1851.
517	7	COOPER (S. F.) Rural Hours. 12mo. 1850.
517	10	——— Rural Hours. 12mo. 1850.
96	18	——— Rambles in England. 12mo. 1853.
175	4	COOPER (T.) Political Economy. 8vo. 1831.

Shelf.	No.	
*480	13	COOPER. History of North America. 16mo. 1797.
107	15	COPWAY (G.) Men and Places. 12mo. 1851.
8	1	——— History of Ojibway Nation. 12mo. 1851.
38	14	CORKRAN (J. F.) Constituent Assembly. 12mo. 1849.
58	1	CORMENIN (Visc. de). Orators of France. 12mo. 1849.
505	6	CORNELL (W. M.) Journal of Health. Vol. 1. 8vo. 1846.
27	8	CORSI (F.) Pietre Antiche. 8vo. 1833.
14	2	CORTES (H.) Despatches. 8vo. 1843.
*626	12	CORVISART (J. N.) On the Heart. 8vo. 1812.
86	5	COSTIGAN (A. W.) Sketches in Portugal. 2 vols. 12mo. 1787.
189	31	COTTER (J. R.) Mass and Rubrics of the Roman Catholic Church. 18mo. 1846.
128	10	COTTIN (Mad. S.) Elizabeth. 16mo. 1853.
111	23	——— Matilda and Malek Adhel. 4 vols. 12mo. 1833.
*470	6	COTTON (J.) On the 13th Chap. of Revelations. 8vo. 1656.
429	5	COTTON (N.) Verse and Prose. 12mo. 1791.
*650	11	COTTON (R. P.) Phthisis and the Stethoscope. 16mo. 1851.
68	9	COTTLE (J.) Reminiscences of Coleridge and Southey. 12mo. 1848.
506	13	COUES (S. E.) Mechanical Philosophy. 8vo. 1851.
170	10	COURT and Camp of Buonaparte. 18mo. 1831.
26	2	COUSIN (V.) Modern Philosophy. 2 vols. 12mo. 1852.
183	6	——— History of Philosophy. 8vo. 1832.
171	25	——— Philosophy of the Beautiful. 16mo. 1849.
185	8	——— Education in Holland. 12mo. 1838.
190	16	——— Report on Public Instruction in Prussia. 18mo. 1835.
185	12	——— JOUFFROY, & CONSTANT. Philosophical Miscellanies. 2 vols. 12mo. 1838.
54	7	COVERDALE (M.) Memorials of. 8vo. 1838.
518	11	COWLEY (A.) Prose Works. 12mo. 1826.
*429	1	——— Works. 3 vols. 8vo. 1710.

Vol. 1. Life; Miscellanies; Anacreontiques; the Mistress; Pindarique Odes; Davideis, books 1, 2.
2. Davideis, books 3, 4; Davideidos, book 1; Verses written on Several Occasions; Advancement of Experimental Philosophy; Discourses in Verse and Prose; Cutter of Coleman Street.
3. Wood's Life of Cowley; Constantia and Philetus; Piramus and Thisbe; Sylva; Love's Riddle; Naufragium Joculare; Plants; Index to Plants.

Shelf.	No.	
*422	4	——— Works. Folio. 1672.
156	4	COWPER (W.) Works. 16mo. 1852.
429	6	——— Poems. 3 vols. 12mo. 1808.
157	7	——— Works. 15 vols. 16mo. 1835–37.

Vol. 1, 2. Life, by Southey.
3. Life; Letters.
4–7, and 15. Letters.
8. Juvenile Poems; Olney Hymns; Anti-Thelyphthora; Minor Poems; Translations from Vincent Bourne.
9. Translations from Madame Guion; the Task; Minor Poems.

Shelf.	No.	
157	7	Cowper (W.) Works, *continued.* 10. Minor Poems; Translations from Vincent Bourne and Milton; Epigrams from Owen; Translations of Greek Verses; and Fables of Gay. 11, 12. Homer's Iliad. 13, 14. Homer's Odyssey.
149	2	——— Poems. 3 vols. 16mo. 1843.
*429	7	——— Poems. 3 vols. 12mo. 1817.
419	12	——— Works. Vol. 1, Bohn's edition. Post 8vo. 1853.
178	12	Cox (F. A.) Baptists in America. 12mo. 1836.
122	19	Cox (S. S.) Buckeye Abroad. 12mo. 1852.
*470	1	Coxe (D.) Description of Florida. 8vo. 1741.
*7	5	Coxe (T.) View of the United States. 8vo. 1794.
398	12	Coxe (W.) History of the House of Austria. 4 vols. post 8vo. 1847–53.
95	16	——— Russian Discoveries between Asia and America. 8vo. 1803.
397	9	——— Memoir of the Duke of Marlborough. 3 vols. post 8vo. 1847–48.
*444	4	——— Memoir of the Duke of Marlborough. 6 vols. 8vo. 1820.
*444	9	——— Atlas to Memoir of the Duke of Marlborough. 4to. n. d.
94	10	——— Travels in Poland, Russia, &c. 5 vols. 8vo. 1792.
33	3	——— Travels in Switzerland. 3 vols. 8vo. 1789.
*444	5	——— Life of Sir Robert Walpole. 4 vols. 8vo. 1816.
*660	5	Crabb (G.) Dictionary of General Knowledge. 12mo. 1830.
*653	2	——— English Synonymes. 8vo. 1853.
173	2	Craig (J.) Elements of Political Science. 3 vols. 8vo. 1814.
*477	14	Craig (N. B.) History of Pittsburgh. 12mo. 1851.
*252	9	Craig (T.) Right of Succession to the Kingdom of Great Britain. Folio. 1703.
490	12	Craik (G. L.) Bacon's Writings. 3 vols. 18mo. 1846–47.
510	2	——— History of British Commerce. 3 vols. 18mo. 1844.
490	11	——— History of Literature in England. 6 vols. 18mo. 1844–45.
550	3	——— Pursuit of Knowledge under Difficulties. 2 vols. 12mo. n. d.
490	13	——— Pursuit of Knowledge under Difficulties. 3 vols. 18mo. 1845.
490	17	——— Spenser and his Poetry. 3 vols. 18mo. 1845.
*452	1	——— and MacFarlane. Pictorial History of England. 8 vols. 8vo. 1847–49.
42	3	——— and MacFarlane. Pictorial History of England. 4 vols. 8vo. 1846–51.
139	5	Cranford. 16mo. 1853.
*29	7	Crantz (D.) History of Greenland. 2 vols. 8vo. 1767.
83	10	Craufurd (Q.) Laws, &c. of Ancient and Modern India. 8vo. 1817.

Shelf.	No.	
*464	9	CRAWFURD (J.) History of Indian Archipelago. 3 vols. 8vo. 1820.
37	17	CREASY (E. S.) Fifteen Decisive Battles. 12mo. 1851.
494	16	CRESSWELL (D.) Supplement to Elements of Euclid. 8vo. 1825.
503	13	——— On Geometry. 8vo. 1819.
98	8	CRICHTON (A.) History of Arabia. 2 vols. 18mo.
90	14	——— and WHEATON (H.) History of Denmark, &c. 2 vols. 18mo. 1850.
79	12	CROCKETT (D.) Life of. 12mo. 1834.
199	15	CROFTON (D.) Genesis and Geology. 12mo. 1853.
539	50	CROKER (J. W.) History of the Guillotine. 12mo. 1853.
170	8	CROKER (T. C.) Fairy Legends and Traditions of Ireland. 12mo. 1838.
88	11	CROLY (Rev. G.) Life and Times of George IV. 18mo. n. d.
486	15	CROMWELL (O.) Letters and Speeches. 2 vols. 16mo. 1845.
121	35	CROSLAND (N.) English Tales and Sketches. 16mo. 1853.
*671	12	CROSSE (J. G.) Urinary Calculus. 4to. 1835.
51	3	CROSWELL (H.) Memoir of Rev. W. Croswell. 8vo. 1853.
48	1	CROWE (E. E.) History of France. 3 vols. 18mo. n. d.
49	3	——— History of France. 3 vols. 18mo. 1830.
177	7	CROWE (F.) Gospel in Central America. 12mo. 1850.
*574	9	CRUVEILHIER (J.) Anatomy. 8vo. 1844.
168	5	CRYSTALINA. 12mo. 1816.
*664	9	CULLEN (Wm.) Nosology. 8vo. 1800.
*402	5	CUMBERLAND (G.) Outlines from the Ancients. 8vo. 1829.
53	5	CUMBERLAND (R.) Memoirs. 8vo. 1806.
66	2	——— Memoirs. 2 vols. 8vo. 1807.
84	11	CUMMING (R. G.) Hunter's Life in South Africa. 2 vols. 12mo. 1850–51.
84	10	——— Hunter's Life in South Africa. 2 vols. 12mo. 1850.
*660	8	CUMMINGS (P.) Dictionary of Congregational Usages. 12mo. 1853.
88	1	CUNNINGHAM (A.) British Painters, Sculptors, &c. 5 vols. 18mo. n. d.
*170	15	——— British Painters, Sculptors, &c. 6 vols. 18mo. 1829–33.
114	9	——— Sir Michael Scott. 3 vols. 8vo. 1828.
443	1	CUNNINGHAM (G. G.) History of England in the Lives of Englishmen. 8 vols. 8vo. 1849–51.
129	27	CUNNINGHAM (J. W.) Velvet Cushion. 18mo. 1815.
*656	4	CURLING (T. B.) On the Rectum. 8vo. 1851.
*554	2	——— and GODDARD. On the Testis. 8vo. 1843.
483	3	CURRAN (J. P.) Speeches. 8vo. 1847.
73	3	CURRIE (W. W.) Life and Writings of J. Currie. 2 vols. 8vo. 1831.
84	2	CURTIS (G. W.) Nile Notes of a Howadji. 16mo. 1852.
108	12	——— Lotus Eating. 12mo. 1852.

Shelf.	No.	
84	1	Curtis (G. W.) The Howadji in Syria. 16mo. 1852.
131	8	——— Potiphar Papers. 12mo. 1853.
12	2	Curwen (S.) Journal and Letters. 8vo. 1842.
186	16	Curtis (G. T.) Inventors' Manual. 12mo. 1851.
*477	24	Cushing (C.) History of Newburyport. 12mo. 1826.
105	13	——— Reminiscences of Spain. 2 vols. 12mo. 1833.
38	7	——— Revolution in France. 2 vols. 12mo. 1833.
180	27	Cushing (L. S.) Manual of Parliamentary Practice. 16mo. 1851.
*344	8	——— Reports. Vol. 6. 8vo. 1853.
38	18	Custine (Marquis de). Empire of the Czar. 3 vols. 12mo. 1843.
507	17	Cutter (C.) Anatomy and Physiology. 12mo. 1846.
67	5	Cutter (W.) Life of Israel Putnam. 12mo. 1847.
505	8	Cuvier (Baron). Index to Animal Kingdom, &c. 8vo. 1835.
496	3	——— Progrès des Sciences Naturelles. 4 vols. 8vo. 1826.
97	2	Curzon (R., Jun.) Monasteries in Levant. 12mo. 1849.
*593	2	Cyclopædia National.

Vol. 1. A—Bau.	Vol. 4. Han—Nor.
2. Bav—Cot.	5. Nor—Sie.
3. Cot—Han.	6. Sie—Zyg.

D.

Shelf.	No.	
394	16	Dallas (G. M.) Memoir of. 8vo. 1853.
435	11	Dalrymple (D.) Annals of Scotland. 3 vols. 8vo. 1819.
435	2	Dalrymple (J.) Memoirs of Great Britain and Ireland. 3 vols. 8vo. 1790.
504	17	Dalton (J.) Meteorological Observations. 8vo. 1834.
*449	1	Dampier (W.) Voyage round the World. 3 vols. 8vo. 1697–1707.
504	14	Dana (J. F.) Chymical Philosophy. 8vo. 1825.
493	19	Dana (J. D.) Mineralogy. 8vo. 1844.
155	13	Dana (R. H.) Poems and Prose Writings. 2 vols. 12mo. 1850.
99	12	Dana (R. H. jun.) Two Years before the Mast. 18mo. 1840.
109	2	——— Two Years before the Mast. 18mo. n. d.
150	1	Dante (A.) La Divina Commedia. 3 vols. 32mo. 1829.
156	2	——— The Vision, translated by Cary. 16mo. 1852.
479	2	Danvers Centennial Celebration. 8vo. 1852.
45	1	D'Anville (J. B.) Compendium of Ancient Geography. 2 vols. 8vo. 1814.
*211	12	Dapper (Dr. O.) Beschryving van gantsch Syrie en Palestyn. Folio. 1677.
*211	11	——— Gedenkwaerdig Bedryf der Nederlandsche Oost-Indische Maetschappye, op de Kuste en in het Keizerrijk van Taising of Sina. Folio. 1670.

Shelf.	No.	
138	8	D'Arblay (Mad. F. B.) Cecilia. 3 vols. 12mo. 1803.
123	12	—— Evelina. 12mo. 1852.
119	18	—— Evelina. 2 vols. 12mo. 1808.
118	2	—— The Wanderer. 5 vols. 12mo. 1814.
104	10	Darby (W.) Tour from New York to Detroit. 8vo. 1819.
108	3	Darwin (C.) Voyage of a Naturalist. 2 vols. 16mo. 1846.
539	1	—— Voyage of a Naturalist. 16mo. 1845.
108	1	—— Voyage of a Naturalist. 2 vols. 16mo. 1852.
504	9	Darwin (E.) Zoonomia. 2 vols. 8vo. 1801.
*422	10	—— Botanic Garden. 4to. 1791.
*447	1	D'Avenant (C.) Works. 5 vols. 8vo. 1771.
*392	2	Davenant (Sir W.) Works. Folio. 1673.
150	12	Davenport (R. A.) History of the Bastile. 18mo. 1839.
170	7	—— Life of Ali Pasha. 18mo. 1837.
160	2	—— Lives of Eminent Individuals. 18mo. 1841.
150	13	—— Narratives of Peril and Suffering. 2 vols. 18mo. 1840.
100	20	—— Narratives of Peril and Suffering. 18mo. n. d.
		Davidson (L. M.) Poetical Remains. 12mo. 1843.
76	1	Davidson (M. M.) Poetical Remains and Biography. 12mo. 1841.
518	9	—— Writings of. 12mo. 1843.
*636	1	Davies (J.) Pathology and Surgery. 8vo. 1841.
70	12	Davies (T.) Life of Garrick. 2 vols. 12mo. 1818.
7	4	Davis (E.) Half Century. 12mo. 1851.
*436	9	Davis (J.) Travels in the United States. 8vo. 1803.
*646	6	Davy (J.) Physiological and Anatomical Researches. 2 vols. 8vo. 1839.
84	14	Davis (J. F.) China during the War. 2 vols. post 8vo. 1852.
510	14	—— The Chinese. 4 vols. 18mo. 1845–46.
99	8	—— The Chinese. 2 vols. 18mo. 1848.
550	4	—— China and its Inhabitants. 2 vols. 12mo. n. d.
54	11	Davis (M. L.) Memoirs of Aaron Burr. 2 vols. 8vo. 1836–52.
123	14	Day (J.) Old Engagement. 12mo. 1852.
129	4	Day (T.) Sanford and Merton. 16mo. 1847.
494	2	Deaf and Dumb, Annals of. 8vo. 1848–49.
8	27	Dearborn (N.) Boston Notions. 16mo. 1848.
*480	12	—— Boston Notions. 16mo. 1848.
14	3	De Bow (J. D. B.) Resources of the Southern and Western States. 3 vols. 8vo. 1852–53.
126	14	De Foe (D.) Robinson Crusoe. 12mo. 1835.
124	16	—— Robinson Crusoe. 12mo. n. d.
170	5	—— Journal of the Plague Year. 18mo. 1839.
131	33	—— Works. 20 vols. 18mo. 1840–41.

Vol. 1, 2. Robinson Crusoe.
3. Captain Singleton.
4. Moll Flanders.
5. Colonel Jack; Apparition of Mrs. Veal.
6. Memoirs of a Cavalier.

Shelf. No.

126 14 De Foe (D.) Works, *continued.*
7. New Voyage round the World.
8. Memoirs of Captain Carleton and Mrs. Davis.
9. History of the Plague in London; the Consolidator.
10. Political History of the Devil.
11. Roxana.
12. System of Magic.
13. History of Apparitions.
14. Religious Courtship.
15, 16. Family Instructor.
17, 18. English Tradesman.
19. Life of Duncan Campbell; Dumb Philosopher; Everybody's Business is Nobody's Business.
20. Life of De Foe, by Chalmers; List of De Foe's Works; Tracts; True-born Englishman.

187 4 Degerando (Baron). Visitor of the Poor. 12mo. 1832.
104 6 Delano (A.) Voyages and Travels. 8vo. 1818.
506 6 Deleuze (J. P. F.) Animal Magnetism. 12mo. 1850.
190 23 Dellon (M.) Inquisition at Goa. 18mo. 1815.
398 7 De Lolme (J. L.) Constitution of England. Post 8vo. 1853.
5 8 Deming (L.) Officers of Vermont. 8vo. 1851.
30 12 De Morgan (A.) Essay on Probabilities. 18mo. 1841.
485 6 Demosthenes. Orations, translated by Leland. 2 vols. 8vo. 1806.
120 2 ——— Orations, translated by Leland. 2 vols. 18mo. 1844.
409 8 ——— Olynthiac, and other Orations, translated by Kennedy. Post 8vo. 1852.
92 10 Denham (D.) Travels in Africa. 8vo. 1826.
500 4 Dennis (G.) Chronicles of the Cid. 18mo. 1845.
464 3 ——— Cities of Etruria, &c. 2 vols. 8vo. 1848.
476 2 Denton (D.) Description of New Netherlands. 8vo. 1845.
168 1 Depping (G. B.) & Michel (F.) Wayland Smith. 12mo. 1847.
525 8 De Quincey (T.) Autobiographic Sketches. 16mo. 1853.
529 7 ——— Biographical Essays. 16mo. 1851.
519 17 ——— Cæsars. 16mo. 1851.
537 7 ——— Essays on Philosophical Writers. 2 vols. 16mo. 1854.
529 20 ——— Essays on the Poets. 16mo. 1853.
529 19 ——— Historical and Critical Essays. 2 vols. 16mo. 1853.
537 6 ——— Letters to a Young Man. 16mo. 1854.
519 12 ——— Life and Manners. 16mo. 1841.
519 14 ——— Literary Reminiscences. 2 vols. 16mo. 1851.
519 15 ——— Miscellaneous Essays. 16mo. 1851.
529 21 ——— Narrative and Miscellaneous Papers. 2 vols. 16mo. 1853.
519 16 ——— Opium Eater. 16mo. 1851.
520 17 ——— Opium Eater. 16mo. 1841.
448 10 Derham (W.) Astro-Theology. 8vo. 1719.
184 16 ——— Physico-Theology. 8vo. 1768.
*401 3 Des Essarts. Dictionnaire de Police. 8 vols. 4to. 1786.
Tome 1. A—Bor.
2. Bor—Cid.
3. Cim—Fem.
4. Fes—Hop.
Tome 5. Hop—Jui.
6. Lab—Mœ.
7. Mon—Pau.
8. Pau—Pol.

Shelf.	No.	
*448	15	DESPOTISM, Progress of, in Africa, Europe, and America. 8vo. 1764.
499	2	DE VERE (M. S.) Comparative Philology. 12mo. 1853.
*594	4	DEWEES (W. P.) On Children. 8vo. 1853.
516	7	DE WETTE (W. N. L.) On Human Life. 2 vols. 12mo. 1842.
181	4	——— On the Old Testament. 2 vols. 8vo. 1850.
179	1	DEWEY (O.) Discourses. 3 vols. 12mo. 1846–52.
6	2	DIAZ (B.) History of the Conquest of Mexico. 2 vols. 8vo. 1844.
53	12	DIBDIN (T.) Reminiscences. 2 vols. 8vo. 1827.
98	2	DICK (T.) Celestial Scenery. 18mo. n. d.
90	1	——— On the Improvement of Society. 18mo. n. d.
497	20	——— On the Improvement of Society. 12mo. n. d.
498	13	——— Practical Astronomer. 16mo. 1846.
98	18	——— Sidereal Heavens. 18mo. n. d.
112	1	DICKENS (C.) Barnaby Rudge. 8vo. 1841.
112	8	——— Christmas Stories. 8vo. 1852.
112	14	——— David Copperfield. 8vo. 1852.
112	15	——— Dombey & Son. 8vo. 1852.
522	3	——— Household Words. 8vo. 1850–53.
112	6	——— Martin Chuzzlewit. 8vo. 1852.
112	13	——— Nicholas Nickleby. 8vo. 1839.
112	7	——— Old Curiosity Shop. 8vo. 1852.
112	4	——— Oliver Twist. 8vo. 1840.
112	5	——— Pickwick Papers. 8vo. 1853.
175	12	DICKENSON (J.) Political Writings. 2 vols. 8vo. 1801.
*663	4	DICTIONARY, English and German. 8vo. 1849.
*650	5	DICTIONNAIRE de Santé. 2 vols. 16mo. 1777.
*650	6	DICTIONNAIRE de Chirurgie. 16mo. 1777.
*650	4	DICTIONNAIRE des Hommes Célèbres. 2 vols. 16mo. 1822.
417	5	DIDRON. Christian Iconography, translated by Millington. Vol. 1. Post 8vo. 1851.
409	9	DIOGENES LAERTIUS. Lives of Eminent Philosophers, translated by Yonge. Post 8vo. 1853.
528	5	D'ISRAELI (I.) Amenities of Literature. 2 vols. 12mo. 1847.
518	12	——— Amenities of Literature. 2 vols. 12mo. 1847.
528	1	——— Amenities of Literature. 2 vols. 12mo. 1841.
512	5	——— Curiosities of Literature. 8vo. 1851.
528	6	——— Curiosities of Literature. 3 vols. 12mo. 1834.
528	2	——— Curiosities of Literature. 3 vols. 12mo. 1834.
528	7	——— Curiosities of Literature. Second series. 2 vols. 12mo. 1834.
528	3	——— Curiosities of Literature. Second series. 2 vols. 12mo. 1834.
528	4	——— Miscellanies of Literature. 3 vols. 12mo. 1841.
528	8	——— Miscellanies of Literature. 3 vols. 12mo. 1841.
90	5	DISTINGUISHED Men of Modern Times. 2 vols. 18mo. n. d.

Shelf.	No.	
77	16	Dix (J.) Life of Chatterton. 16mo. 1851.
85	14	Dix (J. A.) Winter in Madeira. 12mo. 1851.
66	15	Dixon (H.) John Howard and Prison World of Europe. 12mo. 1850.
57	4	Dixon (W. H.) William Penn. 12mo. 1851.
*437	1	Dobrizhoffer (M.) Abipones of Paraguay. 3 vols. 8vo. 1822.
78	19	Dobson (S.) Life of Petrarch. 2 vols. 18mo. 1809.
500	17	Dodd (G.) British Manufactures. 6 vols. 18mo. 1844–51.
167	5	Dodd (W.) Beauties of Shakespeare. 2 vols. 12mo. 1752.
*556	4	Dodsley's Old Plays. 12 vols. 8vo. 1825–27.

Vol. 1. Prefaces; Historia Histrionica; God's Promises; the Four P's; Ferrex and Porrex; Damon and Pithias; New Costume.
2. Gammer Gurton's Needle; Alexander and Campaspe; Tancred and Gismunda; Cornelia; Edward II.
3. George à Greene; Pinner of Wakefield; First Part of Jeronymo; Spanish Tragedy; Honest Whore.
4. Malcontent; All Fools; Eastward Hoe; Revenger's Tragedy; Dumb Knight.
5. Miseries of Inforced Marriage; Lingua; Merry Devil of Edmonton; a Mad World, my Masters; Ram Alley.
6. Roaring Girl; Widow's Tears; White Devil; the Hog hath lost his Pearl; Four Prentices of London.
7. Green's Tu Quoque; Albumazar; Woman Kill'd with Kindness; Match at Midnight; Fuimus Troes; True Trojans.
8. Wounds of Civil War; the Heir; Friar Bacon and Friar Bungay; Jew of Malta; the Wits.
9. Will Summer's Last Will and Testament; Microcosmus; Muse's Looking-Glass; City Match; Queen of Arragon.
10. Antiquary; the Goblins; the Ordinary; Jovial Crew; Old Couple.
11. Chronicle of Edward the First; Mayor of Quinborough; Grim, the Collier of Croydon; City Night Cap; Parson's Wedding.
12. Adventures of Five Hours; Elvira; the Widow; Chichevache and Bycorne; the World and the Chylde; Apius and Virginia; Additional Notes; Index.

*392	1	Dollman (F. T.) Ancient Pulpits. 4to. 1849.
6	7	Domestic Industry, Convention of the Friends of. 8vo. 1831.
40	15	Donovan (M.) On Chemistry. 18mo. 1832.
40	2	——— Domestic Economy. 2 vols. 18mo. 1830.
75	10	Doubourg (J. H.) Life of Cheverus. 12mo. 1839.
*464	2	Douce (F.) Dance of Death. 8vo. 1833.
475	12	Douglass (W.) British Settlements in North America. 2 vols. 8vo. 1755.
*596	7	——— British Settlements in North America. 2 vols. 8vo. 1760.
89	8	Dover (Lord). Life of Frederick II. 2 vols. 18mo. 1848.
503	8	Downing (A. J.) Cottage Residences. 8vo. 1853.
493	20	——— Country Houses. 8vo. 1851.
496	4	——— Fruit and Fruit Trees. 12mo. 1852.
502	10	——— Landscape Gardening. 8vo. 1850.
493	18	——— Rural Essays. 8vo. 1853.
*646	14	Downing (C. T.) Neuralgia. 8vo. 1851.
89	2	Drake, Cavendish, and Dampier. Voyages. 18mo. n. d.
79	13	Drake (B.) Life of Black Hawk. 16mo. 1838.

Shelf.	No.	
*626	4	DRAKE (D.) Diseases of the Valley of North America. 8vo. 1850.
154	8	DRAKE (J. R.) Culprit Fay, &c. 8vo. 1836.
121	31	DRAKE (N.) Noontide Leisure. 12mo. 1824.
2	4	DRAKE (S. G.) Book of the Indians. 8vo. 1841.
7	18	—— Indian Captivities. 12mo. 1852.
159	3	DRAMA, British; with Biography of Authors. 9 vols. 18mo. 1817.

Vol. 1. George Barnwell; Isabella, or the Fatal Marriage; Grecian Daughter; Gamester; Maid of Mariendorpt.
2. Constant Couple; City Wives' Confederacy; All for Love.
3. The Chances; All in the Wrong; Orphan; Tamerlane.
4. The Beaux Stratagem; She Would and She Would Not; Provoked Husband; Careless Husband.
5. Alzira; Way to Keep Him; Oroonoko; Clandestine Marriage.
6. Rule a Wife and Have a Wife; Tamerlane; Country Girl; Way of the World; Richelieu.
7. Zara; Busy Body; Miser; Gamesters.
8. School for Fathers; Maid of the Mill; Beggar's Opera; Love in a Village; Woman's Wit.
9. Every Man in his Humor; the Mistake; Brothers; the Minor; Love Chase.

Shelf.	No.	
*157	6	DRAMATICUS Thesaurus. 2 vols. 12mo. 1724.
539	5	DRINKWATER (J.) Siege of Gibraltar. 16mo. 1844.
189	4	DROZ (J.) Art of being Happy. 12mo. 1832.
*584	6	DRUITT (R.) Modern Surgery. 8vo. 1853.
167	19	DRUMMOND (W.) Poems. 16mo. 1833.
157	3	DRYDEN (J.) Fables. 12mo. 1745.
159	8	—— Poems and Translations. 2 vols. 18mo. 1777.
148	6	—— Poetical Works. 5 vols. 16mo. 1843–44.
95	17	DUANE (W.) Visit to Colombia. 8vo. 1826.
*402	3	DU BARTAS. Diuine Weekes and Workes. Folio. n. d.
*508	7	DUCATEL (J. T.) Practical Toxicology. 12mo. 1833.
*428	8	DUCK (S.) Poems. 8vo. 1737.
*664	11	DUDEVANT (L. H.) Tableau Analytique. 8vo. 1803.
62	8	DUER (W. A.) Life of the Earl of Stirling. 8vo. 1847.
100	21	—— Jurisprudence of the United States. 18mo. n. d.
*395	5	DU HALDE (P.) History of China. 4 vols. 8vo. 1741.
14	14	DUHRING (H.) Remarks on the United States. 12mo. 1833.
538	6	DUMAS (A.) Pictures of France. 12mo. n. d.
538	13	—— Pictures of France. 12mo. n. d.
131	24	—— Memoirs of a Physician. 2 vols. 16mo. 1847.
35	2	DUMAS (C. M.) Memoirs of his Own Time. 2 vols. 12mo. 1839.
*470	2	DUMMER (J.) Defence of New England Charters. 8vo. 1765.
449	7	DUNCAN (J.) Entomology. Nat. Lib. 6 vols. 16mo. n. d.

Vol. 1. Introduction; Memoir of Swammerdam and De Geer.
2. Memoir of Werner; British Butterflies.
3. Memoir of Madame Merian; British Moths, Sphinxes, &c.
4. Memoir of Lamarck; Foreign Butterflies.
5. Memoir of Latreille; Exotic Moths.
6. Memoir of Ray; Beetles.

Shelf.	No.	
*574	8	DUNGLISON (R.) Human Physiology. 2 vols. 8vo. 1850.
*554	1	——— Medical Dictionary. 8vo. 1853.
*584	12	——— New Remedies. 8vo. 1851.
49	1	DUNHAM (S. A.) History of Denmark, Sweden, and Norway. 3 vols. 18mo. 1839.
29	2	——— History of Germanic Empire. 3 vols. 18mo. 1834–35.
29	3	——— History of Middle Ages. 4 vols. 18mo. 1833–34.
29	1	——— History of Poland. 18mo. 1831.
49	2	——— History of Spain and Portugal. 5 vols. 18mo. 1832.
49	6	——— Literary and Scientific Men of Great Britain. 3 vols. 18mo. 1836.
5	7	DUNLAP (W.) History of the American Theatre. 8vo. 1832.
15	5	——— History of the American Theatre. 8vo. 1832.
13	8	——— History of the New Netherlands. 2 vols. 8vo. 1839–40.
26	10	——— History of the Arts of Design. 2 vols. 8vo. 1834.
*444	2	——— Life of C. B. Brown. 8vo. 1815.
27	5	DUNLOP (J.) History of Fiction. 2 vols. 12mo. 1842.
95	14	DUNN (H.) Guatimala. 8vo. 1828.
38	4	DU PAN (J. M.) History of Destruction of the Helvetic Union. 12mo. 1799.
*445	7	DU PAN (Mallet). Mémoires et Correspondances. Par A. Sayous. 8vo. 1851.
482	7	DU PONCEAU (P. S.) Chinese Writing. 8vo. 1838.
516	2	DWIGHT (J. S.) Poems translated from Goethe and Schiller. 12mo. 1839.
183	3	DWIGHT (M. A.) Mythology. 8vo. 1849.
68	13	DWIGHT (T.) Character of Thomas Jefferson. 12mo. 1839.
171	9	——— History of the Hartford Convention. 8vo. 1833.
103	12	DWIGHT (Timothy). Travels in New England and New York. 4 vols. 8vo. 1821–22.
90	12	DWIGHT (T. jun.) History of Connecticut. 18mo. n. d.
*427	1	DYCE (A.) On Collier's and Knight's edition of Shakspeare. 8vo. 1844.
*436	4	DYER (G.) Privileges of the University of Cambridge. 2 vols. 8vo. 1824.
189	13	DYER (J.) Character, &c. of Mary Dyer. 12mo. 1819.
65	12	DYER (T. H.) Life of Calvin. 12mo. 1850.
498	16	DYER'S Companion. 16mo. 1851.

E.

Shelf.	No.	
82	3	EARL (G. W.) Eastern Seas. 8vo. 1837.
417	4	EATON (C. A.) Rome in the Nineteenth Century. 2 vols. Post 8vo. 1852.
58	10	EATON (J. H.) Life of A. Jackson. 12mo. 1828.

Shelf.	No.	
74	1	EATON (Gen. W.) Life of. 8vo. 1813.
516	3	ECKERMAN (J. P.) Conversations with Goethe. 12mo. 1839.
177	19	EDDY (D. C.) Heroines of the Missionary Enterprise. 16mo. 1850.
68	12	EDGEWORTH (C. S.) Memoirs of the Abbe Edgeworth. 12mo. 1815.
129	6	EDGEWORTH (M.) Frank. 2 vols. 16mo. 1848.
111	11	——— Helen. 3 vols. post 8vo. 1834.
132	2	——— Parents' Assistant. 12mo. 1850.
132	1	——— Rosamond. 12mo. 1844.
132	3	——— Tales and Novels. 10 vols. 12mo. 1852.
		Vol. 1. Castle Rackrent; on Irish Bulls; on Self-Justification; Moral Tales. 2. Moral Tales. 3. Popular Tales. 4. Manœuvring; Almeria; Vivian. 5. Absentee; Madame de Fleury; Emilie de Coulanges; Modern Griselda. 6. Belinda. 7. Leonora; Letters; Patronage. 8. Patronage and Comic Dramas. 9. Harrington; Thoughts on Bores; Ormond. 10. Helen.
186	13	EDGEWORTH (M. & R. L.) Practical Education. 12mo. 1849.
185	2	——— Practical Education. 2 vols. 8vo. 1801.
185	7	EDGEWORTH (R. L.) On Education. 8vo. 1812.
73	9	——— Memoirs of. 8vo. 1821.
*315	4	EDINBURGH Annual Register, 1819–20. 2 vols. 8vo. 1823.
		——— Review. 99 vols. 8vo. 1814–52.
*605	2	Vols. 1–14.
*615	1	,, 15–36.
*625	1	,, 37–58.
*635	1	,, 59–80.
*645	1	,, 81–96.
*645	2	Index to Vols. 1–20.
*645	3	Index to Vols. 21–50.
*645	4	Index to Vols. 51–80.
170	1	EDMONDS (C. R.) Life and Times of Washington. 2 vols. 18mo. 1835–36.
181	5	EDMONDS (J. W.) & DEXTER (G. T.) Spiritualism. 8vo. 1853.
*314	3	EDUCATION Society. Quarterly Register and Journal. 8vo. 1830.
*314	4	——— Journal of. 3 vols. 8vo. 1826.
187	12	——— Hints for the Improvement of. 12mo. 1826.
*404	12	EDUCATIONAL Documents of Connecticut. 8vo. 1853.
*462	4	EDWARDS (B.) Historical Survey of Island of St. Domingo. 4to. 1797.
70	24	EDWARDS (B. B.) Biography of Self-taught Men. 2 vols. 18mo. 1850.
*660	7	——— Missionary Gazetteer. 12mo. 1832.
*392	7	EDWARDS (E.) Anecdotes of Painters. 4to. 1808.

Shelf.	No.	
*432	1	EDWARDS (F. E.) Eocene Mollusca. 4to. 1849.
97	19	EDWARDS (F. S.) Doniphan's Campaign in Mexico. 12mo. 1847.
188	12	EDWARDS (J.) Against Chauncy. 12mo. 1824.
65	4	——— Memoirs of D. Brainerd. 8vo. 1822.
183	10	——— On the Will. 8vo. 1831.
192	7	——— Works. 4 vols. 8vo. 1852. Vol. 1. Memoirs; Farewell Sermon; On Communion; Reply to Williams; History of the Work of Redemption; Marks of a Work of the Spirit of God; Observations on Important Doctrines; Life of Brainerd. 2. On the Will; Dissertations on Original Sin; Divine Decrees and Election; Efficacious Grace; Faith. 3. Religious Affections; Surprising Conversions; Revival in New England; On Prayer; Perseverance of Saints; Pre-Existence of Christ's Human Soul; Mysteries of Scripture; Observations upon Scripture; Theological Questions; Six Occasional Sermons. 4. Sermons.
539	2	EDWARDS (W. H.) Voyage up the Amazon. 16mo. 1847.
79	1	EGERTON (W.) Memoirs of Anne Oldfield. 12mo. 1731.
118	11	ELECTION (The). 16mo. 1840.
490	2	ELEPHANT (The). 18mo. 1844.
100	2	——— Natural History of. 18mo. n. d.
26	1	ELIOT (S.) History of Liberty. 2 vols. 8vo. 1853.
39	5	——— History of Liberty, Passages from. 16mo. 1847.
*465	3	——— History of Liberty, Rome. 2 vols. 8vo. 1849.
8	17	ELIOT (S. A.) Sketch of the History of Harvard College. 16mo. 1848.
171	49	ELIOT (W. G.) Lectures to Young Men. 12mo. 1854.
8	9	ELLET (E. F.) Domestic History of the American Revolution. 12mo. 1850.
69	9	——— Women of the American Revolution. 3 vols. 12mo. 1853.
487	1	——— Characters of Schiller. 12mo. 1839.
*473	6	ELLICOTT (A.) Journal. 4to. 1814.
*203	3	ELLIOT (J.) Debates. 4 vols. 8vo. 1827–30.
337	3	——— Diplomatic Code. 8vo. 1827.
339	12	ELLIS (C.) Law of Insurance and Annuities. 8vo. 1832.
408	2	ELLIS (G.) Early English Metrical Romances. Post 8vo. 1848.
156	9	——— Specimens of Early English Poets. 3 vols. 16mo. 1845.
550	5	——— Elgin Marbles, &c., in British Museum. 2 vols. 12mo. 1846.
18	9	——— Embassy to China. 8vo. 1818.
550	6	——— Townley Gallery of Sculpture. 2 vols. 12mo. n. d.
*448	5	ELLIS (H.) Voyage to Hudson's Bay. 8vo. 1748.
180	2	ELLIS (R.) British Tariff for 1843–44. 12mo. 1843.
33	5	ELLIS (W.) History of Madagascar. 2 vols. 8vo.
105	14	——— Polynesian Researches. 4 vols. 12mo. 1833.

Shelf.	No.	
442	4	Elmes (J.) Life of Sir C. Wren. 4to. 1823.
60	27	Elton (C. A.) Roman Emperors. 12mo. 1825.
528	9	Emerson (R. W.) Essays. 2 vols. 12mo. 1852.
528	10	—— Nature, Addresses, and Lectures. 12mo. 1850.
527	4	—— Representative Men. 12mo. 1850.
*15	4	Emerson (W.) History of the First Church, Boston. 8vo. 1812.
7	19	Emery (S. H.) Ministry of Taunton. 2 vols. 12mo. 1853.
550	1	Eminent Men, Biographies of. 4 vols. 12mo. n. d.
*596	2	Emmery (H. C.) Statistique des Eaux de la Ville de Paris. 8vo. 1840.
*411	4	Encyclopedia, American. 7 vols. 4to. 1805–11.
*643	1	Encyclopedia Americana. 14 vols. 8vo. 1850.

Vol. 1. A—Bat.
2. Bat—Cat.
3. Cat—Cra.
4. Cra—Eve.
5. Eve—Gre.
6. Gre—Ind.
7. Ind—Lin.
Vol. 8. Lin—Mon.
9. Mon—Pen.
10. Pen—Rev.
11. Rev—Ste.
12. Ste—Vis.
13. Vis—Zwi.
14. Supplement.

391	8	—— Another Copy. 13 vols. 8vo. 1842.
		Encyclopedia Britannica. 21 vols. 4to. 1842.
*662	8	Vols. 1– 5.
*672	1	„ 6–17.
*682	1	„ 18–21.

Vol. 1. Diss.; Index.
2. A—Ana.
3. Ana—Ast.
4. Ast—Bor.
5. Bor—Cal.
6. Cal—Clo.
7. Clo—Dia.
8. Dia—Eng.
9. Eng—Fra.
10. Fra—Gro.
11. Gro—Hyd.
Vol. 12. Hyd—Kyr.
13. Lab—Mag.
14. Mag—Mex.
15. Mey—Nav.
16. Nav—Pan.
17. Pan—Pla.
18. Pla—Quo.
19. Rab—Scu.
20. Scu—Sur.
21. Sur—Zym.

		Encyclopédie Méthodique. 197 vols. 4to. 1782–1828.
542	1	Agriculture. 7 vols.

Vol. 1. Aal—Azu.
2. Bab—Cet.
3. Cha—Cyt.
4. Dac—Hys.
Vol. 5. Ibé—Pom.
6. Pom—Zuc.
7. Aal—Zan.

542	2	Amusemens des Sciences. Abc—Vol.
632	6	Anatomie. Planches.
542	3	Antiquités. 5 vols.

Vol. 1. A—Chl.
2. Chl—Fyl.
3. G—Mec.
Vol. 4. Med—Plu.
5. Plu—Zyt.

632	7	Antiquités. Texte.
642	1	Antiquités. Planches. 2 vols.

Vol. 1. 1—190.
Vol. 2. 191—380.

542	4	Architecture. 3 vols.

Vol. 1. Aba—Col.
2. Col—Mut.
Vol. 3. Nac—Zot.

Shelf.	No.	
		ENCYCLOPÉDIE MÉTHODIQUE, *continued.*
552	1	Art Oratoire. Abe—Zon.
632	6	Art Oratoire. Planches.
552	2	Artillerie. Aci—Zin.
552	3	Art Militaire. 4 vols.

Vol. 1. A—Con.
2. Con—Gue.
Vol. 3. Gue—Zig.
4. Abr—Vol. Suppl.

552	4	Arts et Métiers. 8 vols.

Vol. 1. Aig—Cha.
2. Cou—Fil.
3. Flo—Ins.
4. Ins—Men.
Vol. 5. Mer—Pla.
6. Par—Pur.
7. Qua—Tab.
8. Tab—Zin.

642	2	Arts et Métiers. Planches. 8 vols.

Vol. 1. Aig—Cui.
2. Dia—Hor.
3. Hor—Mon.
4. Mos—Tour.
5. Tour—Vou; Marine.
6. Bon—Vel; Manufactures et Arts.
7. Art Militaire, Armes ; Art Militaire, Equitation ; Art Héraldique ; Mathématiques ; Machines Hydrauliques; Optique, Perspective, Astronomie ; Histoire Naturelle ; Verrerie.
8. Planches [concernant le Chanvre, le Coton, la Laine, le Poil, et la Soie ; concernant l'Emploi des Peaux et Cuirs ; Pelleterie, Huile, Savon, Teinture, Impression. Planches du Dictionnaire des Amusemens des Sciences et des Arts.

552	5	Assemblée Nationale. Abs—Aur.
642	3	Atlas. 2 vols.
552	6	Beaux Arts. Vol. 1. Aca—Pei.
562	1	Beaux Arts. Vol. 2. Pei—Ver.
642	4	Beaux Arts. Planches.
562	2	Botanique, 8 vols. Supplement, 5 vols.

Vol. 1. Aal—Cho.
2. Cic—Gor.
3. Gor—Mau.
4. Mau—Pan.
5. Pan—Pyx.
6. Qua—Sci.
7. Sci—Tra.
8. Tre—Zuc.

SUPPLEMENT.
Vol. 1. Aba—Bur.
2. Caa—Gyr.
3. Hab—Mor.
4. Mor—Ryn.
5. Sab—Xyl.

652	1	Botanique Texte. 3 vols.
652	2	Botanique Planches. 4 vols.

Vol. 1. 1—250.
2. 251—500.
Vol. 3. 501—750.
4. 751—1000.

562	4	Chasses. Aba—Zou.
652	3	Chasses. Planches.
562	5	Chimie. Vol. 1. A—Air.
572	1	Chimie. Vols. 2—6.

Vol. 2. Al—Car.
3. Car—Chi.
4. Chr—Mep.
Vol. 5. Mep—Pyr.
6. Qua—Zym.

652	4	Chimie. Planches.

Shelf. No.

ENCYCLOPÉDIE MÉTHODIQUE, *continued.*

572 2 Chirurgie. 2 vols.

Vol. 1. Aba—Kys. | Vol. 2. Lac—Zig.

652 5 Chirurgie. Planches.

572 3 Commerce. 3 vols.

Vol. 1. A—Cys. | Vol. 3. Kab—Zor.
2. D—Ize.

652 6 Coquilles et Vers. Planches. 3 vols.

Vol. 1. 1— 95. | Vol. 3. 315—488.
2. 96—314.

572 4 Economie Politique. 4 vols.

Vol. 1. Aba—Cza. | Vol. 3. Imp—Pro.
2. Dac—Imp. | 4. Pru—Sue.

572 5 Encyclopediana. A—Zeu.

652 7 Entomologie. Planches. 2 vols.

Vol. 1. 1—268. | Vol. 2. 269—397.

652 8 Erpétologie. Planches.

572 6 Equitation, &c. Aba—Tom.

582 1 Finances. 3 vols.

Vol. 1. Abo—Dun. | Vol. 3. Mag—Yve.
2. Eau—Lyo.

582 2 Forêts et Bois. Acc—Utr.

582 3 Géographie Ancienne. 3 vols.

Vol. 1. Aba—Gra. | Vol. 3. Rom—Zyr.
2. Græ—Rom.

582 4 Géographie Moderne. 3 vols.

Vol. 1. Aai—Hol. | Vol. 3. Rie—Zwy.
2. Hom—Rie.

582 5 Géographie Physique. 5 vols.

Vol. 1. Ard—Woo. | Vol. 4. Eau—Noy.
2. Aa—Azo. | 5. Oas—Zur.
3. Baa—Dyl.

662 1 Géographie Physique. Planches.

592 1 Grammaire et Littérature. 3 vols.

Vol. 1. Aba—Esp. | Vol. 3. Par—Str.
2. Esp—Par.

592 2 Histoire. 6 vols.

Vol. 1. Aba—Cas. | Vol. 4. Naa—Sce.
2. Cas—Gra. | 5. Sau—Zyp.
3. Gra—Myt. | 6. Supplement.

592 3 Histoire Naturelle. Vols. 1—7.

Vol. 1. Quadrupèdes, A—Z. Oiseaux, A—Eve.
2. Oiseaux, Fai—Vip.
3. Poissons; Insectes, Discours Préliminaire.
4. Insectes: Abe—Bom.
5. „ Bom—Cin.
6. „ Cir—Gyr.
7. „ Han—Mou.

Shelf. No.

ENCYCLOPÉDIE MÉTHODIQUE, *continued.*

602 1 Histoire Naturelle. Vols. 8—10.

Vol. 8. Insectes: Mou—Pan.
9. „ Pap—Pap.
10. „ Par—Zyg.

602 2 Histoire Naturelle des Vers. 3 vols.

Vol. 1. Abe—Con.
2. Aca—Myt.
Vol. 3. Nac—Zoo.

602 3 Histoire Naturelle des Zoophytes. Abr—Zoo.

662 2 Histoire Naturelle. Ichthyologie. Planches.

662 3 Histoire Naturelle. Mammalogie. Texte.

662 4 Histoire Naturelle. Mammalogie. Planches.

662 5 Histoire Naturelle. Ornithologie. Texte. 3 vols.

662 6 Histoire Naturelle. Ornithologie. Planches.

602 4 Jurisprudence. Vols. 1—9.

Vol. 1. Aba—Bay.
2. Bea—Com.
3. Com—Dom.
4. Don—Gul.
5. Hab—May.
Vol. 6. Mef—Pri.
7. Pro—Tax.
8. Tem—Zew.
9. La Police et les Municipalités. Aba—Cut.

612 1 Jurisprudence. La Police et les Municipalités. Dan—Voi.

612 2 Logique, Metaphysique, et Morale. 4 vols.

Vol. 1. Logique et Metaphysique. Abs—Mem.
2. Met—Sys. Morale. Aba—Dev.
3. Dig—Ost.
4. Par—Uti. Supplement.

612 3 Manufactures. 4 vols.

Vol. 1. Att—Reg.
2. Reg—Toi. Supplement.
3. Art—Tau. Vocabulaire et Appendix.
4. Aba—Zan. Teinture, Huiles, et Savons.

612 4 Marine. 3 vols.

Vol. 1. Aba—Des.
2. Des—Mur.
Vol. 3. Nad—Zop.

612 5 Mathématiques. 4 vols.

Vol. 1. Aba—Ext.
2. Fac—Rud.
Vol. 3. Sag—Zon. Jeux.
4. Jeux.

622 1 Médecine. 13 vols.

Vol. 1. A—Ali.
2. Alk—And.
3. Ang—Blu.
4. Boa—Cly.
5. Coa—Env.
6. Epa—Gyr.
7. Hab—Jus.
Vol. 8. Kaa—Maz.
9. Mea—Mer.
10. Mes—Nou.
11. Noy—Pht.
12. Phy—Sel.
13. Sem—Zyt.

622 2 Musique. 2 vols.

Vol. 1. A—Gym.
Vol. 2. H—Za.

632 1 Pêches. Aba—Zin.

652 3 Pêches. Planches.

632 2 Philosophie. 3 vols.

Vol. 1. Aca—Col. Vol. 2. Con—Ind. Suppl. Car.
Vol. 3. Ine—Zen.

Shelf.	No.	
		ENCYCLOPÉDIE MÉTHODIQUE, *continued.*
632	3	Physique. 4 vols.
		Vol. 1. Aba—Buf. 2. Aba—Dys. Vol. 3. Eau—Max. 4. Mau—Zym.
662	7	Physique. Planches.
632	4	Système Anatomique. 4 vols.
		Vol. 1. Aba—Zyg. 2. Quadrupedes. Vol. 3. Mammifères et Oiseaux. 4. Reptiles, Poissons, &c.
632	5	Théologie. 3 vols.
		Vol. 1. Aar—Eze. 2. Fab—Nys. Vol. 3. Obe—Zwi.
*312	2	ENGINEER (Civil) and Architect's Journal. 4 vols. 4to. 1837–41.
44	5	ENGLAND, Beauties of. 2 vols. 8vo. 1776.
*470	7	——— Geography and History of. 8vo. 1765.
28	3	——— Remarkable Events in History of. 2 vols. 18mo. 1838.
189	6	ENGLAND (J.) Explanation of Ceremonies at Rome. 12mo. 1833.
180	19	——— Explanation of Furniture, &c., of Romish Church. 12mo. n. d.
514	4	ENGLISH Forests and Forest Trees. 8vo. 1853.
83	12	ENGLISH (G. B.) Expedition to Dongola and Sennaar. 8vo. 1823.
188	13	——— Grounds of Christianity. 12mo. 1813.
84	4	EOTHEN. 12mo. 1850.
435	6	EPICTETUS, translated by Mrs. Carter. 2 vols. 8vo. 1807.
105	11	ERMAN (A.) Travels in Siberia. 2 vols. 12mo. 1850.
*394	15	ESCHENBURG (J. J.) Manual of Classical Literature. 8vo. 1850.
*584	9	ESQUIROL (E.) On Insanity. 8vo. 1845.
522	1	ESSAYISTS, Modern British. 8 vols. 8vo. 1848–51.
		Vol. 1. Macaulay. 2. Alison. 3. Sydney Smith. 4. Wilson. 5. Carlyle. 6. Jeffrey. 7. Talfourd and Stephens. 8. Mackintosh.
*594	7	ESSAYS on the Puerperal Fever. 8vo. 1850.
175	9	——— on Various Subjects. 8vo. 1822.
186	9	——— on Various Subjects. 8vo. 1822.
*404	6	ETHNOLOGICAL Society's Transactions. 2 vols. 8vo. 1845–48.
499	16	EUCLID's Elements, Simson's edition. 8vo. 1806.
505	1	EULER (L.) Letters of. 2 vols. 8vo. 1802.
89	16	——— Letters of. 2 vols. 18mo. n. d.
167	16	EUPHROSYNE. 12mo. 1776.
120	9	EURIPIDES, translated by Potter. 3 vols. 18mo. 1852.
409	10	——— translated by Buckley. 2 vols. post 8vo. 1850.

Shelf.	No.	
5	4	Européan and North American Railway Convention at Portland. 8vo. 1850.
24	14	Eusebius' Ecclesiastical History, Council of Nice. 8vo. 1836.
150	18	Eustace (J. C.) Tour through Italy. 3 vols. 18mo. 1841.
*436	3	——— Tour through Italy. 4 vols. 8vo. 1821.
38	8	Eustaphieve (A.) Resources of Russia. 12mo. 1813.
*12	5	Evans (C.) Trial of S. Chase. 8vo. 1805.
492	12	Evans (O.) Mill-wright and Miller's Guide. 8vo. 1850.
429	2	Evans (T.) Old Ballads. 4 vols. post 8vo. 1810.
24	9	Evelyn (J.) History of Religion. 2 vols. post 8vo. 1850.
67	15	——— Life of Mrs. Godolphin. 12mo. 1847.
*271	8	Evening Gazette. Folio. 1815–16.
175	2	Everett (A. H.) America. 8vo. 1827.
528	11	——— Essays. 2 vols. 12mo. 1845–46.
176	1	——— On Population. 8vo. 1823.
44	8	——— Survey of Europe. 8vo. 1822.
189	9	Everett (E.) Defence of Christianity. 12mo. 1814.
186	14	——— Importance of Practical Education. 12mo. n. d.
482	3	——— Orations and Speeches. 2 vols. 8vo. 1850.
482	4	——— Orations and Speeches. 2 vols. 8vo. 1850.
*626	5	Evers (P.) Comparative Anatomy. 8vo. 1841.
493	4	Ewbank (T.) On Hydraulics. 8vo. 1850.
*430	1	Examen du Fatalisme. 3 vols. 12mo. 1757.
503	10	Examinations, Classical. 8vo. 1830.
*422	11	Exhibition of Works of Industry of All Nations, 1851. 8vo. 1852.
422	12	——— Industry of all Nations in 1851. 8vo. 1852.
508	1	——— of 1851. Lectures on the Results. 12mo. 1852.

F.

Shelf.	No.	
84	6	Fabens (J. W.) Camel Hunt. 12mo. 1853.
183	9	Faber (G. S.) View of the Prophecies. 8vo. 1809.
148	10	Falconer (W.) Poetical Works. 16mo. 1836.
159	4	——— Shipwreck, &c. 18mo. 1838.
177	12	Farley (S.) Discourses and Essays. 12mo. 1851.
104	17	Farnham (T. J.) Travels in California. 8vo. 1852.
158	4	Farquhar (G.) Works. 12mo. 1772.
122	11	Fay (T. S.) Dreams and Reveries of a Quiet Man. 2 vols. 12mo. 1832.
95	12	Fearon (H. B.) Sketches of America. 8vo. 1819.
4	4	Federalist. 8vo. 1852.
197	2	Fellowes (R.) Christian Philosophy. 8vo. 1803.
197	6	——— Religion without Cant. 8vo. 1801.
*472	6	Fellows (W. D.) Sketches of the latter part of Charles I.'s Reign. 4to. 1828.

Shelf.	No.	
*477	13	FELT (J. B.) Annals of Salem. 2 vols. 12mo. 1845–49.
*477	9	——— History of Ipswich, Essex, and Hamilton. 8vo. 1834.
475	2	——— History of Massachusetts Currency. 8vo. 1839.
75	16	——— Memorials of W. S. Shaw. 12mo. 1852.
67	19	FELTON (C. C.) Memoir of Rev. J. S. Popkin. 12mo. 1852.
506	9	FEMALES' Encyclopedia. 8vo. 1830.
129	15	FÉNÉLON (F. S. de la M.) Adventures of Telemachus. 18mo. 1853.
129	16	——— Adventures of Telemachus. 18mo. 1853.
140	18	——— Les Aventures de Télémaque. 4 vols. 18mo. 1796.
90	17	——— Lives of Ancient Philosophers. 18mo. n. d.
138	13	——— Dialogues des Morts. 12mo. 1805.
*646	7	FENNER (E. D.) Southern Medical Reports. 2 vols. 8vo. 1850–51.
49	7	FERGUS (H.) History of United States. 2 vols. 18mo. 1830.
32	4	FERGUSON (A.) History of the Roman Republic. 8vo. 1849.
110	11	——— History of the Roman Republic. 18mo. n. d.
176	3	——— History of Civil Society. 8vo. 1819.
499	18	FERGUSON (J.) Astronomy. 8vo. 1809.
493	21	FERGUSSON (W.) Professional Life. 8vo. 1846.
*554	10	FERGUSSON (W.) Practical Surgery. 8vo. 1853.
135	14	FERRIER (S.) Destiny. 16mo. 1852.
121	13	——— Inheritance. 3 vols. 8vo. 1825.
506	18	FESSENDEN (T. G.) Complete Farmer. 12mo. 1853.
166	4	——— Democracy Unveiled. 12mo. 1805.
507	18	——— New American Gardener. 12mo. 1831.
508'	12	FETIS (F. J.) Music Explained. 16mo. 1842.
78	15	FEUERBACH (A. von). Caspar Hauser. 18mo. 1832.
633	7	FIELD Book. Sports, &c. 8vo. 1833.
*473	5	FINANCIAL Register of the United States. 2 vols. 8vo. 1838
*583	3	FINDLAY (A. G.) Classical Atlas. 8vo. 1853.
*583	2	——— Modern Atlas. 8vo. 1853.
41	16	FINLAY (G.) Byzantine Empire. 8vo. 1853.
41	15	——— Greece under the Romans. 8vo. 1844.
41	17	——— Greece and the Empire of Trebizond. 8vo. 1851.
155	1	FINLAY (J.) Scottish Ballads. 12mo. 1808.
*671	11	FISHER (J. D.) Small Pox, Varioloid, &c. 4to. 1834.
*653	1	FISHER (R. S.) Gazetteer of the United States. 8vo. 1853.
340	3	FISHER (R. T.) Law of Wills. 12mo. 1837.
507	25	FITCH (S. S.) On Consumption. 12mo. 1848.
*469	28	FITCH (T.) On the Stamp Act. 8vo. 1766.
105	4	FLAGG (E.) Venice, the City of the Sea. 2 vols. 12mo. 1853.
*168	7	FLATMAN (T.) Poems and Songs. 12mo. 1686.
*633	1	FLEMING & TIBBINS's French Dictionary. 8vo. 1852.
176	4	FLETCHER (A.) Political Works. 8vo. 1732.
88	16	FLETCHER (J.) History of Poland. 18mo. n. d.
182	3	FLETCHER (J.) Checks to Antinomianism. 4 vols. 8vo. 1819.

Shelf.	No.	
172	12	FLETCHER (J.) Studies on Slavery. 8vo. 1852.
121	42	FLIM Flams. 3 vols. 12mo. 1805.
14	10	FLINT (T.) The Mississippi Valley. 8vo. 1833.
103	13	——— Ten Years in the Mississippi Valley. 8vo. 1826.
507	8	FLORA, Toilet of. 12mo. 1784.
28	1	FLORIAN (J. P. C. de). Gonzalve de Cordoue. 18mo. 1828.
110	3	——— Moors of Spain. 18mo. n. d.
18	13	FLORIDA, East, Notices of. 12mo. 1822.
199	1	FOLLEN (C.) Works. 5 vols. 12mo. 1842.
526	6	——— Works. 5 vols. 12mo. 1842. Vol. 1. Life; Poems. 2. Sermons. 3. Lectures on Moral Philosophy; Psychology. 4. Schiller's Life and Dramas; Don Carlos; Wallenstein; Mary Stuart; William Tell; &c. 5. Future State of Man; History; Funeral Oration on Spurzheim; Slavery; Peace and War.
158	22	FOLLEN (E. L.) Poems. 12mo. 1839.
188	14	——— Selections from Fenelon. 16mo. 1851.
129	7	——— Well-spent Hour. 16mo. 1848.
*469	31	FONBLANQUE (A.) England under Seven Administrations. 3 vols. 12mo. 1837.
87	12	FOOTE (H. S.) Texas and Texans. 2 vols. 12mo. 1841.
154	2	FOOTE (S.) Works. 2 vols. 8vo. 1799. Vol. 1. Taste; Englishman in Paris; the Knights; Englishman Returned from Paris; the Author; Mayor of Garrat; the Orators; the Minor; the Lyar, and the Patron. 2. The Commissary; Lame Lover; the Bankrupt; the Cozeners; the Maid of Bath; Devil upon Two Sticks; Nabob; Trip to Calais; and the Capuchin.
435	4	FORBES (Major). Eleven Years in Ceylon. 2 vols. 8vo. 1840.
*613	3	FORBES (J.), TWEEDIE, and others. Cyclopædia of Practical Medicine. 4 vols. 8vo. 1852. Vol. 1. Abd—Emm. | Vol. 3. Inf—Rap. 2. Emp—Inf. | 4. Ref—Yaw.
*636	9	——— On the Chest. 8vo. 1824.
85	1	——— Physicians' Holiday. 12mo. 1852.
*433	1	FORBES (J. D.) Norway and its Glaciers. 8vo. 1853.
16	13	FORBES (J. G.) Sketches of East Florida. 8vo. 1821.
85	13	FORD (R.) Spaniards and their Country. 12mo. 1850.
539	3	——— Gatherings from Spain. 16mo. 1846.
188	17	FORDYCE (J.) Sermons to Young Women. 12mo. 1809.
		FOREIGN Quarterly Review. 37 vols. 8vo. 1827–46.
*302	1	Vols. 1–22. 8vo. 1827–39.
*303	1	,, 23–37. 8vo. 1839–46.
122	7	FORSAKEN (The). 2 vols. 12mo. 1831.
80	2	FORSTER (J.) Life of Oliver Goldsmith. 8vo. 1848.
62	12	——— Statesmen of the Commonwealth. 8vo. 1846.
40	1	FOSTER (J.) and others. Lives of British Statesmen. 7 vols. 18mo. 1831–39.

Shelf.	No.	
483	15	FORSYTH (J.) Antiquities, Arts, &c., in Italy. 8vo. 1818.
45	8	FORSYTH (W.) Captivity of Napoleon at St. Helena. 3 vols. 8vo. 1853.
41	1	—— Captivity of Napoleon at St. Helena. 2 vols. 12mo. 1853.
49	8	FOSBROKE (T. D.) and others. Arts, Manners, &c. of Greeks and Romans. 2 vols. 18mo. 1833.
530	13	FOSTER (J.) Essays. 16mo. 1851.
488	5	—— Essays. 12mo. 1851.
398	5	—— Lectures. 2 vols. post 8vo. 1853.
397	13	—— Life and Correspondence. 2 vols. post 8vo. 1852.
530	12	—— On Popular Ignorance. 12mo. 1821.
530	14	—— On Popular Ignorance. 16mo. 1850.
486	4	FOSTER (Mrs.) European Literature. 12mo. 1850.
189	33	FOUNTAIN of Living Waters. 16mo. 1851.
499	17	FOWLER (O. S.) Home for All. 12mo. 1854.
*443	5	FOX (C. J.) Memorials and Correspondence. 2 vols. 8vo. 1853.
67	1	—— Memorials and Correspondence. 2 vols. 12mo. 1853.
*472	2	—— Reign of James II. 4to. 1808.
189	17	FOX (T. B.) Ministry of Jesus Christ. 16mo. 1840.
*691	18	FRANCE. Brevets d'Invention. 10 vols. 4to. 1850–52.
180	28	—— Code Civil des Français. 18mo. 1804.
*586	5	—— Collection Officielle des Ordonnances de Police. Vols. 2, 3, 4. 1844–45.
*650	3	—— Gazetteer of. 3 vols. 12mo. 1793.
*656	9	FRANCIS (D. J. T.) Change of Climate. 12mo. 1853.
62	2	FRANKLIN (B.) Autobiography. 8vo. 1849.
518	1	—— Familiar Letters. 12mo. 1833.
75	2	—— Life. 12mo. 1853.
54	5	—— Memoirs. 2 vols. 8vo. 1840.
98	14	—— Memoirs. 2 vols. 18mo. n. d.
488	4	—— Select Works, Sargent's edition. 12mo. 1853.
514	1	—— Works. 10 vols. 8vo. n. d.
403	1	—— Works. 10 vols. 8vo. 1840.

Vol. 1. Autobiography; Life continued, by Sparks.
2. Essays on Religious and Moral Subjects, and the Economy of Life; Essays on Politics, Commerce, and Political Economy.
3. Essays and Tracts, Historical and Political, before the American Revolution; Constitution and Government of Pennsylvania.
4. Essays and Tracts continued.
5. Political Papers during and after the American Revolution; Letters and Papers on Electricity.
6. Letters and Papers on Philosophical Subjects.
7. Correspondence: Part 1. Private Letters to the Time of the Author's First Mission to England, 1725–57. Part 2. Letters, Private and Official, from the Time of the Author's First Mission to England to the Beginning of the American Revolution, 1757–75.

Shelf. No.

FRANKLIN (B.) Works, *continued.*

8. Correspondence: Part 2 continued, 1757–75. Part 3. Letters, Private and Official, from the Beginning of the Revolution to End of the Author's Mission to France, 1775–85; Appendix; Fragment of Polybius, on the Athenian Government; Memoir of Sir John Dalrymple.
9. Correspondence: Part 3 continued; Journal of the Negotiation of the Treaty of Peace.
10. Correspondence: Part 3 continued; Part 4. Private Letters, from the Termination of the Author's Mission to France to the End of his Life, 1785–90; Supplement; Indexes; Chronological List of the Author's Writings.

103 10 FRANKLIN (J.) Journey to Polar Sea. 8vo. 1824.
*392 22 FRASER (J. B.) Journey into Khorasan. 4to. 1825.
98 10 ——— History of Persia. 18mo. n. d.
100 18 ——— History of Mesopotamia and Assyria. 18mo. n. d.
515 1 FREDERIC II. Posthumous Works. 13 vols. 8vo. 1789–91.

Vol. 1. History of My Own Times.
2. Seven Years' War.
3. War continued.
4. Memoirs from the Peace of Hubertsburg to the Partition of Poland; the Bavarian War of 1778.
5. Political, Philosophical, and Satirical Miscellanies.
6, 7, 8. Letters between Frederic II. and Voltaire.
9. Letters between Frederic II. and M. Jordan.
10. Letters between Frederic II. and the Marquis D'Argens.
11. Letters between Frederic II. and M. D'Alembert.
12. Letters between Frederic II. and Messrs. D'Alembert, De Condorcet, Grimm, and D'Arget.
13. Letters between Frederic II., the Prince of Prussia, and General Fouquet; Miscellanies.

155 9 FREE (J.) Poems. 8vo. 1751.
184 5 FREEMAN (J.) Sermons. 8vo. 1812.
*340 6 FREEMAN (S.) Town Officer. 12mo. 1808.
106 17 FREMONT (J. C.) Travels in California. 8vo. 1849.
*474 11 FRENCH (B. F.) Historical Memoirs of Louisiana. 8vo. 1853.
*474 12 ——— Historical Collections of Louisiana. Part 1. 8vo. 1846.
*474 13 ——— Historical Collections of Louisiana. Part 3. 8vo. 1851.
167 15 FRENEAU (P.) Poems. 2 vols. 12mo. 1809.
519 19 FRIENDS in Council. 12mo. 1849.
42 5 FROISSART (J.) Chronicles of England, France, &c. 8vo. 1853.
83 15 FRONTIER Lands of the Christian and Turk. 2 vols. 8vo. 1853.
54 2 FROST (J.) Pictorial Life of Andrew Jackson. 8vo. 1853.
66 12 ——— Life of General Taylor. 12mo. 1847.
15 7 ——— Pictorial History of United States. 2 vols. 8vo. 1847.
97 4 ——— Travels in Africa. 12mo. 1848.
14 1 ——— Remarkable Events in History of America. 2 vols. 8vo. 1852.

Shelf.	No.	
12	6	Frothingham (R. jun.) History of Siege of Boston. 8vo. 1851.
*475	1	——— History of Siege of Boston. 8vo. 1851.
171	19	Fruits of Leisure. 12mo. 1852.
483	1	Fry (E.) Pantographia. 8vo. 1799.
397	14	Fuller (A.) Works. Post 8vo. 1852.
604	3	Fuller (H. W.) Rheumatism. 8vo. 1854.
180	23	Fuller (R.) & Wayland (F.) Domestic Slavery. 18mo. 1847.
54	6	Fuller (T.) History of Worthies of England. 3 vols. 8vo. 1840.
110	19	Furniss (W.) Waraga. 12mo. 1850.

G.

Shelf.	No.	
7	3	Gage (T.) History of Rowley. 12mo. 1840.
*477	12	——— History of Rowley. 12mo. 1840.
*480	5	Gage (T.) Survey of the West Indies. 12mo. 1677.
*656	5	Gairdner (W.) On the Gout. 12mo. 1851.
*656	2	Gairdner (W. T.) Bronchitis. 8vo. 1850.
660	15	Galignani (A. & W.) Paris Guide. 18mo. 1825.
18	11	Gallatin (A.) On the North-east Boundary. 8vo. 1843.
189	32	Gallaudet (T. H.) Child's Book on the Soul. 16mo. 1847.
189	15	——— Youth's Book on Natural Theology. 12mo. 1833.
*201	2	Galliat (V.) Hotel de Ville de Paris. Folio. 1846.
666	14	Gallois (M. Le). On Life. 8vo. 1813.
*664	7	Gallup (J. A.) Institutes of Medicine. 2 vols. 8vo. 1839.
121	37	Galt (J.) Ayrshire Legatees. 12mo. 1823.
121	14	——— Ayrshire Legatees. 12mo. 1821.
134	6	——— Eben Erskine. 3 vols. post 8vo. 1833.
121	38	——— Eben Erskine. 2 vols. 12mo. 1833.
140	5	——— Entail. 2 vols. 12mo. 1823.
121	27	——— Lawrie Todd. 2 vols. 12mo. 1830.
69	11	——— Life of Cardinal Wolsey. Post 8vo. 1846.
88	6	——— Life of Lord Byron. 18mo. n. d.
154	9	——— Poems. 8vo. 1833.
140	4	——— Provost. 12mo. 1822.
131	16	——— Rothelan. 2 vols. 12mo. 1825.
111	12	——— Southennan. 3 vols. 12mo. 1830.
121	33	——— Spae Wife. 2 vols. 12mo. 1824.
127	5	——— Stanley Buxton. 3 vols. 12mo. 1832.
121	39	——— Stanley Buxton. 2 vols. 12mo. 1833.
137	17	——— Stolen Child. 16mo. 1833.
127	1	——— Stories of the Study. 3 vols. post 8vo. 1833.
178	20	Gammell (W.) History of American Baptist Missions. 12mo. 1851.
175	7	Ganilh (C.) Political Economy. 8vo. 1812.

Shelf.	No.	
503	19	GARDINER (W.) Music and Friends. 2 vols. 8vo. 1838.
*663	7	GARDNER (C. K.) Dictionary of the Army of the United States. 12mo. 1853.
65	10	GARLAND (H. A.) Life of John Randolph. 2 vols. 12mo. 1851.
*446	5	——— Life of John Randolph. 2 vols. 12mo. 1851.
173	10	GARRISON (W. L.) African Colonization. 8vo. 1832.
538	8	GAUTIER (T.) Wanderings in Spain. Post 8vo. 1853.
167	9	GAY (J.) Works. 3 vols. 12mo. 1772.
12	1	GAYARRE (C.) History of Louisiana. 8vo. 1851.
*470	18	GEE (J.) Trade, &c. of Great Britain. 18mo. 1760.
140	6	GENLIS (S. F.) Alphonso and Dalinda. 16mo. 1799.
138	11	——— Alphonse, où le Fils Naturel. 2 vols. 16mo. 1824.
131	17	——— Knights of the Swan. 3 vols. 12mo. 1796–97.
121	41	——— New Moral Tales. 12mo. 1825.
131	18	——— Rival Mothers. 2 vols. 12mo. 1801.
121	43	——— Sinclair. 12mo. 1813.
131	29	——— Zuma. 18mo. 1818.
137	5	GENTLEMAN Jack. 2 vols. 12mo. 1837.
189	18	GENTLEMAN'S Religion. 18mo. 1737.
		——— Magazine. 137 vols. 8vo. From 1731 to 1850.
*548	1	From 1731—1747.
*558	1	,, 1748—1763.
*568	1	,, 1764—1778.
*578	1	,, 1779—1789.
*588	1	,, 1789, part 2, to 1796.
*598	1	,, 1797—1804.
*608	1	,, 1805—1812.
*618	1	,, 1813—1820.
*628	1	,, 1821—1828.
*638	1	,, 1829—1837.
*648	1	,, 1837—1844.
*658	1	,, 1845—1850.
*404	3	GEOLOGISTS and Naturalists. Association Reports, 1840–42. 8vo. 1843.
69	15	GEORGE (A.) Queens of Spain. 2 vols. 12mo. 1850.
*544	4	GERHARD (W. W.) Diseases of the Chest. 8vo. 1850.
137	14	GHOST-HUNTER and his Family. 12mo. 1833.
57	11	GIBBON (E). Autobiography. 12mo. 1846.
36	1	——— Decline and Fall of the Roman Empire. 6 vols. 12mo. 1851.
*456	1	——— Decline and Fall of the Roman Empire. 6 vols. 8vo. 1846.
2	6	GIBBS (G.) Administrations of Washington and Adams. 2 vols. 8vo. 1846.
23	4	GIESELER (J. C. L.) Ecclesiastical History. 2 vols. 8vo. 1849.
444	6	GIFFORD (J.) Life of Pitt. 6 vols. 8vo. 1809.

Shelf.	No.	
172	4	GILBART (J. W.) On Banking. 8vo. 1851.
177	16	GILES (H.) Discourses on Life. 16mo. 1851.
519	13	——— Lectures and Essays. 2 vols. 16mo. 1851.
178	13	GILFILLAN (G.) Bards of the Bible. 12mo. 1851.
494	10	GILLESPIE (W. M.) On Road Making. 8vo. 1850.
*44	2	GILLIES (J.) History of Ancient Greece. 4 vols. 8vo. 1787.
35	9	——— History of Ancient Greece. 4 vols. 8vo. 1814.
53	6	——— Reign of Frederick II. 8vo. 1789.
124	3	GILMAN (C.) New England Bride and Southern Matron. 12mo. 1852.
122	13	——— Southern Matron. 12mo. 1852.
539	51	GILSON (A.) Czar and Sultan. 12mo. 1853.
539	52	——— Czar and Sultan. 16mo. 1853.
493	10	GIRAUD (J. P. jun.) Birds of Long Island. 8vo. 1844.
185	6	GISBORNE (T.) Duties of Men. 2 vols. 8vo. 1800.
38	6	GLEASON (B.) Remembrancer. 12mo. 1814.
539	16	GLEIG (G. R.) British Army at Washington and New Orleans. 16mo. 1847.
170	18	——— British Empire in India. 4 vols. 18mo. 1830–35.
137	3	——— Chelsea Pensioners. 3 vols. post 8vo. 1829.
115	10	——— Country Curate. 2 vols. post 8vo. 1830.
88	9	——— History of the Bible. 2 vols. 18mo. n. d.
539	43	——— Life of Robert, first Lord Clive. 16mo. 1848.
539	45	——— Life of Sir Thomas Munro. 16mo. 1849.
73	1	——— Life of Warren Hastings. 3 vols. 8vo. 1841.
111	5	——— Light Dragoon. 2 vols. 8vo. 1844.
49	9	——— Lives of British Military Commanders. 3 vols. 18mo. n. d.
539	4	——— Sales's Brigade in Affghanistan. 12mo. 1846.
111	17	——— Self-Devotion. 3 vols. post 8vo. 1844.
539	46	——— Story of the Battle of Waterloo. 16mo. 1847.
97	18	GOBAT (S.) Residence in Abyssinia. 12mo. 1851.
*404	11	GODMAN (J. D.) American Natural History. 3 vols. 8vo. 1826.
666	5	——— Addresses. 8vo. 1829.
*633	9	GODWIN (P.) Universal Biography. 12mo. 1852.
138	3	GODWIN (W.) Cloudesley. 2 vols. 12mo. 1830.
*442	10	——— Life of Chaucer. 2 vols. 4to. 1803.
*442	2	——— Life of E. and J. Phillips. 4to. 1815.
*403	4	GODWYN (F.) Annales of England. Folio. 1630.
92	5	GŒDE (C. A. G.) A Foreigner's Opinion of England. 8vo. 1822.
400	5	GOETHE (J. W.) Autobiography. 2 vols. post 8vo. 1848–49.
399	6	——— Dramatic Works. Post 8vo. 1850.
165	8	——— Faust, translated by Hayward. 16mo. 1851.
135	2	——— Faust, translated by Hayward. 16mo. 1840.
146	2	——— Faust, part 2. 16mo. 1842.
135	8	——— Wilhelm Meister. 2 vols. 16mo. 1851.

Shelf.	No.	
530	25	GOLDSMITH (O.) Essays, with Life. 16mo. n. d.
47	4	——— History of England. 4 vols. 12mo. 1792.
39	12	——— History of Greece. 12mo. 1822.
45	6	——— History of Greece. 2 vols. 8vo. 1821.
44	3	——— History of Greece. 2 vols. 8vo. 1820.
44	10	——— History of Rome. 2 vols. 8vo. 1821.
		——— History of Rome. 2 vols. 8vo. 1797.
516	10	——— Miscellaneous Works. 4 vols. 12mo. 1850.

Vol. 1. The Bee; Essays; Present State of Polite Learning in Europe; Prefaces and Introductions.
2. Citizen of the World; Introduction to the Study of Natural History.
3. Vicar of Wakefield; Biographies of Voltaire; Richard Nash; Parnell and Bolingbroke; Miscellaneous Criticism.
4. Poems; Miscellaneous Pieces; Good-natured Man; She Stoops to Conquer; the Grumbler; Criticism relating to Poetry and the Belles Lettres; Index.

Shelf.	No.	
*522	6	——— Miscellaneous Works. 8vo. 1850.
156	14	——— Poems. 12mo. 1800.
149	3	——— Poems. 16mo. 1851.
115	11	——— Vicar of Wakefield. 12mo. 1851.
139	16	——— Vicar of Wakefield. 18mo. n. d.
494	11	GOOD (J. M.) Book of Nature. 8vo. 1850.
105	3	GOODELL (W.) Thirty Years in the East. 12mo. 1853.
43	2	GOODMAN (G.) Court of James I. 2 vols. 8vo. 1839.
483	16	GOODRICH (C. A.) Select British Eloquence. 8vo. 1853.
8	5	——— History of United States. 12mo. 1853.
32	10	GOODRICH (S. G.) History of All Nations. 2 vols. 8vo. 1851.
*656	1	GOODSIR (J. & H. D. S.) Anatomical and Pathological Observations. 8vo. 1845.
*396	1	GORDON (D.) History of Trials and Executions for High Treason. 3 vols. 8vo. 1760.
*353	8	GORDON (T. F.) Digest of United States Laws. 8vo. 1827.
18	14	——— History of America. 2 vols. 16mo. 1831.
14	9	——— History of New Jersey. 8vo. 1834.
*476	3	GORDON (W.) History of the American War. 4 vols. 8vo. 1788.
116	8	GORE (C. F.) Manners of the Day. 3 vols. 12mo. 1830.
111	6	——— Men of Capital. 3 vols. 12mo. 1846.
137	2	——— Peers and Parvenus. 3 vols. 12mo. 1846.
121	5	——— Polish Tales. 3 vols. 12mo. 1833.
111	1	——— Popular Member. 3 vols. 12mo. 1844.
56	9	GÖRGEI (A.) My Life and Acts in Hungary. 16mo. 1852.
*633	2	GORTON (J. Biographical Dictionary. 4 vols. 8vo. 1851.

Vol. 1. Aa—Exp.	Vol. 3. Nad—Vul.
2. Fab—Myl.	4. Wac and Supplement.

Shelf.	No.	
530	3	GOSTICK (J.) German Literature. 12mo. 1849.

Shelf.	No.	
492	1	Gould (A. A.) Naturalist's Library. 8vo. 1851.
*660	10	Gould (J.) Dictionary of Painters, &c. 2 vols. 16mo. 1838.
		Vol. 1. A—L. | Vol. 2. M—Z.
*344	2	Gow (N.) On Partnerships. 8vo. n. d.
*650	8	Graglia (C.) Italian Dictionary. 16mo. 1851.
*660	12	Graham (G. F.) English Synonymes. 12mo. 1851.
486	5	——— English Synonymes. 12mo. 1847.
67	8	Graham (I.) Life and Writings. 12mo. 1843.
12	7	Grahame (J.) History of the United States. 2 vols. 8vo. 1850.
530	18	Grant (A.) Letters from the Mountains. 12mo. 1809.
77	4	——— Memoirs of an American Lady. 12mo. 1846.
520	3	Grant (R.) British Senate. 2 vols. 12mo. 1838.
520	2	——— Great Metropolis. 12mo. 1837.
188	10	——— Metropolitan Pulpit. 12mo. 1839.
530	8	——— Recollections of House of Commons. 12mo. 1836.
530	9	——— Recollections of House of Lords. 12mo. 1836.
529	17	——— Walks in the World of Literature. 2 vols. 12mo. 1840.
134	5	Grattan (T. C.) Agnes de Mansfeldt. 3 vols. 12mo. 1835.
121	19	——— High-ways and By-ways. 3 vols. 12mo. 1840.
121	10	——— High-ways and By-ways. 3 vols. 12mo. 1835.
48	2	——— History of the Netherlands. 18mo. 1843.
49	10	——— History of the Netherlands. 18mo. 1830.
121	22	——— Legends of the Rhine. 2 vols. 12mo. 1833.
121	30	——— Traits of Travel. 2 vols. 12mo. 1829.
100	4	Graves (A. J.) Woman in America. 18mo. n. d.
*544	8	Graves (R. J.) & Gerhard. Clinical Medicine. 8vo. 1848.
*646	18	Gray's Supplement to the Pharmacopœia. 8vo. 1848.
498	9	Gray (A.) Elements of Chemistry. 12mo. 1842.
505	7	Gray (Asa). Botanical Text Book. 8vo. 1850.
497	3	——— Botanical Text Book. 12mo. 1842.
496	9	——— Manual of Botany. 12mo. 1848.
147	3	Gray (T.) Works. 5 vols. 16mo. 1836–43.

Vol. 1. Life; Poems.
2. Essay on the Poetry of Gray; Letters.
3. Letters.
4. Letters; Criticism on Architecture and Painting during a Tour in Italy.
5. Mathias's Letter on the Death of Nicholls; Reminiscences of Gray, by Nicholls; Correspondence of Gray with Nicholls; Correspondence of Brown and Nicholls relative to Gray; Letters of Nicholls; Notes by Mitford; Gray's Notes on Walpole's Lives of the Painters; Extracts from a Poem on the Letters of the Alphabet; Observations on English Metre, Pseudo-Rhythm, Use of Rhyme, and on the Poems of Lydgate.

*469	6	Great Britain, Appeal to the Justice and Interests of the People of. 8vo. 1776.

Shelf.	No.	
*469	17	Great Britain. Appeal (second), &c. 8vo. 1775.
*291	2	—— British Museum. Commissioners' Report. Folio. 1836.
*291	3	—— British Museum. Commissioners' Report. Folio. 1850.
*291	4	—— British Museum. Commissioners' Report. Index. Folio. 1850.
*291	15	—— Commercial Tariffs, Resources, and Trade. Brazil. Folio. 1847.
*291	14	—— Commercial Tariff, &c. Hayti, and Foreign West Indies. Folio. 1847.
*291	17	—— Commercial Tariff, &c. India, Ceylon, &c. Folio. 1848.
*291	13	—— Commercial Tariff, &c. Mexico. Folio. 1846.
*291	16	—— Commercial Tariff, &c. Spanish American Republics. Folio. 1847.
*291	12	—— Commercial Tariff, &c. United States. Folio. 1846.
*291	18	—— Commercial Tariff, &c. Appendixes. Folio. 1850.
		—— Commons' Journal. 1547—1826. 81 vols. folio.
*541	1	From 1547—1697. Vols. 1-11.
*551	1	,, 1697—1741. ,, 12-23.
*561	1	,, 1741—1772. ,, 24-33.
*571	1	,, 1772—1788. ,, 34-43.
*581	1	,, 1788—1798. ,, 44-54.
*591	1	,, 1799—1809. ,, 55-63.
*601	1	,, 1809—1818. ,, 64-73.
*611	1	,, 1818—1826. ,, 74-81.
*631	2	Index of vols. 1- 7. Folio. 1785.
*631	3	Index of vols. 8-11. Folio. 1780.
*631	4	Index of vols. 12-17. Folio. 1778.
*631	5	Index of vols. 18-34. Folio. 1778.
*631	6	Index of vols. 35-45. Folio. 1796.
*641	2	Index of vols. 56-75. Folio. 1825.
*651	2	—— Commons' Reports. 1812-24. Bogs in Ireland, Public Works, Linen Trade. Folio. 1824.
*291	6	—— General Index to the Bills, Reports, &c., printed by order of the House of Commons. 1845-50. Folio. 1850.
*469	2	—— Interest of, with regard to her Colonies, considered. 8vo. 1761.
*469	21	—— Interest of, with regard to her Colonies, considered. 8vo. 1761.
*291	5	—— Minutes of Committee of Council on Education, with Plans for School Houses. Folio. 1840.
		—— Parliamentary Papers, from 1820, vol. 3, to 1826-27, vol. 26. 144 vols. Folio.
*541	2	1820. Vols. 3-12. Index to 1820, vol. 12.
*541	2	1821. ,, 1- 6.

Shelf.	No.	
		GREAT BRITAIN. Parliamentary Papers, *continued.*
*551	2	1821. Vols. 7–21.
*561	2	1821. ,, 22–23. Index to 1821, vol. 23.
*561	2	1822. ,, 1–14.
*571	2	1822. ,, 15–22. Index to 1822, vol. 22.
*571	2	1824. ,, 1–8.
*581	2	1824. ,, 9–21.
*591	2	1824. ,, 22–24. Index to 1824, vol. 24.
*591	2	1825. ,, 1–11.
*601	2	1825. ,, 12–15. Vols. 17–26.
*611	2	1825. ,, 27. Index to 1825, vol. 27.
*611	2	1826. ,, 1–13. Vols. 15, 16.
*611	2a	1826. ,, 14.
*621	2	1826. ,, 17–29. Index to 1826, vol. 29.
*631	7	1826–27. Vols. 1–13.
*641	4	1826–27. ,, 14–26. Index to 1826–27, vol. 26.
*651	9	——— Parliamentary Papers. Children's Employment Commission. Parts 1, 2. 2 vols. folio. 1842.
*651	10	——— Parliamentary Papers. Commissioners of Inquiry for South Wales. Folio. 1844.
*651	5	——— Parliamentary Papers. Despatches of Sir F. B. Head on Canada. Folio. 1839.
*651	6	——— Parliamentary Papers. Earl of Durham on British North America. Folio. 1839.
*651	8	——— Parliamentary Papers. Grand Jury Presentment in Ireland. Folio. 1842.
*651	3	——— Parliamentary Papers. Grievances complained of in Canada. Folio. 1837.
*651	4	——— Parliamentary Papers. Lower and Upper Canada. Folio. 1838.
*651	7	——— Parliamentary Papers. North American Boundary A. Folio. 1838.
*452	4	——— Parliamentary Papers. North American Boundary. Parts 1 and 2. Correspondence. Folio. 1840.
*651	11	——— Parliamentary Papers. Revenue, Population, Commerce of the United Kingdom. Folio. 1844.
*291	10	——— Plans of Buckingham Palace. Folio. 1847.
*291	11	——— Plans of Buckingham Palace. Folio. 1847.
*291	7	——— Public Works, Ireland. Sixteenth Report of the Board of Public Works. Folio. 1848.
*252	7	——— Reports of Commissioners on Criminal Law. Folio. 1834–43.
		——— Reports from Committees of the House of Commons, 1715 to 1803. 16 vols. folio.
*621	1	Vols. 1–11.
*631	1	,, 12–16. Vol. 16. General Index, from 1715 to 1803.
*291	8	——— Report of Committee on Public Libraries. 1 vol. folio. 1849.

Shelf.	No.	
*291	19	Great Britain. Report of Committee on Public Libraries. Folio. 1849.
291	9	—— Report of Committee on Public Libraries. Folio. 1850.
409	3	Greek Anthology, translated by Burges. Post 8vo. 1852.
509	26	Greeley (H.) Art and Industry at the Crystal Palace. 12mo. 1853.
96	3	—— Glances at Europe. 12mo. 1851.
525	13	—— Hints toward Reforms. 12mo. 1850.
*604	11	Green (H.) On Bronchitis. 8vo. 1852.
*614	10	—— Pathology of Croup. 12mo. 1852.
150	17	Green (S.) Life of Mahomet. 18mo. 1840.
102	2	Green (T. J.) Journal of Texian Expedition against Mier. 8vo. 1845.
37	7	Greene (G. W.) Historical Studies. 12mo. 1850.
8	8	—— Middle Ages. 12mo. 1851.
126	6	Greene (N.) Tales from the German. 2 vols. 12mo. 1837.
12	4	Greenhow (R.) Oregon and California. 8vo. 1845.
13	2	—— Oregon and California. 8vo. 1845.
*16	8	—— Oregon and California. 8vo. 1844.
*474	10	Greenleaf (M.) Statistical View of Maine. 8vo. 1816.
198	1	Greenleaf (S.) On the Four Evangelists. 8vo. 1846.
518	5	Greenwood (Rev. F. W. P.) Miscellaneous Writings. 12mo. 1846.
177	6	—— Sermons. 2 vols. 12mo. 1844.
177	18	—— Sermons on Consolation. 16mo. 1847.
109	19	Gregg (J.) Commerce of the Prairies. 2 vols. 12mo. 1850.
*594	9	Gregory (G.) Eruptive Fevers. 8vo. 1851.
398	1	Gregory (O.) Evidences of the Christian Religion. Post 8vo. 1851.
77	23	—— Memoirs of J. M. Good. 12mo. 1832.
502	19	—— Mathematics. 8vo. 1852.
497	13	Gregory (W.) Animal Magnetism. 12mo. 1851.
*586	6	Grenville (R. & G.) Papers and Correspondence. 4 vols. 8vo. 1852.
500	13	Gresham (T.) Life. 18mo. 1845.
524	5	Griffin (E. D.) Remains. 2 vols. 8vo. 1831.
127	7	Griffin (G.) Invasion. 4 vols. 12mo. 1832.
121	11	—— Rivals. 3 vols. 12mo. 1830.
*604	21	Griffin (W. & D.) On the Spinal Cord. 8vo. 1834.
*594	10	Griffith (R. E.) Medical Botany. 8vo. 1847.
*594	11	—— Universal Formulary. 8vo. 1850.
*614	6	Griffith, Rees, & Markwick. On the Blood and Urine. 12mo. 1848.
*392	6	Griffiths (J. W.) Marine Architecture. 4to. 1851.
128	9	Grimm, Brothers. Household Stories. 2 vols. 12mo. 1853.
131	13	—— German Popular Tales. 2 vols. 12mo. 1853.
93	7	Griscom (J.) Year in Europe. 2 vols. 8vo. 1823.

Shelf.	No.	
98	3	Griscom (J. H.) Animal Mechanism and Physiology. 18mo. n. d.
507	15	——— Uses and Abuses of Air. 12mo. 1850.
110	18	Griswold (C. D.) Isthmus of Panama. 12mo. 1852.
162	2	Griswold (R. W.) Female Poets of America. 8vo. 1852.
*163	4	——— Poets and Poetry of America. 8vo. 1851.
163	2	——— Poets and Poetry of America. 8vo. 1850.
163	6	——— Poets and Poetry of America. 8vo. 1842.
162	4	——— Poets and Poetry of England. 8vo. 1852.
512	8	——— Prose Writers of America. 8vo. 1847.
164	15	——— Sacred Poets of England and America. 8vo. 1850.
138	12	Grivel (M.) L'Ile Inconnue. 2 vols. 12mo. 1812.
*664	8	Gross (S. D.) Pathological Anatomy. 2 vols. 8vo. 1839.
*413	4	——— Pathological Anatomy. 8vo. 1845.
*466	2	Grote (G.) History of Greece. 10 vols. 8vo. 1849–52.
25	8	——— History of Greece. 10 vols. 12mo. 1851–53.
*339	14	Grotius (H.) De Jure Belli. 8vo. 1773.
180	1	Guide (American's). Declaration of Independence, Constitutions, &c. 12mo. n. d.
176	21	Guizot (F.) Democracy in France. 12mo. 1849.
70	8	——— Essay on Washington. 12mo. 1851.
28	8	——— History of Civilization. 4 vols. 12mo. 1852.
176	19	——— History of Civilization. 12mo. 1848.
39	1	——— History of the English Revolution. 12mo. 1846.
47	8	——— History of the English Revolution. 12mo. 1851.
398	9	——— Origin of Representative Government. Post 8vo. 1852.
66	16	Guizot (F). Corneille and his Times. 12mo. 1852.
164	7	——— Shakespeare and his Times. 12mo. 1852.
131	19	Guizot (Madame). Moral Tales. 16mo. 1852.
63	3	Gurley (R. R.) Life of Jehudi Ashmun. 8vo. 1835.
189	28	Gurney (J. J.) Essay on Love to God. 18mo. 1840.
196	8	——— Evidences, &c. of Christianity. 8vo. 1825.
180	12	——— Evidences, &c. of Christianity. 12mo. 1829.
189	29	——— Hints on Portable Evidence of Christianity. 16mo. 1833.
196	9	——— On the Society of Friends. 8vo. 1824.
92	7	——— Winter in the West Indies. 8vo. 1841.
576	2	Gutch (J.) Collectanea Curiosa. 2 vols. 8vo. 1781.
97	1	Gutzlaff (C.) Voyages along the Coast of China. 12mo. 1833.
506	5	Guyot (A.) Earth and Man; Physical Geography. 12mo. 1851.
497	7	——— Earth and Man; Physical Geography. 12mo. 1849.
*593	4	Gwilt (J.) Encyclopædia of Architecture. 8vo. 1842.
*636	10	Guthrie (G. J.) On Arteries. 8vo. 1830.
*626	5	——— Compound Fractures of the Extremities.

H.

Shelf.	No.	
135	12	HADDON HALL, Evenings at. 12mo. 1851.
70	23	HAINES (C. G.) Memoir of Emmet. 16mo. 1829.
530	19	HALE (M.) Advice to his Grandchildren. 12mo. 1823.
*271	1	HALE (N.) Boston Weekly Messenger. Folio. 1820–23.
90	3	HALE (S.) History of the United States. 2 vols. 18mo. n. d.
129	17	HALE (S. J.) Keeping House and House-keeping. 18mo. 1845.
131	10	——— Liberia, or Mr. Peyton's Experiments. 16mo. 1853.
432	5	——— Woman's Record. 8vo. 1853.
*470	16	HALES (J. G.) Survey of Boston. 16mo. 1821.
477	16	HALIBURTON (T. C.) History of Nova Scotia. 2 vols. 8vo. 1829.
126	1	——— Yankee Stories. 12mo. n. d.
109	14	HALL (B.) Journal on the Coasts of Chili, &c. 12mo. 1824.
87	3	——— Schloss Hainfeld. 18mo. 1836.
109	15	——— Travels in North America. 2 vols. 12mo. 1829.
83	9	——— Voyage to the West Coast of Corea, &c. 8vo. 1818.
76	3	HALL (E. B.) Memoir of Mary L. Ware. 12mo. 1853.
118	13	HALL (J.) Legends of the West. 12mo. 1833.
124	17	——— Legends of the West. 12mo. 1853.
8	11	——— The West, its Commerce and Navigation. 12mo. 1848.
121	18	——— Wilderness and War Path. 12mo. 1846.
154	6	HALL (Jos.) Satires, and other Poems. 8vo. 1838.
*594	15	HALL (M.) Nervous System and its Diseases. 8vo. 1836.
397	1	HALL (R.) Miscellaneous Works. Post 8vo. 1849.
200	17	——— Works, with Life. 6 vols. 16mo. 1851.

Vol. 1. Memoir, by Gregory; Letters and Circular Letters.
2. Sermons, Charges, and Reviews.
3. Works on Terms of Communion.
4. Tracts, Political and Miscellaneous.
5. Sermons; Notes of Sermons.
6. Sermons; Fragments; Miscellaneous Pieces; Index.

Shelf.	No.	
121	44	HALL (S. C.) Buccaneer. 2 vols. 12mo. 1833.
121	26	——— Lights and Shadows of Irish Life. 2 vols. 12mo. 1838.
121	28	——— Marian. 2 vols. 12mo. 1840.
122	1	——— Sketches of Irish Character. 8vo. 1853.
46	2	——— Stories and Studies from History of England. 2 vols. 16mo. 1847.
121	29	——— Uncle Horace. 2 vols. 12mo. 1838.
190	18	HALL (S. R.) Instructor's Manual. 18mo. 1852.
*455	2	HALLAM (H.) Constitutional History of England. 2 vols. 8vo. 1846.
43	6	——— Constitutional History of England. 8vo. 1853.

Shelf.	No.	
*455	4	HALLAM (H.) History of the Middle Ages, with Supplement. 3 vols. 8vo. 1846–48.
43	10	——— History of the Middle Ages. 8vo. 1853.
*455	3	——— Literature of Europe. 3 vols. 8vo. 1847.
43	5	——— Literature of Europe. 2 vols. 8vo. 1851.
149	8	HALLECK (F. G.) Alnwick Castle, and other Poems. 12mo. 1845.
165	13	——— Alnwick Castle, and other Poems. 12mo. 1845.
98	13	——— Selections from British Poets. 2 vols. 18mo. n. d.
*347	2	HALLETT (B. F.) Trial of E. K. Avery. 8vo. 1833.
55	1	HALLS (J. J.) Life of Henry Salt. 2 vols. 8vo. 1834.
1	2	HAMILTON (A.) Works. 7 vols. 8vo. 1851. Vol. 1. Correspondence. 2. Political Miscellanies. 3. Papers as Secretary of the Treasury. 4. Cabinet Papers. 5. Cabinet Papers; Military Papers; Correspondence. 6. Correspondence, and Political Papers. 7. Political and Law Papers; Index.
140	15	HAMILTON (E.) Cottagers of Glenburnie. 18mo. 1808.
187	14	——— Letters on Education. 2 vols. 12mo. 1825.
190	6	——— Letters on Education. 2 vols. 12mo. 1825.
440	7	——— Popular Essays. 2 vols. 16mo. 1817.
189	23	HAMILTON (J.) Life in Earnest. 16mo. 1850.
60	22	——— Memoir of Lady Colquhoun. 12mo. 1853.
177	20	——— Royal Preacher. 16mo. 1853.
95	1	HAMILTON (J. P.) Travels through Columbia. 2 vols. 8vo. 1827.
450	13	HAMILTON (R.) Amphibious Carnivora. (Nat. Lib. 25). 16mo. n. d.
449	10	——— British Fishes. (Nat. Lib. 36, 37). 2 vols. 16mo. 1832.
450	11	——— Whales. (Nat. Lib. 26). 16mo. 1852.
106	15	HAMILTON (T.) Men and Manners in America. 8vo. 1833.
39	7	——— Peninsular Campaigns. 3 vols. 12mo. 1831.
13	9	HAMMOND (J. D.) Political History of New York. 2 vols. 8vo. 1842.
24	11	HAMOND (J.) Guide to the Scriptures. 8vo. 1727.
*574	7	HANDY (W. R.) Text Book of Anatomy. 8vo. 1854.
76	13	HANNA (W.) Life of Thomas Chalmers. 4 vols. 12mo. 1851–52.
*413	1	HANSARD's Parliamentary Debates. Third series, vols. 123–128. November 4, 1852, to July 8, 1853. 6 vols. 8vo. 1853.
80	9	HANSON (J. H.) Louis XVII. and Rev. E. Williams. 12mo. 1854.
126	3	HARDENBERG (F. von). Henry of Ofterdingen. 12mo. 1842.
55	2	HARDY (F.) Life of Earl of Charlemont. 2 vols. 8vo. 1812.
181	9	HARE (J. C.) Mission of the Comforter. 12mo. 1854.
*469	20	HARPER (R. G.) On the Dispute between United States and France. 8vo. 1798.

Shelf.	No.	
485	20	HARPER (R. G.) Select Works. 2 vols. 8vo. 1814.
*469	19	——— Speech at Annapolis, Jan. 20, 1814. 8vo. 1814.
*584	7	HARRIS (C. A.) Dictionary of Dental Science. 8vo. 1849.
*584	8	——— Principles and Practice of Dental Surgery. 8vo. 1853.
485	8	HARRIS (J.) Hermes. 8vo. 1786.
506	14	——— On Art. 8vo. 1754.
179	11	HARRIS (John). Great Commission. 12mo. 1842.
179	15	——— Man Primeval. 12mo. 1852.
179	2	——— Pre-Adamite Earth. 12mo. 1851.
73	2	HARRIS (T. M.) Biography of J. Oglethorpe. 8vo. 1841.
18	4	——— Constitutions of Masons. 4to. 1798.
*106	11	——— Tour to the Alleghany Mountains. 12mo. 1805.
492	16	HARRIS (T. W.) On Insects of New England. 8vo. 1852.
477	19	HARRIS (W. T.) Epitaphs from Burying Ground in Cambridge. 12mo. 1845.
556	1	HARTLEY (D.) Observations on Man. 3 vols. 8vo. 1791.
189	8	——— Truth of the Christian Religion. 12mo. 1808.
*478	3	HARVARD Lyceum in 1810–11. 8vo. 1811.
525	1	——— Lyceum in 1810–11. 8vo. 1811.
*478	4	——— Register, 1827–28. 8vo. 1828.
*393	7	——— University, Catalogue of Maps and Charts. 8vo. 1831.
*393	8	——— University, Catalogue of Library. 5 vols. 8vo. 1830–34.
*626	2	HASSALL (A. H.) Microscopic Anatomy. 2 vols. 8vo. 1851.
94	3	HASSELQUIST (F.) Travels in the Levant. 8vo. 1766.
86	6	HAUSSEZ (Baron de). Great Britain in 1833. 12mo. 1833.
80	1	HAVEN (N. A.) Remains, with Memoir by George Ticknor. 8vo. 1827.
530	22	HAWKESWORTH (J.) and others. Adventurer. 2 vols. 16mo. n. d.
18	3	HAWKS (F. L.) Ecclesiastical History of United States. 2 vols. 8vo. 1836–39. Vol. 1. Virginia. | Vol. 2. Maryland.
82	9	——— Monuments of Egypt. 8vo. 1850.
126	13	HAWKSTONE. 2 vols. 12mo. 1849.
136	8	HAWTHORNE (N.) Blithedale Romance. 16mo. 1852.
121	36	——— House of the Seven Gables. 16mo. 1851.
70	7	——— Life of Franklin Pierce. 16mo. 1852.
136	4	——— Scarlet Letter. 16mo. 1851.
131	21	——— Tangle Wood Tales. 16mo. 1853.
135	5	——— Twice-told Tales. 2 vols. 16mo. 1851.
539	47	HAY (J. H. D.) Western Barbary. 16mo. 1844.
*563	3	HAYDEN (J.) Dictionary of Dates. 8vo. 1851.
51	11	HAYDON (B. R.) Autobiography. 2 vols. 12mo. 1853.
539	44	HAYGARTH (H. W.) Bush Life in Australia. 16mo. 1848.
56	7	HAYLEY (W.) Life of Milton. 8vo. 1797.

Shelf.	No.	
165	1	HAYLEY (W.) Poems and Plays. 6 vols. 16mo. 1788.
		Vol. 1. Essay on Painting; Epistles; Odes; Occasional Verses. 2. Essay on History in Three Epistles to Edward Gibbon. 3. On Epic Poetry, in Five Epistles. 4. Notes to the Third, Fourth, and Fifth Epistles of an Essay on Epic Poetry. 5. Triumphs of Temper; the Happy Prescription, a Comedy. 6. Marcella; the Two Connoisseurs; Lord Russel; the Mausoleum.
*660	1	HAYWARD (J.) Gazetteer of Massachusetts. 12mo. 1849.
*660	2	——— Gazetteer of New Hampshire. 12mo. 1849.
*660	3	——— Gazetteer of Vermont. 12mo. 1849.
*462	12	HAZARD (S.) United States Statistics. 6 vols. 4to. 1840–42.
100	14	HAZEN (E.) Technology. 2 vols. 18mo. 1850.
487	9	HAZLITT (W.) Characters of Shakespeare's Plays. 12mo. 1845.
487	8	——— Dramatic Literature of the Age of Elizabeth. 12mo. 1845.
57	3	——— Life of Bonaparte. 4 vols. 12mo. 1852.
526	2	——— Miscellaneous Works. 5 vols. 12mo. 1848.
		Vol. 1. Table Talk; Opinions on Books, Men, and Things. Parts 1, 2. 2. Table Talk; Opinions on Books, Men, and Things. Second Series. Part 1, 2. 3. Dramatic Literature of the Age of Elizabeth. Characters of Shakspeare's Plays. 4. English Comic Writers; English Poets. 5. Spirit of the Age, or Contemporary Portraits.
94	6	HEAD (F. B.) Bubbles from the Brunnens of Nassau. 12mo. 1834.
126	11	——— Emigrant. 16mo. 1847.
85	7	——— Faggot of French Sticks. 16mo. 1852.
539	48	——— Journey across Pampas and Andes. 12mo. 1846.
90	8	——— Life of Bruce. 18mo. n. d.
160	1	——— Life of Bruce. 18mo. 1838.
539	49	——— Stokers and Pokers. 12mo. 1849.
108	10	HEADLY (J. T.) Adirondack. 1851.
76	5	——— Guard of Napoleon. 12mo. 1851.
86	10	——— Italy, Alps, and the Rhine. 12mo. 1851.
74	9	——— Napoleon and his Marshals. 2 vols. 12mo. 1851.
10	7	——— Second War with England. 2 vols. 12mo. 1853.
74	8	——— Washington and his Generals. 2 vols. 12mo. 1851.
*422	3	HEARNE (S.) Journey from Prince of Wales Port to Northern Ocean. 4to. 1795.
*586	1	HEARNE (T.) Works. 4 vols. 8vo. 1810.
		Vols. 1, 2. Robert of Gloucester's Chronicle. 3, 4. Peter Langtoft's Chronicle.
*448	1	HEATH (W.) Memoirs. 8vo. 1798.
539	42	HEBER (R.) Journey to India. 2 vols. 16mo. 1844.
110	20	——— Journey to India. 2 vols. 16mo. 1829.
72	10	——— Life. 2 vols. 8vo. 1830.
167	7	——— Poems. 16mo. 1841.

Shelf.	No.	
52	8	HEDGE (F. H.) Prose Writers of Germany. 8vo. 1852.
46	13	HEEREN (A. H. L.) Ancient Greece. 8vo. 1847.
46	12	——— Ancient History. 8vo. 1847.
46	11	——— Historical Researches. 2 vols. 8vo. 1846.
46	14	——— Politics and Trade of the Carthaginians, &c. 8vo. 1850.
46	10	——— Political History of Europe. 8vo. 1846.
156	6	HEMANS (F. D.) Complete Works. 2 vols. 16mo. 1851.
156	1	——— Complete Works. 2 vols. 16mo. 1852.
157	2	——— Poems. 2 vols. 18mo. 1828.
157	1	——— Poems. 2 vols. 18mo. 1827.
117	1	HEMDEM (A. I.) Turkish Evening Entertainments. 12mo. 1850.
*470	12	HENNEPIN (L.) Discoveries. 8vo. 1698.
90	19	HENRY (C. S.) History of Philosophy. 2 vols. 18mo. n. d.
408	3	HENRY of Huntingdon, Chronicle of. Post 8vo. 1853.
448	3	HENRY, Prince of Wales, Memoir of. 8vo. 1760.
457	3	HENRY (R.) History of Great Britain. 12 vols. 8vo. 1823.
16	18	HENRY (W. S.) Campaign Sketches of the War with Mexico 12mo. 1847.
49	12	HENSLOW (J. S.) Botany. 18mo. 1836.
138	5	HENTZ (Mrs.) Tadeuskund. 12mo. 1825.
464	1	HERBERT (A.) Cyclops Christianus. 8vo. 1849.
443	7	HERBERT (E.) Life of. 8vo. 1826.
146	4	HERBERT (G.) Life and Writings. 12mo. 1851.
506	17	HERBERT (H. W.) American Game. 12mo. 1853.
70	1	——— Captains of the Old World. 12mo. 1851.
504	2	——— Frank Forester's Field Sports. 2 vols. 8vo. 1852.
504	4	——— Frank Forester's Fish and Fishing. 8vo. 1851.
*392	19	HERDER (J. G.) Philosophy of the History of Man. 4to. 1800.
486	17	——— Spirit of Hebrew Poetry. 2 vols. 12mo. 1833.
109	7	HERIOT (G.) Travels through the Canadas. 12mo. 1813.
*470	11	——— Travels through the Canadas. 12mo. 1813.
119	14	HERODOTUS. Translated by Beloe. 3 vols. 18mo. n. d.
410	1	——— Translated by Cary. Post 8vo. 1852.
35	5	HERON (R.) History of Scotland. 6 vols. 8vo. 1794.
94	8	——— Journey through Scotland. 2 vols. 8vo. 1793.
*430	3	HERRICK (R.) Hesperides, &c. 2 vols. 16mo. 1846.
49	13	HERSCHEL (J. F. W.) Astronomy. 18mo. 1834.
508	2	——— Astronomy. 12mo. 1836.
494	5	——— Astronomy. 8vo. 1849.
497	25	——— Study of Natural Philosophy. 12mo. 1851.
49	11	——— Study of Natural Philosophy. 18mo. 1830.
499	19	HERSHBERGER (H. R.) Horsemanship. 12mo. 1844.
92	12	HERVÉ (F.) Residence in Greece and Turkey. 2 vols. 8vo. 1837.
190	3	HERVEY (G. W.) Rhetoric of Conversation. 12mo. 1853.

Shelf. No.

188 15 Hervey (J.) Theron and Aspasia. 3 vols. 12mo. 1767.

520 4 Hervey (T. K.) Book of Christmas. 12mo. 1845.

28 19 Hetherington (W. M.) Westminster Assembly of Divines. 12mo. 1853.

10 1 Hewes (G. R. T.) Memoirs of, with Traits of Tea Party. 18mo. 1835.

99 5 Higgins (W. M.) The Earth. 18mo. n. d.

184 6 Hildreth (R.) Despotism in America. 12mo. 1840.

15 1 ——— History of the United States. 6 vols. 8vo. 1849–52.

171 29 ——— Theory of Politics. 12mo. 1853.

13 12 Hildreth (S. P.) Pioneer History. 8vo. 1848.

515 4 Hill (A.) Works. 4 vols. 8vo. 1757.

*448 4 ——— Works. 4 vols. 8vo. 1753.

Vol. 1, 2. Letters.
3. Poems.
4. Poems, and Essay on the Art of Acting.

56 1 Hill (J.) Life of Hugh Blair. 8vo. 1808.

87 17 Hillard (G. S.) Six Months in Italy. 2 vols. 16mo. 1853.

167 10 Hillhouse (J. A.) Dramas, and other Works. 2 vols. 16mo. 1839.

Vol. 1. Demetria; Hadad; Percy's Masque.
2. Judgment; Sachem's Wood; Discourses; Hermit of Warkworth.

347 2 Hilliard (F.) Digest of Pickering's Reports. Vols. 8—1[illegible]. 8vo. 1837.

339 5 ——— Elements of Law. 8vo. 1835.

507 11 Hind (J. R.) On the Solar System. 12mo. 1852.

550 7 Hindoos. India: its Government, Religion, &c. 2 vols. 12mo. n. d.

106 3 Hines (G.) Oregon, its History, &c. 12mo. 1851.

196 12 Hints to the Public on Evangelical Preaching. 8vo. 1808.

28 2 Historic Sketches of Spain and Portugal. 18mo. 1835.

500 7 Historical Parallels. 3 vols. 18mo. 1846.

History, Universal. 60 vols. 8vo. 1779–84.

*458 3 Vols. 1—15.

*459 1 ,, 16—38.

*460 1 ,, 39—60.

Vol. 1. Creation; Deluge; Egypt; Moabites; Syrians.
2. Phœnicians; Jews.
3. Jews; Assyria; Babylon; Phrygia.
4. Medes; Persians; Scythians; Mysians; Lydians.
5. Fabulous Times; Athenians; Lacedæmonians.
6. Thebes; Sicily; Syracuse.
7. Syracuse; Macedonia.
8. Macedonia; Syria; Egypt; Armenia; Pontus.
9. Cappadocia; Persia; Rome.
10–13. Roman History.
14. Rome; Constantinople; Eastern and Western Empire.
15. Constantinople; Carthage.
16. Carthage; Arabia; Spain; Gaul.
17. Germans; Britons; Hunns, &c.; Ostrogoths.
18. Turks; Indians; Chinese; Etruscans.
19. Life of Mahommed; Arabs.

Shelf. No.

HISTORY, Universal, *continued.*

20. Arabs.
21. Arabs; Turks; Seljukians.
22. Seljukians; Moguls; Tartars.
23. Moguls, &c.; Hindustan.
24. Hindustan.
25. Eastern Tartary; China; Japan.
26. East India Settlements.
27. India Settlements; Othman Empire.
28. Othman Empire; Jews.
29. Jews; Africa; Egypt; African Islands.
30. African Islands; Abyssinia; Hottentots.
31. Africa; Ethiopia; Angola, &c.
32. Africa; Barbary; Morocco; Algiers.
33. Algiers; Tunis; Tripoli; Malta.
34, 35. Spain.
36. Spain; Portugal.
37. Portugal; Navarre; France.
38, 39. France.
40. Italy.
41. Italy; Venice.
42. Venice; Naples.
43. Naples; Genoa; Germany.
44. Germany.
45. Germany; Holland.
46. Holland; Denmark.
47. Denmark; Sweden.
48. Sweden; Poland.
49. Poland; Prussia; Russia.
50. Russia; Hungary; Geneva, &c.
51. Mecklenburg; Tuscany; Milan.
52. Milan; Savoy; America.
53. America.
54. America and Asia.
55. Asia; Africa; and Europe.
56. America.
57, 58. England.
59. Scotland.
60. Ireland.

181 11 HITCHCOCK (E.) Elementary Geology. 12mo. 1853.
509 24 ——— Outline of the Geology of the Globe. 8vo. 1853.
507 16 ——— On Diet, Regimen, and Employment. 12mo. 1830.
177 8 ——— Religion of Geology. 12mo. 1851.
*472 1 HITCHINS (F.) History of Cornwall. 2 vols. 4to. 1824.
180 8 HOBART (J. H.) Apology for Apostolic Order and its Advocates. 12mo. 1844.
189 27 ——— Christian Manual. 16mo. 1844.
180 13 ——— Christian Manual. 12mo. 1853.
188 6 ——— Companion to the Altar. 12mo. 1850.
180 17 HOBART (N.) Life of Swedenborg. 12mo. 1850.
434 2 HOBBES (T.) Works. 11 vols. 8vo. 1839–45.

Vol. 1. Logic; First Grounds of Philosophy; of the Proportions of Motions and Magnitudes; of Physics, or the Phenomena of Nature.
2. Philosophical Rudiments concerning Government and Society.
3. Of Man; Commonwealth; of a Christian Commonwealth; of the Kingdom of Darkness.
4. Tripos, in three Discourses: 1st. Human Nature; 2d. Law; 3d. Liberty and Necessity. Answer to Bishop Bramhall's Book; Historical Narration concerning Heresy, and the Punishment thereof; Considerations upon the Reputation, Loyalty, Manners, and Religion of Thomas Hobbes; Answer to Sir William Davenant's Preface before "Gondibert;" Letter to Howard.

Shelf. No.

434 2 Hobbes (T.) Works, *continued.*

5. Liberty, Necessity, and Chance.
6. Dialogue upon the Common Laws of England; Behemoth; Whole Art of Rhetoric; Art of Sophistry.
7. Seven Philosophical Problems; Decameron Physiologicum; Proportion of a Straight Line to half the Arc of a Quadrant; Six Lessons to the Professors of the Mathematics; Marks of the Absurd Geometry, &c. of Dr. Wallis; Extract of a Letter from Henry Stubbe; Papers against Dr. Wallis; Considerations on the Answer of Dr. Wallis; Letters, and other Pieces.
8, 9. Translation of Eight Books of Thucydides.
10. Translation of Homer's Iliad and Odyssey.
11. Index.

164 14 Hobhouse (J.) Illustrations of Childe Harold. 8vo. 1818.
*660 9 Hoblyn (R. D.) Dictionary of Scientific Terms. 12mo. 1850.
*426 6 Hoccleve (T.) Poems. 4to. 1796.
131 2 Hoffman (D.) Cartaphilus, the Wandering Jew. 2 vols. 8vo. 1853.
140 10 Hofland (B.) Moral Tales. 16mo. 1852.
140 8 ——— Domestic Tales. 16mo. 1852.
139 9 ——— Visit to London. 4 vols. 12mo. 1814.
138 6 Hogg (J.) Three Perils of Man. 3 vols. 12mo. 1822.
80 6 Holcroft (T.) Memoirs of. 3 vols. 18mo. 1816.
472 8 Holgate (J. B.) American Genealogy. 4to. 1851.
626 9 Holland (H.) Medical Notes. 8vo. 1839.
160 3 Holland, Family Tour through. 18mo. 1831.
30 2 Holland (J.) Manufactures in Metals. 3 vols. 18mo. 1849.
85 16 Holland (Lord). Foreign Reminiscences. 12mo. 1851.
519 7 ——— Foreign Reminiscences. 12mo. 1851.
160 6 Hollings (J. F.) Life of Cicero. 18mo. 1839.
150 14 ——— Life of Gustavus Adolphus. 18mo. 1838.
16 4 Holmes (A.) Annals of America. 2 vols. 8vo. 1829.
*463 7 ——— Annals of America. 2 vols. 8vo. 1805.
*446 1 ——— Life of Ezra Stiles. 8vo. 1798.
70 16 Holmes (E.) Life of Mozart. 16mo. 1845.
507 28 Holmes (O. W.) On Homœopathy. 12mo. 1842.
*664 13 ——— On Homœopathy. 12mo. 1842.
164 1 ——— Poems. 16mo. 1852.
158 18 ——— Poems. 16mo. 1846.
93 9 Holmes (W. R.) Shores of the Caspian. 8vo. 1845.
70 11 Holstein (H. L. V. D.) Memoir of La Fayette. 12mo. 1824.
178 3 Holyoke (E. A.) Duties we owe to God. 8vo. 1830.
189 7 Home (H. Lord Kames). Art of Thinking. 12mo. 1818.
485 13 ——— Elements of Criticism. 8vo. 1853.
484 10 ——— Elements of Criticism. 2 vols. 8vo. 1823.
483 14 Homer. Iliad, edited by Felton, Flaxman's Designs. 8vo. 1833.
410 2 ——— Iliad, translated by Buckley. Post 8vo. 1853.

Shelf.	No.	
538	22	HOMER. Iliad, translated by Pope, Flaxman's Designs. 2 vols. 12mo. 1853.
483	6	—— Iliad, translated by Cowper. 8vo. 1850.
482	8	—— Iliad and Odyssey, translated by Pope. 8vo. 1853.
120	14	—— Iliad and Odyssey, translated by Pope. 3 vols. 18mo. n. d.
*426	3	—— Iliad and Odyssey, translated by Pope, edited by Wakefield. 11 vols. 8vo. 1796.
409	11	—— Odyssey, translated by Buckley. Post 8vo. 1851.
538	21	—— Odyssey, translated by Pope, Flaxman's Designs. 12mo. 1853.
*485	16	—— Enquiry into the Life and Writings of. 8vo. 1736.
123	3	HOMME (L') de Desir. 8vo. 1790.
77	21	HOOD (E. P.) Life of John Milton. 16mo. 1852.
190	15	—— Self-Education. 18mo. 1852.
530	21	—— Uses of Biography. 18mo. 1852.
28	7	HOOD (G.) History of Music in New England. 12mo. 1846.
121	32	HOOD (T.) Hood's Own. 12mo. 1852.
165	16	—— Poems. 12mo. 1852.
121	24	—— Prose and Verse. 12mo. 1852.
114	11	—— Tylney Hall. 3 vols. 8vo. 1834.
529	6	—— Up the Rhine. 2 vols. 12mo. 1852.
519	11	—— Whims and Oddities. 12mo. 1852.
519	10	—— Whimsicalities. 12mo. 1852.
111	7	HOOK (T.) Maxwell. 3 vols. 12mo. 1830.
*563	1	HOOK (W. F.) Church Dictionary. 8vo. 1854.
465	6	HOOKE (N.) Roman History. 11 vols. 8vo. 1806.
195	7	HOOKER (R.) Works. 2 vols. 8vo. 1851.
*594	13	HOOPER (R.) Medical Dictionary. 8vo. 1849.
*544	7	HOPE (J.) Diseases of the Heart. 8vo. 1846.
193	3	HOPKINS (M.) Evidences of Christianity. 8vo. 1846.
178	4	—— Essays and Discourses. 8vo. 1847.
470	5	HOPKINS (S.) On the Future State. 12mo. 1783.
484	8	HORACE, translated by Boscawen. 8vo. 1793.
484	11	—— translated by Boscawen. 8vo. 1797.
486	8	—— translated by Dunster. 8vo. 1719.
487	17	—— translated by Francis. 4 vols. 18mo. 1756.
120	10	—— translated by Francis. 2 vols. 18mo. 1808.
409	12	—— translated by Smart. Post 8vo. 1853.
487	20	—— translated by Smart. 2 vols. 18mo. n. d.
192	3	HORNE (G.) Works. 2 vols. 8vo. 1853.

Vol. 1. Life of Dr. Horne; Letters; Poems; Essays; Commentary on the Psalms.
2. Discourses; Life and Death of John the Baptist; Letters on Infidelity; Letters.

Shelf.	No.	
51	1	HORNER (F.) Memoirs and Correspondence, by L. Horner. 2 vols. 8vo. 1853.

Shelf.	No.	
*574	6	HORNER (W. E.) Anatomy and Histology. 2 vols. 8vo. 1851.
504	18	HOSACK (D.) Essays on Medical Science. 2 vols. 8vo. 1824.
442	5	——— Memoir of De Witt Clinton. 4to. 1829.
*554	6	——— Practice of Physic. 8vo. 1838.
*502	3	HOSKING (W.) On Architecture. 4to. 1852.
*606	1	HOVEY (C. M.) Horticultural Magazine (vols. 1, 2, entitled American Gardeners' Magazine). 18 vols. 8vo. 1835–52.
148	3	HOWARD (H.) Poems. 16mo. 1831.
*479	1	HOWE (H.) Historical Collections of Virginia. 8vo. 1852.
37	3	HOWE (S. G.) Greek Revolution. 12mo. 1828.
157	8	HOWE (Mrs. S. G.) Passion Flowers. 16mo. 1854.
117	2	HOWITT (M.) The Artist-Wife. 12mo. n. d.
167	21	——— Ballads, and other Poems. 12mo. 1848.
117	4	——— Heir of Wast Wayland. 12mo. 1851.
129	22	——— Hope on, Hope Ever. 18mo. 1851.
131	26	——— My Own Story. 18mo. 1851.
129	23	——— My Uncle the Clock-Maker. 18mo. 1845.
164	16	——— Milman and Keats's Poetical Works. 8vo. 1840.
129	21	——— Sowing and Reaping. 18mo. 1851.
129	25	——— Which is the Wiser. 18mo. 1852.
129	24	——— Who shall be Greatest. 18mo. 1851.
115	6	——— Wood Leighton. 3 vols. 12mo. 1836.
117	19	——— Wood Leighton. 16mo. 1847.
129	26	——— Work and Wages. 18mo. 1850.
126	4	HOWITT (W.) Country Year Book. 12mo. 1850.
124	5	——— Hall and Hamlet. 12mo. 1847.
525	6	——— Homes and Haunts of British Poets. 2 vols. 12mo. 1847–51.
525	5	——— Homes and Haunts of British Poets. 2 vols. 12mo. 1847.
94	5	——— Rural Life of England. 2 vols. 12mo. 1838.
522	5	——— Student Life of Germany. 8vo. 1842.
417	6	HOWITT (W. & M.) Stories of English and Foreign Life. Post 8vo. 1853.
478	13	HUBBARD (W.) History of New England. 8vo. 1815.
97	12	HUC (M.) Travels in Tartary, Thibet, and China. 2 vols. 16mo. 1852.
538	28	——— Travels in Tartary, Thibet, and China. 2 vols. 12mo. n. d.
538	9	——— Travels in Tartary, Thibet, and China. 2 vols. 12mo. n. d.
78	7	HUDSON (D.) History of Jemima Wilkinson. 12mo. 1821.
164	9	HUDSON (H. W.) Lectures on Shakespeare. 2 vols. 12mo. 1848.
164	10	——— Lectures on Shakespeare. 2 vols. 12mo. 1848.
499	4	HUFELAND (C. W.) Art of Prolonging Life. 16mo. 1854.
506	16	HUFF (G.) Electro-Physiology. 12mo. 1853.

Shelf.	No.	
178	5	HUG (J. L.) Introduction to New Testament. 8vo. 1836.
*650	16	HUGHES (H. M.) On Auscultation. 12mo. 1846.
498	15	HUGHES (W. C.) Miller and Millwrights' Assistant. 16mo. 1851.
137	19	HUGO (V.) Slave King. 12mo. 1833.
497	2	HUMBOLDT (A. Von) Aspects of Nature. 12mo. 1850.
496	7	——— Cosmos. 4 vols. 12mo. 1851–52.
418	9	——— Cosmos. 4 vols. post 8vo. 1849–52.
41	2	——— Researches on the Ancient Inhabitants of America. 2 vols. 8vo. 1814.
418	10	——— Travels in America. 3 vols. post 8vo. 1852–53.
89	15	——— Travels in America and Asiatic Russia. 18mo. n. d.
418	11	——— Views of Nature. Post 8vo. 1850.
47	13	HUME (D.) History of England. 6 vols. 12mo. 1851.
42	4	HUME, SMOLLETT, & FARR. History of England. 3 vols. 8vo. n. d. Vol. 1. From Invasion of Julius Cæsar to 1688. 2. 1688—1760. 3. 1760—1847.
46	15	HUME, SMOLLETT, & MILLER. History of England. 4 vols. 8vo. 1832. Vol. 1. To 1558. 2. 1558—1688. 3. 1688—1760. 4. 1760—1820.
130	3	HUMOR, Wit, and Wisdom. 18mo. 1849.
70	18	HUMPHREYS (D.) Life of General Putnam. 12mo. 1818.
69	3	——— Life of Putnam. 12mo. 1851.
524	11	——— Miscellaneous Works. 8vo. 1804.
418	12	HUMPHREYS (H. N.) Coin Collectors' Manual. 2 vols. post 8vo. 1853.
176	20	HUNT (F.) Library of Commerce. 12mo. 1845.
		——— Merchants' Magazine. 29 vols. 8vo. 1839–53.
*313	1	Vols. 1–18.
*314	1	,, 19–29.
518	3	HUNT (F. K.) Fourth Estate. 2 vols. 12mo. 1850.
158	7	HUNT (J.) Hours of Reflection. 12mo. 1845.
68	7	HUNT (L.) Autobiography. 2 vols. 12mo. 1850.
519	8	——— Book for a Corner. 2 vols. 12mo. 1852.
517	3	——— Essays and Miscellanies. 12mo. 1851.
155	5	——— Imagination and Fancy. 12mo. 1848.
168	9	——— Imagination and Fancy. 12mo. 1845.
526	7	——— Men, Women, and Books. 2 vols. 12mo. 1847.
153	12	——— Poetical Works. 8vo. 1832.
127	10	——— Stories from the Italian Poets. 12mo. 1846.
498	10	HUNT (R.) Elementary Physics. 16mo. 1851.
62	3	HUNTER (H.) Sacred Biography. 8vo. 1844.

Shelf.	No.	
*564	6	HUNTER (J.) Works. 4 vols. 8vo. 1841. Vol. 1. Life, by Ottley; Principles of Surgery. 2. Diseases of the Human Teeth; Venereal Disease. 3. The Blood; Inflammation, and Gun-shot Wounds. 4. Animal Œconomy; Notes by Owen.
104	9	HUNTER (J. D.) Indian Tribes West of the Mississippi. 8vo. 1823.
507	6	HUNTINGDON (D.) View of the Fine Arts. 12mo. 1851.
190	9	HURD (R.) Dialogues with Letters. 3 vols. 12mo. 1765.
190	13	HUTCHESON (F.) On Beauty and Virtue. 16mo. 1772.
*656	6	HUTCHINSON (J.) On the Spirometer. 8vo. 1852.
196	11	HUTCHINSON (L.) On the Christian Religion. 8vo. 1817.
400	11	——— Memoirs of Colonel Hutchinson. Post 8vo. 1848.
*454	8	HUTCHINSON (T.) Collection of Papers relative to the History of the Colony of Massachusetts Bay. 8vo. 1769.
*478	11	——— History of Massachusetts. 2 vols. 8vo. 1795.
*454	9	——— History of the Colony and Province of Massachusetts Bay. 3 vols. 8vo. Vol. 1. 1764. | Vol. 2. 1767. | Vol. 3. 1828.
*430	7	HYTA (G. P. de). Guerras de Grenada. 2 vols. 16mo. 1833.

I.

Shelf.	No.	
90	11	ICELAND, Greenland, and Faroe Islands. 18mo. 1851.
122	6	IDLE Man. 8vo. 1821–22.
509	13	IGNORANCE, Social Evils of. Popular Tumults. 18mo. 1847.
*18	7	IMLAY (G.) Topographical Description of Western Territory of North America. 8vo. 1793.
160	19	IMPOSTURE, &c., Sketches of. 18mo. 1840.
158	1	INCHBALD (E.) Theatre. 16mo. n. d. First Love; The Jew; Wheel of Fortune; Way to Keep Him; Grecian Daughter.
159	10	——— Theatre. 16mo. n. d. Deserted Daughter; Road to Ruin; Such Things Are; To Marry, or Not to Marry.
159	11	——— Theatre. 16mo. n. d. Speed the Plough; Cure for the Heart-ache; School of Reform; Wild Oats.
159	12	——— Theatre. 16mo. n. d. Mountaineers; John Bull; Poor Gentleman; Dramatist.
*3	7	INCHIQUIN, the Jesuit's Letters. 8vo. 1810.
*271	4	INDEPENDENT Chronicle. Folio. 1808.
*493	15	INDIANA. Reports of Board of Agriculture. 8vo. 1852–53.

Shelf.	No.	
76	7	INDIVIDUALS of American History, Lives of. 3 vols. 12mo. n. d.
15	2	INGERSOLL (C. J.) History of Second War with Great Britain. 4 vols. 8vo. 1845–52.
336	9	INGERSOLL (E.) Abridgment of the Acts of Congress. 8vo. 1825.
85	22	INGLIS (H. D.) Journey throughout Ireland. 12mo. 1838.
96	6	——— Ireland in 1834. 2 vols. 12mo. 1835.
539	41	IRBY (C. L.) & MANGLES (J.) Travels in Egypt, Nubia, &c. 16mo. 1844.
430	8	IRIARTE (T. de). Fabulas. 18mo. 1826.
483	9	IRISH Eloquence. Speeches of Philips, Curran, Grattan, and Emmett. 8vo. 1850.
550	8	INSECT Architecture. 12mo. n. d.
505	15	——— Life, Episodes of. 3 vols. 8vo. 1849–51.
550	9	——— Miscellanies. 12mo. n. d.
550	10	——— Transformation. 12mo. n. d.
88	5	INSECTS, Natural History of. 2 vols. 18mo. 1843.
160	24	——— Natural History of. 2 vols. 18mo. 1829.
28	9	INVENTIONS (Wonderful), History of. 16mo. n. d.
509	20	IRON, Manufacture of. 16mo. 1837.
53	8	IRVING (D.) Life and Writings of George Buchanan. 8vo. 1807.
87	13	IRVING (J. T. jun.) Indian Sketches. 2 vols. 12mo. 1835.
7	14	IRVING (T.) Conquest of Florida. 12mo. 1851.
517	22	IRVING (W.) Alhambra. 12mo. 1851.
527	16	——— Alhambra. 12mo. 1851.
517	17	——— Astoria. 12mo. 1851.
527	10	——— Astoria. 12mo. 1850.
103	14	——— Astoria. 2 vols. 8vo. 1836.
517	18	——— Bonneville's Adventures. 12mo. 1851.
527	12	——— Bonneville's Adventures. 12mo. 1851.
109	18	——— Bonneville's Adventures. 2 vols. 12mo. 1837.
517	14	——— Bracebridge Hall. 12mo. 1851.
527	8	——— Bracebridge Hall. 12mo. 1851.
539	40	——— Bracebridge Hall. 16mo. 1845.
517	13	——— Columbus and his Companions. 3 vols. 12mo. 1851.
527	7	——— Columbus and his Companions. 3 vols. 12mo. 1851.
160	14	——— Columbus, Abridged. 18mo. 1841.
160	9	——— Companions of Columbus. 18mo. 1831.
517	21	——— Conquest of Grenada. 12mo. 1851.
527	15	——— Conquest of Grenada. 12mo. 1851.
517	16	——— Crayon Miscellany. 12mo. 1851.
527	11	——— Crayon Miscellany. 12mo. 1851.
517	11	——— History of New York. Knickerbocker. 12mo. 1851.
527	5	——— History of New York. Knickerbocker. 12mo. 1851.

Shelf.	No.	
160	10	Irving (W.) History of New York. Knickerbocker. 18mo. 1836.
517	20	——— Mahomet and his Successors. 2 vols. 12mo. 1851.
527	14	——— Mahomet and his Successors. 2 vols. 12mo. 1851.
517	19	——— Oliver Goldsmith. 12mo. 1851.
527	13	——— Oliver Goldsmith. 12mo. 1851.
539	38	——— Oliver Goldsmith. 16mo. 1849.
90	4	——— Oliver Goldsmith. 2 vols. 18mo. n. d.
160	11	——— Salmagundi. 18mo. 1839.
517	12	——— Sketch Book. 12mo. 1851.
527	6	——— Sketch Book. 12mo. 1851.
170	11	——— Sketch Book. 2 vols. 18mo. 1838.
517	15	——— Tales of a Traveller. 12mo. 1851.
527	9	——— Tales of a Traveller. 12mo. 1851.
539	39	——— Tales of a Traveller. 16mo. 1848.
*512	2	——— Works, complete. 2 vols. 8vo. 1834.
179	21	Isham (W.) Mud Cabin. 12mo. 1853.
164	6	Italian Comedies. 12mo. 1849.
75	19	Ivimey (J.) Life of John Milton. 12mo. 1833.
*475	15	Izard (R.) Correspondence of. 12mo. 1844.
*392	17	Jackson (C. T.) Geology and Mineralogy of New Hampshire. 4to. 1844.
*666	1	Jackson (J.) Theory and Practice of Physic. 2 parts 8vo. 1825–27.
*666	2	——— Theory and Practice of Physic. Part 1. 8vo. 1825.
97	11	Jackson (J. G.) Morocco, &c. 12mo. 1810.
*636	15	Jackson (S.) Principles of Medicine. 8vo. 1832.
67	10	Jackson (W.) Man of Sorrows. 12mo. 1842.
196	4	Jahn (J.) Biblical Archæology. 8vo. 1853.
26	13	——— History of Hebrew Commonwealth. 8vo. n. d.
103	2	James (E.) Expedition to the Rocky Mountains. 3 vols. 8vo. 1823.
117	9	James (G. P. R.) Ancient Regime. 3 vols. 12mo. 1841.
116	5	——— Arabella Stuart. 3 vols. 12mo. 1844.
116	9	——— Beauchamp. 3 vols. 12mo. 1848.
128	5	——— Castle of Ehrenstein. 3 vols. 12mo. 1847.
127	4	——— Convict. 3 vols. 12mo. 1847.
114	10	——— Dark Scenes in History. 3 vols. 12mo. 1849.
116	7	——— De L'Orme. 3 vols. 12mo. 1830.
111	8	——— Desultory Man. 3 vols. 12mo. 1836.
114	12	——— False Heir. 3 vols. 12mo. 1843.
115	5	——— Heidelberg. 3 vols. 12mo. 1848.
121	2	——— Henry Masterton. 3 vols. 12mo. 1832.
88	13	——— History of Chivalry. 18mo. n. d.
116	1	——— King's Highway. 3 vols. 12mo. 1840.
99	2	——— Life of Charlemagne. 18mo.
74	5	——— Life of Henry the Fourth. 2 vols. 12mo. 1847.
407	3	——— Life of Louis the Fourteenth. 2 vols. post 8vo. 1851.

Shelf.	No.	
30	3	James (G. P. R.) Lives of Eminent Foreign Statesmen. 5 vols. 18mo. 1833–38.
115	8	—— Margaret Graham. 2 vols. 12mo. 1848.
128	8	—— Morley Ernstein. 3 vols. 12mo. 1843.
114	2	—— Russell. 3 vols. 12mo. 1847.
518	8	James (H.) Lectures and Miscellanies. 12mo. 1852.
188	21	James (J. A.) On Christian Duty. 16mo. 1852.
189	19	—— Church Member's Guide. 16mo. 1848.
180	7	—— Christian Professor. 12mo. 1838.
89	4	Jameson (A.) Celebrated Female Sovereigns. 2 vols. 18mo, n. d.
510	18	—— Early Italian Painters. 2 vols. 18mo. 1845.
15	9	Jamestown, Voyage of the. 8vo. 1847.
54	1	Janney (S. M.) Life of William Penn. 8vo. 1852.
550	14	Jardine (D.) Criminal Trials; Gunpowder Plot. 2 vols. 12mo. n. d.
		Jardine (W.) Birds of Great Britain and Ireland. 4 vols. 16mo. n. d.
449	13	—— Vols. 1, 2. (Nat. Lib. vols. 1, 2.)
450	1	—— ,, 3, 4. (Nat. Lib. vols. 3, 4.)
449	11	—— Fishes of the Perch Family. (Nat. Lib. vol. 38.) 16mo. 1852.
450	4	—— Gallinaceous Birds. (Nat. Lib. vol. 14.) 16mo. n. d.
450	1	—— Game Birds. (Nat. Lib. vol. 8.) 16mo. n. d.
450	1	—— Humming Birds. (Nat. Lib. vols. 6, 7.) 2 vols. 16mo. n. d.
450	6	—— Lions, Tigers, &c. (Nat. Lib. vol. 16.) 16mo. n. d.
450	12	—— Monkeys. (Nat. Lib. vol. 27.) 16mo. n. d.
450	9	—— Ruminating Animals. (Nat. Lib. vols. 21, 22.). 2 vols. 16mo. n. d.
450	1	—— Sun Birds. (Nat. Lib. vol. 5.) 16mo. n. d.
450	9	—— Thick-skinned Quadrupeds. (Nat. Lib. vol. 23.) 16mo. n. d.
29	5	Jarves (J. J.) History of Hawaiian Islands. 8vo. 1847.
22	4	Jarvis (Rev. S. F.) Chronological Introduction to History of the Church. 8vo. 1845.
62	9	Jay (W.) Life of John Jay. 2 vols. 8vo. 1833.
7	13	—— Review of the Mexican War. 12mo. 1849.
7	15	—— Review of the Mexican War. 12mo. 1849.
176	8	—— Writings on Slavery. 12mo. 1853.
184	15	Jay (W.) Sermons. 8vo. 1805.
183	14	Jebb (J.) Works. 3 vols. 8vo. 1787.
51	7	Jefferson (T.) Memoirs, Correspondence, &c. 4 vols. 8vo. 1829.
65	6	—— Memoirs of. 2 vols. 8vo. 1809.
10	4	—— Notes on Virginia. 16mo. 1802.
478	9	—— Notes on Virginia. 8vo. 1801.
*252	8	Jefferys (T.) History of the French Dominions. Folio. 1760.

Shelf.	No.	
*402	10	JEFFRIES (J.) Narrative of Two Aerial Voyages. 4to. 1786.
183	12	JENYNS (S.) Works. 2 vols. 8vo. 1791.
131	20	JEWSBURY (G. E.) History of an Adopted Child. 16mo. 1853.
187	9	JEWSBURY (M. J.) Letters to the Young. 12mo. 1835.
137	13	——— Three Histories. 12mo. 1831.
*453	8	JEWETT (C. C.) On Public Libraries of the United States. 8vo. 1851.
96	11	JEWETT (I. A.) Passages in Foreign Travel. 2 vols. 12mo. 1838.
96	12	——— Passages in Foreign Travel. 2 vols. 12mo. 1838.
109	3	JEWITT (J. R.) Adventures. 12mo. 1849.
97	14	JOCELYN (Lord). Chinese Expedition. 12mo. 1841.
97	15	——— Chinese Expedition. 12mo. 1841.
*613	4	JOHNSON (C. W.) Farmer's Encyclopedia. 8vo. 1848.
660	17	JOHNSON (J.) Typographia. 2 vols. 18mo. 1824.
*650	18	JOHNSON (James). On Indigestion. 12mo. 1831.
*663	1	JOHNSON (S.) English Dictionary. 8vo. 1828.
*391	5	——— English Dictionary. 8vo. 1852.
99	14	——— Life and Writings. 2 vols. 18mo. 1844.
78	11	——— Lives of the English Poets. 16mo. 1831.
79	2	——— Lives of the Poets. 3 vols. 16mo. 1811.
139	15	——— Rasselas. 16mo. 1806.
140	11	——— Rasselas. 18mo. 1850.
74	2	——— Religious Life and Death. 12mo. 1850.
*656	7	JOHNSON (W.) Diseases of Young Women. 12mo. 1849.
*593	3	JOHNSTON (A. K.) Dictionary of Geography. 8vo. 1852.
507	20	JOHNSTON (J. F. W.) Chemistry and Geology applied to Agriculture. 12mo. n. d.
497	9	——— Lectures on Agriculture. 12mo. 1850.
106	9	——— Notes on North America. 2 vols. post 8vo. 1851.
52	1	JOHNSTONE (J.) Life of Samuel Parr. 2 vols. 8vo. 1829.
27	2	JOMINI (Baron de). History of the Campaign of Waterloo. 12mo. 1853.
503	5	JONES (A.) The Electric Telegraph. 8vo. 1852.
2	2	JONES (G.) Ancient America, 8vo. 1843.
155	7	JONES (Henry). Poems. 12mo. 1749.
*478	8	JONES (H.) Present State of Virginia. 8vo. 1724.
*650	10	JONES (H. B.) Animal Electricity. 16mo. 1852.
*646	16	——— Gravel and Gout. 8vo. 1842.
*660	16	JONES (S.) Biographical Dictionary. 12mo. 1805.
497	22	JONES (Silas). Practical Phrenology. 12mo. 1836.
348	3	JONES (W.) On Bailments. 8vo. 1804.
22	3	JOSEPHUS (F.) Works. 8vo. 1851.
22	6	——— Works. 2 vols. 4to. 1823.
516	4	JOUFFROY (T.) Introduction to Ethics. 2 vols. 12mo. 1840.
*316	2	JOURNAL of the Times. Vol. 1. 8vo. 1818.
505	5	——— of Health. 8vo. 1830.
139	12	JOURNEY to the World Under Ground. 12mo. 1742.

Shelf.	No.	
110	17	Joutel. Voyage of La Salle to Gulf of Mexico. 8vo. 1714.
507	5	Joyce (J.) Introduction to the Arts and Sciences. 12mo. 1852.
507	4	——— Scientific Dialogues. 12mo. 1852.
106	10	Juan (Don G.) Voyage to South America. 2 vols. 8vo. 1758.
124	14	Judd (Rev. S.) Margaret. 2 vols. 12mo. 1851.
165	15	——— Philo. 12mo. 1850.
135	6	——— Richard Edney. 12mo. 1850.
469	10	Judson (A. T.) Comments on the Trial of Dr. Fuller. 8vo. 1831.
180	10	Judson (E.) Kathayan Slave. 16mo. 1853.
78	14	Judson (E. C.) Memoir of S. B. Judson. 18mo. 1851.
400	1	Junius. 2 vols. 8vo. 1850.
485	1	——— with Notes by R. Heron. 2 vols. 8vo. 1804.
		——— 2 vols. 8vo. 1833.
181	6	——— Essay on, by Waterhouse. 8vo. 1831.
119	15	Juvenal. Translated by Charles Badham. 18mo. n. d.
409	13	——— Persius, Sulpicia, and Lucilius. Satires, translated by Evans and Gifford. 8vo. 1852.
*432	10	——— Translated by Gifford. 4to. 1802.

K.

Shelf.	No.	
*271	14	Kæmpfer (E.) History of Japan. 2 vols. folio. 1727.
*447	5	Kalm (P.) Travels in North America. 3 vols. 8vo. 1770–71.
508	24	Kater (Capt. H.) Mechanics. 16mo. 1838.
30	5	——— Mechanics. 18mo. 1849.
105	1	Kay (S.) Travels in Caffraria. 12mo. 1833.
37	5	Keate (G.) Pelew Islands. 8vo. 1789.
75	4	Keats (J.) Life, Letters, &c. 12mo. 1848.
165	17	——— Poetical Works. 12mo. 1846.
165	18	——— Poetical Works. 12mo. 1846.
183	8	Keble (J.) Christian Year. 8vo. 1849.
408	4	Keightley (T.) Fairy Mythology. 8vo. 1850.
99	4	——— History of England. 5 vols. 18mo. 1840.
38	11	——— History of Greece. 12mo. 1835.
37	9	——— History of Rome. 12mo. 1839.
38	3	——— History of Roman Empire. 12mo. 1841.
180	26	——— Mythology for Schools. 18mo. 1852.
30	4	——— Outlines of History. 18mo. 1850.
*454	13	Keith (W.) History of British Plantations in America. 4to. 1738.
53	11	Kelly (M.) Reminiscences. 2 vols. 8vo. 1826.
506	8	Kelt (T.) Mechanics' Text-Book. 12mo. 1850.
200	16	Kempis (T. à). Imitation of Christ. 16mo. 1850.

Shelf.	No.	
106	4	KENDALL (G. W.) Santa Fe Expedition. 2 vols. 12mo. 1850.
*506	10	KENNEDY (E.) Obstetric Auscultation. 12mo. 1843.
123	11	KENNEDY (G.) Dunallan. 12mo. n. d.
129	11	——— Father Clement. 16mo. 1851.
121	17	KENNEDY (J. P.) Horse Shoe Robinson. 12mo. 1852.
75	3	——— Life of William Wirt. 2 vols. 12mo. 1852.
123	18	——— Swallow Barn. 12mo. 1851.
27	6	KENNETT (B.) Romæ Antiquæ Notitia. 8vo. 1763.
333	2	KENT (J.) Commentaries on American Law. 4 vols. 8vo. 1851.
508	19	KENTISH (T.) Treatise on a Box of Instruments. 16mo. 1852.
153	2	KENYON (J.) Poems. 8vo. 1838.
155	11	——— A Day at Tivoli. 8vo. 1849.
95	18	KEPPEL (G.) Journey from India to England. 8vo. 1827.
97	22	KEPPEL (H.) Expedition to Borneo. 16mo. 1846.
449	6	KER (J. B.) Archæology of Popular Phrases and Nursery Rhymes. 2 vols. 12mo. 1837.
149	7	KETTELL (S.) Specimens of American Poetry. 3 vols. 12mo. 1829.
54	3	KETTELL (T.) Life of Admiral A. Keppell. 2 vols. 8vo. 1842.
418	13	KIDD (J.) Adaptation of External Nature to Man. Post 8vo. 1852.
180	25	KIDDER (D. P.) Mormonism, and the Mormons. 16mo. 1852.
472	7	KING (C.) Memoir of the Construction of the Croton Aqueduct. 4to. 1843.
190	10	KING (P.) History of the Apostles' Creed. 12mo. 1804.
46	3	KING (W.) Anecdotes of his own Times. 12mo. 1819.
199	13	KIP (W. F.) Christmas Holidays at Rome. 12mo. 1846.
199	14	——— Early Conflicts of Christianity. 12mo. 1850.
100	9	KIPPIS (A.) Cook's Voyages Round the World. 18mo. n. d.
*221	1	——— Biographia Britannica. 5 vols. folio. 1778–93.
		Vol. 1. A—Bat. 2. Bat—Bull. 3. Bull—Coke. 4. Col—Dav. 5. Dav—Fast.
418	14	KIRBY (W.) Habits and Instincts of Animals. 2 vols. post 8vo. 1853.
494	9	KIRBY'S Wonderful Museum. 5 vols. 8vo. 1820.
179	9	KIRK (E. N.) Sermons. 12mo. 1840.
*404	9	KIRKBRIDE (T. S.) Reports of the Pennsylvania Insane Hospital, 1846–50. 8vo. 1851.
87	10	KIRKLAND (C. M.) Holidays Abroad. 2 vols. 12mo. 1849.
123	5	——— New Home—Who'll Follow. 12mo. 1850.
164	5	——— Spenser and the Fairy Queen. 12mo. 1847.
121	18	——— Western Clearings. 12mo. 1845.
509	1	KITCHENER (W.) Art of Prolonging Life. 18mo. 1823.

Shelf.	No.	
508	10	KITCHENER (W.) Cook's Oracle. 12mo. 1822.
508	29	——— Economy of the Eyes. 16mo. 1824.
*603	2	KITTO (J.) Cyclopædia of Biblical Literature. 2 vols. 8vo. 1852.
		Vol. 1. A—H. | Vol. 2. I—Z.
510	21	——— Lost Senses. 2 vols. 18mo. 1845–53.
510	10	——— Physical Geography of the Holy Land. 18mo. 1848.
417	7	——— Scripture Lands, with Biblical Atlas. 8vo. 1850.
87	1	——— Uncle Oliver's Travels in Persia. 18mo. n. d.
38	20	KLAPKA (Gen.) War in Hungary. 2 vols. 12mo. 1850.
74	3	KLENCKE (Prof.) Lives of the Brothers Humboldt. 12mo. 1853.
485	19	KLIPSTEIN (L. F.) Analecta Anglo-Saxonica. 2 vols. 12mo. 1849.
486	10	——— Anglo-Saxon Grammar. 12mo. 1848.
507	14	KNAPEN (D. M.) Mechanic's Assistant. 12mo. 1850.
494	15	KNAPP (F.) Chemical Technology. 2 vols. 8vo. 1848.
63	5	KNAPP (S. L.) Lawyers, Statesmen, and Men of Letters. 8vo. 1821.
*63	6	——— Lawyers, Statesmen, and Men of Letters. 8vo. 1821.
510	1	KNIGHT (C.) Capital and Labor. 18mo. 1853.
603	8	——— Cyclopædia of Industry. 8vo. 1851.
633	6	——— Cyclopædia of London. 8vo. 1851.
526	3	——— Half-hours with the Best Authors. 4 vols. 12mo. 1851.
510	20	——— Volume of Varieties. 18mo. 1844.
500	5	——— Life of William Caxton. 18mo. 1844.
*252	4	KNOLLES (R.) Historie of the Turkes. Folio. 1631.
125	3	KNORRING (Baroness). Peasant and Landlord. 12mo. 1848.
78	20	KNOWLES (J. D.) Memoir of Mrs. A. H. Judson. 18mo. 1831.
38	5	KNOX (J. P.) History of St. Thomas. W. T. 12mo. 1852.
524	1	KNOX (Rev. V.) Elegant Extracts. 6 vols. 8vo. 1826.
		Vol. 1. Prose, Moral and Religious, Classical and Historical. 2. Prose, Orations; Characters and Letters; Narratives and Dialogues. 3. Letters, Ancient, Classical and Modern. 4. Letters. 5. Poetry, Sacred, Moral, Didactic, &c. 6. Poetry, Dramatic and Miscellaneous; Epigrams, Songs, &c.
195	9	——— Works. 7 vols. 8vo. 1824.
		Vol. 1. Essays. 2. Essays; Winter Evenings. 3. Winter Evenings. 4. Liberal Education; Tract on the Degradation of Grammar Schools. 5. Personal Nobility; Spirit of Despotism; and Antipolemus. 6. Sermons. 7. Christian Philosophy; On the Lord's Supper.

Shelf.	No.	
		Kohl (J. G.) Ireland. 8vo. 1844.
32	6	Kohlrausch (F.) History of Germany. 8vo. 1850.
455	8	——— History of Germany. 8vo. 1852.
82	2	Kolff (D. H. jun.) Voyages of the Dutch Brig Dourga. 8vo. 1840.
184	1	Koran, translated by Sale. 8vo. 1853.
*432	6	——— translated by Sale. 4to. 1734.
87	2	Kotzebue (A. M.) Life and Exile to Siberia. 3 vols. 18mo. 1806.
*395	12	Krabbendam (J.) Catharina Rembrands, of het Beleg van Alkmaar in 1573. 8vo. 1835.
*636	14	Kramer (G.) Maladies de l'Oreille. 8vo. 1848.
28	15	Kugler (F.) History of Painting. 12mo. 1842.
499	15	——— Hand Book of Painting. 2 vols. 8vo. 1851.
509	29	Kurten (P.) Manufacture of Soap. 12mo. 1854.

L.

Shelf.	No.	
45	4	Laborde (A. de). View of Spain. 5 vols. 8vo. 1809.
496	2	Lacépede (B. G. E. de). Histoire Naturelle. 5 vols. 8vo. 1819. Tome 1. Les Quadrupèdes Ovipares. 2–5. Les Poissons.
502	7	Lacroix (S. F.) Plane and Spherical Trigonometry. 8vo. 1826.
125	6	Lady Willoughby, Diary of. 16mo. 1851.
92	13	Laing (S.) Notes of a Traveller. 8vo. 1846.
68	5	Lafayette (Gen.) Complete History of. 12mo. 1851.
*604	6	Lallemand (M.) Spermatorrhœa. 8vo. 1853.
400	2	Lamartine (A. de). French Revolution in 1848. Post 8vo. 1849.
38	17	——— French Revolution in 1848. 12mo. 1849.
400	9	——— Girondists. 3 vols. post 8vo. 1849–50.
186	12	——— Past, Present, and Future. 12mo. 1850.
36	2	——— Restoration of Monarchy. 4 vols. 12mo. 1851–53.
518	13	Lamb (C.) Elia. 12mo. 1851.
523	8	——— Elia. 8vo. 1835.
155	2	——— English Dramatic Poets. 12mo. 1848.
155	3	——— English Dramatic Poets. 12mo. 1845.
525	12	——— Sketches and Letters. 12mo. 1849.
490	15	——— Tales from Shakespeare. 2 vols. 18mo. 1844–46.
118	14	——— Tales from Shakespeare. 16mo. 1851.
525	4	——— Works, with Life. 2 vols. 12mo. 1851.
525	3	——— Works, with Life. 2 vols. 12mo. 1838.
519	4	——— Works, with Life. 4 vols. 12mo. 1850.

Shelf.	No.	
539	29	LAMPING (C.) French in Algiers. 16mo. 1845.
512	1	LAND we Live in (The). 4 vols. 8vo. n. d.
89	5	LANDER (R. & J.) Expedition to the Niger. 2 vols. 18mo. n. d.
160	17	——— Expedition to the Niger. 2 vols. 18mo. 1838.
510	13	LANE (E. W.) Arabian Tales. 18mo. 1845.
95	5	——— Modern Egyptians. 2 vols. 12mo. 1836.
510	12	——— Modern Egyptians. 3 vols. 18mo. 1846.
*550	12	——— Modern Egyptians. 2 vols. 12mo. n. d.
167	4	LANGHORNE (J.) Poetical Works. 2 vols. 16mo. 1804.
139	18	——— Theodosius and Constantia. 2 vols. 18mo. 1770.
498	24	LANGSTROTH (L. L.) On the Hive and Honey Bee. 12mo. 1853.
550	11	LANKESTER (Dr.) Vegetable Substances used for Food. 12mo. n. d.
107	22	LANMAN (C.) Letters from the Alleghany Mountains. 12mo. 1849.
90	16	LANMAN (J. H.) History of Michigan. 18mo. n. d.
28	14	LANZI (L.) History of Painting. 2 vols. 12mo. 1831.
399	5	——— History of Painting. 3 vols. post 8vo. 1847.
*382	2	LA PLACE. Mécanique Céleste, translated, with a Commentary, by Nathaniel Bowditch. 4 vols. 4to. 1829–39.

Vol. 4 contains a Memoir of Dr. Bowditch, by his son.

30	6	LARDNER (D.) Arithmetic. 18mo. 1834.
30	10	——— Electricity, &c. 2 vols. 18mo. 1841.
30	7	——— Geometry. 18mo. 1840.
30	8	——— Heat. 18mo. 1833.
30	9	——— Hydrostatics. 18mo. 1831.
492	5	——— Lectures on Science and Art. 2 vols. 8vo. 1851.
		——— Lectures on Science and Art. 2 vols. 8vo. 1851.
485	22	——— Railway Economy. 12mo. 1850.
493	14	——— Steam Engine. 8vo. 1849.
193	4	LARDNER (N.) Works. 10 vols. 8vo. 1838.

Vol. 1. Life, by Kippis; Credibility of the Gospel History, part 1.
2. Credibility, &c. continued, A.D. 71—247.
3. Credibility, &c. A.D. 248—306.
4. Credibility, &c. A.D. 306—401.
5. Credibility, &c. A.D. 405—1325; Recapitulation; History of the Apostles and Evangelists.
6. History, continued; Jewish Testimonies; Ancient Heathen Testimony.
7. Testimony of Ancient Heathens.
8. Testimony, continued; History of Heretics.
9. Sermons.
10. Tracts; on Epistles ascribed to Clement of Rome; on Ward's Dissertations. Indexes.

78	10	LARRABEE (W. C.) Wesley and his Coadjutors. 2 vols. 16mo. 1851.
*666	16	LARREY (D. J.) On Wounds. 8vo. 1832.
*604	5	LA ROCHE (R.) Pneumonia and Malaria. 8vo. 1854.

Shelf.	No.	
486	20	Latham (R. G.) English Grammar. 12mo. 1852.
483	10	——— Germania of Tacitus. 8vo. 1851.
487	3	——— Hand Book of the English Language. 12mo. 1852.
486	7	——— Hand Book of the English Language. 12mo. 1851.
486	16	——— Man and his Migrations. 12mo. 1852.
484	4	——— On the English Language. 8vo. 1850.
107	13	Latrobe (C. J.) Rambler in Mexico. 12mo. 1836.
28	17	Laurent (P. E.) Ancient Geography. 8vo. 1840.
95	9	Laurie (T.) Dr. Grant and the Nestorians. 12mo. 1853.
505	4	Lavoisier (A. L.) Elements of Chemistry. 2 vols. 8vo. 1802.
51	17	Lawrence (M. W.) Light on the Dark River. 12mo. 1854.
*671	2	Lawrence (T.) Cabinet of Gems. 4to. 1837.
*650	17	Lawrence (W.) Comparative Anatomy, Physiology, &c. Post 8vo. 1848.
*584	2	——— Diseases of the Eye. 8vo. 1854.
*626	3	——— On Ruptures. 8vo. 1843.
*636	3	——— Venereal Diseases of the Eye. 8vo. 1830.
*391	3	Lawson (J. P.) Bible Cyclopædia. 3 vols. 8vo. n. d. Vol. 1. Scripture Gazetteer, A—Ez. 2. Gazetteer, F—Z; Scripture Natural History; Index. 3. Scripture Biography.
105	8	Layard (A. H.) Discoveries at Nineveh. 12mo. 1852.
82	7	——— Discoveries among Ruins of Babylon and Nineveh. 8vo. 1853.
84	12	——— Discoveries among the Ruins of Nineveh and Babylon. 12mo. 1853.
82	6	——— Nineveh and its Remains. 2 vols. 8vo. 1850.
97	8	——— Nineveh and its Remains. 2 vols. 12mo. 1851.
82	4	Leake (W. M.) Travels in the Morea. 3 vols. 8vo. 1830.
*636	7	Lebert (H.) Maladies Scrofuleuses et Tuberculeuses. 8vo. 1849.
*636	8	——— Physiologie Pathologique. 2 vols. 8vo. 1845.
*413	5	——— Physiologie Pathologique, Atlas. 8vo. 1845.
*70	21	Lee (C.) Memoirs. 12mo. 1792.
110	4	Lee (C. A.) Geology. 18mo. n. d.
69	2	Lee (Mrs. E. B.) Memoirs of J. and J. S. Buckminster. 12mo. 1849.
65	5	——— Memoirs of J. and J. S. Buckminster. 12mo. 1851.
140	1	——— Naomi. 12mo. 1848.
118	3	Lee (Mrs. G. G.) Delusion. 16mo. 1840.
77	18	——— Life of Cranmer. 16mo. 1852.
77	19	——— Life of Martin Luther. 16mo. 1852.
77	17	——— Lives of Old Painters. 16mo. 1852.
80	15	——— Pierre Toussaint. 12mo. 1854.
121	40	——— Stories from Life. 16mo. 1850.
16	6	Lee (H.) War in the South. 8vo. 1827.
515	6	Lee (H. F.) Sculpture and Sculptors. 2 vols. 12mo. 1854.

Shelf.	No.	
*650	20	Lee (R.) Ovarian and Uterine Diseases. 12mo. 1853.
*604	22	Lefevre (G.) On the Nerves. 12mo. n. d.
650	9	Leigh (S.) Road Book. 18mo. 1831.
183	2	Leighton (R.) Complete Works. 8vo. 1852.
252	2	Leland (T.) Philip of Macedon. 4to. 1761.
92	2	Lemaistre (J. G.) Travels through France, Italy, &c. 3 vols. 8vo. 1806.
110	14	Leonard (P.) Western Coast of Africa. 12mo. 1833.
140	13	Le Sage (A. R.) Gil Blas. 3 vols. 18mo. n. d.
129	2	——— Roland l'Amoureux. 2 vols. 12mo. 1783.
485	23	Leslie (E.) Behaviour Book. 12mo. 1853.
88	10	Leslie (J.) and others. Discovery, &c. in Polar Regions. n. d.
73	4	Lester (C. E.) Artists of America. 8vo. 1846.
176	23	——— Condition and Fate of England. 2 vols. 12mo. 1842.
176	14	——— Glory and Shame of England. 2 vols. 12mo. 1842.
52	13	——— Life and Voyages of Americus Vespucius. 8vo. 1846.
*475	10	Letters to the Ministry, from Gov. Bernard, &c. 8vo. 1769.
*6	11	——— from House of Representatives, Massachusetts Bay. 8vo. 1768.
*440	5	——— of Love and Gallantry. 12mo. 1718.
108	5	Levasseur (A.) Lafayette in America. 2 vols. 12mo. 1829.
122	5	Lever (C.) Charles O'Malley. 2 vols. 8vo. 1841.
500	16	Lewes (G. H.) History of Philosophy. 4 vols. 18mo. 1852.
490	23	——— Spanish Drama. 18mo. 1846.
5	1	Lewis (A.) History of Lynn. 8vo. 1844.
100	16	Lewis (M.) & Clark's Expedition. 2 vols. 18mo. 1847.
73	6	Lewis (M. G.) Life and Correspondence. 2 vols. 8vo. 1839.
539	19	——— Residence among the Negroes in West Indies. 16mo. 1845.
131	28	——— Ambrosio, or the Monk. 18mo. 1822.
*664	10	Lewis (W.) Materia Medica. 2 vols. 8vo. 1791.
184	3	Liberal Preacher. 2 vols. 8vo. 1831–33.
		Library of Useful Knowledge. 21 vols. 8vo.
499	10	America and the West Indies, Geography of. 8vo. 1841.
41	6	American Revolution. 8vo. n. d.
499	9	Animal Mechanics. 8vo. n. d.
499	12	Arithmetic and Algebra, Processes of. 8vo. n. d.
499	13	Assurance Offices, London. 8vo. n. d.
41	6	Bacon's Novum Organon, Account of. 8vo. n. d.
499	9	Brewing, Art of. 8vo. n. d.
41	9	Busk (M. M.) Spain and Portugal. 8vo. 1814.
499	11	De Morgan (A.) Differential and Integral Calculus. 8vo. 1842.
499	9	——— Spherical Trigonometry. 8vo. n. d.
499	7	Geometry: Plane, Solid, and Spherical. 8vo. 1830.
41	5	Greece, History of. 8vo. 1829.

Shelf.	No.	
		LIBRARY of Useful Knowledge, *continued.*
499	9	Hopkins (W.) Trigonometry. 8vo. 1833.
499	9	Iron, Treatise on. 8vo. n. d.
499	13	Jones (D.) Annuities. 2 vols. 8vo. 1843.
499	13	Life Assurances, Legal Decisions on. 8vo. n. d.
499	5	Lindley (J.) Botany. 8vo. 1838.
74	16	Lives of Eminent Persons. 8vo. 1833.
499	6	Long (G.) Geography of Great Britain. 8vo. n. d.
499	9	Mathematics, The Study and Difficulties of. 8vo. n. d.
499	5	M'Culloch (J. R.) Commerce. 8vo. n. d.
41	4	Merivale (C.) Rome, Augustan Age. 8vo. 1843.
41	6	Müller (K. O.) Literature of Ancient Greece. 8vo. 1840.
499	5	Murphy (R.) Algebraical Equations. 8vo. 1839.
499	14	Natural Philosophy. 3 vols. 8vo. 1834.
		Vol. 1. Heat, Hydraulics, and Hydrostatics; Light (Double Refraction and Polarization of); Mechanics; Optics; Pneumatics; Science (Objects, Advantages, and Pleasures of). 2. Electricity; Electro-Magnetism; Galvanism; Magnetism; Natural Philosophy (Popular Introductions to); Newton's Optics; Optical Instruments; Thermometer and Pyrometer. 3. Astronomy; Geography (Mathematical and Physical); Navigation.
499	9	Physiology, Animal and Vegetable. 8vo. n. d.
499	9	Probability, Essay on. 8vo. n. d.
499	9	Science, Objects, Advantages, &c. of. 8vo. n. d.
41	7	Smedley (E.) France, A.D. 843—1529. 8vo. 1836.
41	4	Switzerland, History of. 8vo. 1840.
41	3	Vaughan (R.) England, 1603—1688. 8vo. 1840.
41	8	Waddington (G.) Church History. 2 vols. 8vo. 1831.
499	12	Waud (S. W.) Algebraical Geometry. 8vo. 1835.
499	8	Youatt (W.) The Horse, &c., a Treatise on Draught. 8vo. 1831.
171	36	LIEBER (F.) Civil Liberty and Self-Government. 2 vols. 12mo. 1853.
37	8	——— Great Events. 12mo. n. d.
176	11	——— Legal and Political Hermeneutics. 12mo. 1839.
173	3	——— Manual of Political Ethics. 2 vols. 8vo. 1847–49.
100	11	——— On Property and Labor. 18mo. 1843.
519	18	——— Reminiscences of Niebuhr, the Historian. 12mo. 1835.
108	9	——— Stranger in America. 2 vols. 12mo. 1835.
503	4	LIEBIG (J.) Works on Chemistry. 8vo. n. d.
*462	3	LIGON (R.) History of Barbadoes. Folio. 1673.
*477	22	LINCOLN (S. jun.) History of Hingham. 12mo. 1827.
505	17	LINDLEY (J.) Theory of Horticulture. 12mo. 1852.
158	10	LINDSAY (D.) Works. 16mo. 1776.
46	5	LINGARD (J.) History of England, Abridged. 12mo. 1836.
41	19	——— History of England. 8 vols. 8vo. 1840.
48	4	——— History of England. 13 vols. 16mo. 1844.

Shelf.	No.	
*447	7	LINNÆUS (C.) Works. 7 vols. 8vo. 1785–87.
469	1	LIOT (W. B.) Panama, Nicaragua. 8vo. 1849.
87	16	LIPPINCOTT (S. J.) (Grace Greenwood.) Haps and Mishaps of a Tour in Europe. 12mo. 1854.
81	9	——— Haps and Mishaps of a Tour in Europe. 12mo. 1854.
137	1	LISTER (T. H.) Herbert Lacy. 3 vols. 12mo. 1825.
*554	12	LISTON (R.) Operations of Surgery. 8vo. 1846.
*564	3	——— Surgery. 8vo. 1846.
*314	7	LITERARY Miscellany. 2 vols. 8vo. 1805–06.
*428	4	——— Museum. 8vo. 1792.
		LITTELL (E.) Living Age. 36 vols. 8vo. 1844–53.
*322	1	Vols. 1—16. 1844–48.
*323	1	,, 17—33. 1848–52.
*324	1	,, 34—36. 1852–53.
176	13	LIVERMORE (A. A.) Review of the Mexican War. 12mo. 1850.
348	5	LIVINGSTON (E.) Penal Law for Louisiana. 8vo. 1833.
392	4	——— Penal Laws for the United States. Folio. 1828.
484	6	LIVIUS (T.) History of Rome, translated by Baker. 3 vols. 8vo. 1823.
120	13	——— History of Rome, translated by Baker. 5 vols. 18mo. n. d.
409	14	——— History of Rome, translated by Spillan and others. 4 vols. post 8vo. 1850–53.
539	35	LIVONIAN Tales. 16mo. 1846.
*203	5	LLOYD (T.) Congressional Register. 3 vols. 8vo. 1789–90.
339	4	——— Trials of Smith and Ogden. 8vo. 1807.
79	9	LLOYD (W. F.) Life of Robert Raikes. 18mo. 1852.
186	20	LOCKE (J.) Essays. 12mo. 1822.
184	9	——— On the Epistles of Paul. 8vo. 1812.
540	1	——— On the Human Understanding. 3 vols. 12mo. 1806.
135	4	LOCKHART (J. G.) Adam Blair. 12mo. 1822.
117	20	——— Adam Blair and Matthew Wald. 16mo. 1843.
155	14	——— Ancient Spanish Ballads. 8vo. 1842.
78	6	——— Life of Sir Walter Scott. 4 vols. 16mo. 1838.
75	15	——— Life of Sir Walter Scott. 7 vols. 12mo. 1839.
135	3	——— Matthew Wald. 12mo. 1824.
88	2	——— Napoleon Buonaparte. 2 vols. 18mo. 1840–43.
122	12	——— Valerius. 2 vols. 12mo. 1835.
456	4	LODGE (E.) Illustrations of British History and Biography. 3 vols. 8vo. 1838.
417	8	——— Portraits of Illustrious Personages of Great Britain. 8 vols. post 8vo. 1849–50.
158	9	LOGAN (J.) Poems. 16mo. 1805.
170	3	LONDON Bridge, Chronicles of. 18mo. 1839.
*231	1	——— Evening Mail, 1845—1853. 15 vols. folio. 1845–53.
*316	1	——— Magazine, 1820—1824. 10 vols. 8vo. 1820–24.

12

Shelf.	No.	
*316	1	LONDON Magazine, New Series. 2 vols. 8vo. 1825.
*393	6	—— Institution, Catalogue of the Library of. 4 vols. 8vo. 1835–52.
529	14	—— Times, Essays from. 16mo. 1852.
529	15	—— Times, Essays from. Second series. 16mo. 1852.
96	9	LONDRES, la Cour et les Provinces d'Angleterre. 2 vols. 8vo. 1816.
500	·6	LONG (G.) Civil Wars of Rome. 5 vols. 18mo. 1844–48.
550	13	—— Egyptian Antiquities in British Museum. 2 vols. 12mo. 1846.
102	1	LONG (S. H.) Expedition to St. Peter's River, &c. 2 vols. 8vo. 1824.
168	10	LONGFELLOW (H. W.) Golden Legend. 16mo. 1852.
136	2	—— Hyperion. 16mo. 1847.
136	3	—— Kavanagh. 16mo. 1851.
136	5	—— Outre-Mer. 16mo. 1852.
164	2	—— Poems. 2 vols. 16mo. 1852.
163	3	—— Poets and Poetry of Europe. 8vo. 1845.
505	18	LOOMIS (E.) Progress of Astronomy. 12mo. 1851.
177	14	LORD (E.) Epoch of Creation. 12mo. 1851.
131	27	LORETTE. 18mo. 1834.
12	11	LORING (J. S.) Hundred Boston Orators. 8vo. 1852.
98	21	LOSSING (B. J.) History of Fine Arts. 18mo. n. d.
2	1	—— Pictorial Field-Book of Revolution. 2 vols. 8vo. 1851–52.
3	4	—— Seventeen Hundred and Seventy-six. 8vo. 1848.
75	14	—— Signers of the Declaration of Independence. 12mo. 1848.
8	18	LOTHROP (S. K.) History of Brattle-street Church. 16mo. 1851.
339	1	—— Proceedings of Ecclesiastical Council, Case of Pierpont. 8vo. 1841.
*603	3	LOUDON (J. C.) Encyclopædia of Agriculture. 8vo. 1844.
*603	6	—— Encyclopædia of Cottage, Farm, and Villa Architecture. 8vo. 1846.
*603	4	—— Encyclopædia of Gardening. 8vo. 1850.
*603	5	—— Encyclopædia of Trees and Shrubs. 8vo. 1842.
496	5	LOUDON (Mrs. J. W.) Gardening for Ladies. 12mo. 1853.
63	15	LOUIS XIV., Secret Memoirs of. 8vo. 1824.
*502	12	LOUIS (P. C. A.) Pathological Researches on Phthisis. 8vo. 1836.
*502	18	—— Anatomical and Pathological Researches. 2 vols. 8vo. 1836.
*664	5	—— Yellow Fever of Gibraltar, 1828. 8vo. 1839.
*604	12	—— Yellow Fever of Gibraltar, 1828. 8vo. 1839.
343	1	LOUISIANA, Civil Code of. 8vo. 1825.
272	11	—— Civil Code of, Additions to. Folio. 1823.
186	18	LOW (S. jun.) Charities of London. 16mo. 1850.

Shelf.	No.	
519	9	LOWELL (J. R.) Biglow Papers. 12mo. 1853.
168	2	——— Conversations on the Old Poets. 16mo. 1846.
166	18	——— Fable for Critics. 12mo. 1848.
158	16	——— Poems. 16mo. 1844.
492	13	LÖWIG (C.) Organic and Physiological Chemistry. 8vo. 1853.
178	2	LOWTH (R.) Lectures on Hebrew Poetry. 8vo. 1829.
410	3	LUCAN, translated by Riley. Post 8vo. 1853.
410	4	LUCRETIUS, translated by Riley, Watson, and Good. Post 8vo. 1851.
69	13	LUTHER (M.) Life of. Post 8vo. 1846.
519	6	——— Table Talk. Post 8vo. 1848.
180	14	——— Sermons. 12mo. 1834.
*314	2	LYCEUM, Boston, January to June, 1827. 8vo. 1827.
506	1	LYELL (C.) Elements of Geology. 12mo. 1839.
493	6	——— Manual of Elementary Geology. 8vo. 1853.
494	4	——— Principles of Geology. 8vo. 1853.
107	14	——— Second Visit to the United States. 2 vols. 16mo. 1850.
106	14	——— Travels in North America. 12mo. 1852.
86	17	LYMAN (T. jun.) A Few Weeks in Paris. 12mo. 1814.
14	13	——— Diplomacy of the United States. 8vo. 1826.
*474	7	——— Diplomacy of the United States. 8vo. 1826.
474	6	——— Diplomacy of the United States. 2 vols. 8vo. 1828.
44	11	——— Political State of Italy. 8vo. 1820.
82	8	LYNCH (W. F.) Expedition to the River Jordan and Dead Sea. 8vo. 1850.
*392	20	LYON (G. F.) Travels in Northern Africa. 4to. 1821.

M.

Shelf.	No.	
7	9	M'CARTNEY (W.) United States. 12mo. 1847.
*554	14	MACAULAY (A.) Dictionary of Medicine. 8vo. 1834.
516	9	MACAULAY (T. B.) Essays. 5 vols. 12mo. 1853.
47	11	——— History of England. 2 vols. 12mo. 1849–50.
457	1	——— History of England. 2 vols. 8vo. 1849.
67	17	M'CLURE (A. W.) Translators Revived. 12mo. 1853.
*626	7	MACCULLOCH (J.) Remittent and Intermittent Diseases. 8vo. 1830.
*623	8	M'CULLOCH (J. R.) Dictionary of Commerce. 2 vols. 8vo. 1851.
*613	2	——— Geographical Dictionary. 2 vols. 8vo. 1851.
623	6	——— Geographical Dictionary. 2 vols. 8vo. 1851.
172	2	——— Interest, Exchange, &c. 8vo. 1851.
172	15	——— Political Economy. 8vo. 1849.
16	1	M'CULLOH (J. H. jun.) Researches on America. 8vo. 1817.

Shelf.	No.	
187	8	MacFarlan (D.) Revivals of the Eighteenth Century. 12mo. n. d.
510	7	MacFarlane (C.) Customs and Sports of South Italy. 18mo. 1846.
84	8	——— Japan. 12mo. 1852.
160	4	——— Lives and Exploits of Banditti and Robbers. 18mo. 1837.
510	6	——— The East. 2 vols. 18mo. 1846–47.
94	2	——— Turkey and its Destiny. 2 vols. 12mo. 1850.
507	24	MacFarlane (R.) History of Propellers, &c. 12mo. 1851.
498	5	——— History of Propellers, &c. 12mo. 1851.
7	6	M'Gee (T. D'A.) Irish Settlers in North America. 12mo. 1851.
6	8	——— Irish Settlers in North America. 8vo. 1852.
28	18	——— Protestant Reformation in Ireland. 12mo. 1853.
450	7	Macgillivray (W.) British Quadrupeds. (Nat. Lib. vol. 17.) 16mo. n. d.
473	2	Macgregor (J.) Commercial Statistics. 5 vols. 8vo. 1847–50.
473	1	——— Progress of America. 2 vols. 8vo. 1847.
399	7	Machiavelli (N.) History of Florence. Post 8vo. 1851.
51	9	Macilwaine (G.) Memoirs of Dr. Abernethy. 12mo. 1853.
123	13	M'Intosh (M. J.) Two Lives. 12mo. 1847.
526	8	——— Woman in America. 12mo. 1850.
108	15	Mackay (A.) Western World. 2 vols. 12mo. 1849.
538	7	Mackay (C.) Extraordinary Popular Delusions. 2 vols. 12mo. 1852.
538	15	——— Extraordinary Popular Delusions. 2 vols. 12mo. 1852.
*623	3	Mackay (R. W. S.) Canada Directory. 8vo. 1851.
4	2	M'Kenney (T. L.) Memoirs of the Indians. 8vo. 1846.
95	11	Mackenzie (A.) Voyage from Montreal to River St. Lawrence. 8vo. 1802.
86	15	Mackenzie (A. S.) American in England. 2 vols. 12mo. 1835.
90	7	——— Life of O. H. Perry. 2 vols. 18mo. n. d.
70	14	——— Life of Paul Jones. 2 vols. 16mo. 1848.
105	16	——— Spain Revisited. 2 vols. 12mo. 1836.
63	2	——— Stephen Decatur. 8vo. 1846.
109	17	——— Year in Spain. 3 vols. 12mo. 1836.
82	14	Mackenzie (G. S.) Travels in Iceland. 4to. 1811.
126	2	Mackenzie (H.) Miscellaneous Works. 12mo. 1853.
131	22	——— Mirror, 1779–80. 2 vols. 12mo. 1793.
663	3	Mackenzie (R.) Five Thousand Receipts. 8vo. 1829.
108	17	Mackinnon (Capt.) Atlantic and Transatlantic Sketches. 2 vols. 8vo. 1852.
523	5	Mackintosh (J.) Miscellaneous Works. 8vo. 1851.
54	4	——— Memoirs of. 2 vols. 8vo. 1853.

Shelf.	No.	
30	11	MACKINTOSH (J.) and others. History of England. 10 vols. 18mo. 1830–40.
104	4	M'LEOD (J.) Voyage of Ship Alceste. 8vo. 1818.
167	11	MACNEILL (H.) Poetical Works. 12mo. 1815.
189	16	M'NEMAR (R.) Kentucky Revival. 12mo. 1808.
497	16	MACNISH (R.) Anatomy of Drunkenness. 12mo. 1835.
498	14	——— Philosophy of Sleep. 12mo. 1834.
455	6	M'SHERRY (J.) History of Maryland. 8vo. 1849.
175	5	M'VICKAR (J.) Political Economy. 8vo. 1825.
55	12	MADDEN (R. R.) United Irishmen. 5 vols. 12mo. 1843–46.
79	5	——— Infirmities of Genius. 12mo. 1833.
344	11	MADDOCK (H.) Chancery Practice. 2 vols. 8vo. 1827.
473	3	MADION FILS (T.) Histoire d'Haiti. 2 vols. 8vo. 1847.
1	4	MADISON (J.) Papers. 3 vols. 8vo. 1840.

Vol. 1. Debates on the Declaration of Independence; Letters preceding the Debates of 1783; Debates in the Congress of the Confederation, Nov. 4, 1782, to Feb. 13, 1783.
2. Debates in the Congress of the Confederation, Feb. 19, 1787, to April 25, 1787; Debates in the Federal Convention, May 14, to Aug. 6, 1787.
3. Debates, &c. continued from Aug. 7, to Sept. 17, 1787.

Shelf.	No.	
539	24	MADRAS, Letters from. 16mo. 1846.
*604	15	MAGENDIE (F.) Physiology. 8vo. 1845.
486	11	MAGLATHLIN (H. B.) Practical Elocutionist. 12mo. 1849.
58	3	MAGOON (E. L.) Living Orators in America. 12mo. 1850.
57	8	——— Orators of American Revolution. 12mo. 1850.
503	7	MAHAN (D. H.) Industrial Drawing. 8vo. 1852.
42	1	MAHON (Lord). History of England. 2 vols. 8vo. 1849.
539	33	——— Historical Essays. 16mo. 1849.
539	25	——— Life of Louis, Prince of Condé. 16mo. 1845.
78	2	——— Life of Louis, Prince of Condé. 12mo. 1845.
46	1	——— The Forty-five. 16mo. 1851.
77	9	MAITLAND (F. L.) Buonaparte on Board the Bellerophon. 12mo. 1826.
122	16	MAITLAND (M.) Passages in the Life of. 12mo. 1851.
96	5	MALCOLM (H.) Travels in Asia. 12mo. 1849.
539	26	MALCOLM (J.) Sketches of Persia. 16mo. 1845.
477	21	MALDEN, Bi-centennial Book of. 12mo. 1850.
*636	6	MALGAIGNE (J. F.) Traité des Fractures. 8vo. 1847.
*211	7	——— Traité des Fractures. Atlas. Folio. 1850.
560	1	MALKIN (J. H.) Historical Parallels. 2 vols. 12mo. 1846.
408	5	MALLET. Northern Antiquities. Post 8vo. 1847.
157	4	MALLET (D.) Works. 3 vols. 12mo. 1759.
39	4	MALLET DU PAN (J.) Destruction of Helvetic Union. 12mo. 1799.
172	18	MALTHUS (T. R.) On Political Economy. 8vo. 1821.
175	6	——— On Political Economy. 8vo. 1821.
490	1	MAMMALIA, History of. 6 vols. 18mo. 1849.
139	11	MAN as He Is. 4 vols. 12mo. 1792.

Shelf.	No.	
*394	16	MANCHESTER Library Report. 4to. 1851.
448	6	MANDEVILLE (B.) Fable of the Bees. 2 vols. 8vo. 1732–33.
*314	6	MANN (H.) Common School Journal. 2 vols. 8vo. 1839–40.
190	2	——— Lectures on Education. 12mo. 1850.
171	34	——— Slavery: Letters and Speeches. 12mo. 1853.
508	30	MANN (J.) American Bird-keeper's Manual. 16mo. 1848.
*428	6	MANNING (F.) Generous Choice, a Comedy. 4to. 1700.
185	3	MANSFIELD (E. D.) American Education. 8vo. 1851.
56	13	——— Life of General Winfield Scott. 12mo. 1846.
6	14	——— Mexican War. 12mo. 1851.
418	15	MANTELL (G. A.) Organic Remains in British Museum. Post 8vo. 1851.
124	19	MANZONI (A.) I Promessi Sposi. 2 vols. 12mo. 1845.
498	12	MARCET (J.) Conversations on Chemistry. 2 vols. 16mo. 1846.
507	23	——— Conversations on Natural Philosophy. 12mo. 1843.
180	16	——— Conversations on Political Economy. 12mo. 1828.
76	15	MARCH (C. W.) Reminiscences of Congress. 12mo. 1851.
465	4	MARCHMONT (Earls of), Selections from the Papers of. 3 vols. 8vo. 1831.
*283	9	MARCOU (J.) Geological Map of the United States, with Text. 2 vols. 8vo. 1853.
124	13	MARGARET Percival in America. 12mo. 1850.
*670	4	MARINERS' Dictionary. 12mo. 1805.
37	10	MARIOTTI (L.) Italy. 2 vols. 12mo. 1841.
47	6	MARKHAM (Mrs.) History of England. 12mo. 1852.
37	15	——— History of France. 12mo. 1848.
546	3	MARLBOROUGH (Duchess of). Private Correspondence. 2 vols. 8vo. 1838.
105	6	MARRYAT (C. B.) Diary in America, second series. 12mo. 1840.
24	10	MARSH (A.) Reformation in France. 2 vols. 12mo. 1851.
128	2	——— Adelaide Lindsay. 3 vols. 12mo. 1850.
115	9	——— Angela. 3 vols. 12mo. 1848.
131	23	——— Emilia Wyndham. 16mo. 1848.
115	1	——— Father Darcy. 2 vols. 12mo. 1846.
121	3	——— Lettice Arnold. 2 vols. 12mo. 1850.
127	6	——— Mordaunt Hall. 3 vols. 12mo. 1849.
121	20	——— Time the Avenger. 3 vols. 12mo. 1851.
138	2	——— The Wilmingtons. 3 vols. 12mo. 1850.
72	2	MARSH (J.) Remains. 8vo. 1843.
480	14	MARSHALL (C.) Diary from 1774 to 1777. 12mo. 1839–49.
*442	9	MARSHALL (J.) Life of Washington. 5 vols. 8vo. 1805–07.
54	10	——— Life of Washington. 2 vols. 8vo. 1840.
*469	14	——— Atlas to Life of Washington. 8vo. n. d.
336	10	——— On the Federal Constitution. 8vo. 1839.
199	11	MARSHALL (T. W.) Polity of the Holy Catholic Church. 12mo. 1844.

Shelf.	No.	
487	18	MARTIALIS (M. V.) Epigrammata. 2 vols. 12mo. 1804.
449	15	MARTIN (W. C. L.) Humming Birds. 12mo. 1852.
490	5	—— History of the Dog. 18mo. 1845.
490	4	—— History of the Horse. 18mo. 1845.
16	14	MARTIN (F. X.) History of North Carolina. 2 vols. 8vo. 1829.
83	3	MARTINEAU (H.) Eastern Life. 8vo. 1848.
510	24	—— Billow and Rock. 18mo. 1846.
121	4	—— Deerbrook. 3 vols. 8vo. 1839.
510	23	—— Feats on the Fiord. 18mo. 1851.
130	4	—— Five Years of Youth. 18mo. 1832.
452	3	—— History of England during the Peace. 2 vols. 8vo. 1850.

Vol. 1. 1815—1830. | Vol. 2. 1830—1846.

Shelf.	No.	
452	2	—— History of the Peace, Introduction to the. 1800–15. 8vo. 1851.
185	11	—— Household Education. 12mo. 1849.
130	1	—— Illustrations of Political Economy. 17 vols. 18mo. 1832–34.
130	2	—— Illustrations of Political Economy. 19 vols. 18mo. 1832–35.

Vol. 1. Life in the Wilds.
2. The Hill and the Valley.
3. Brooke and Brooke Farm.
4. Demerara.
5. Ella of Garveloch.
6. Weal and Woe in Garveloch.
7. A Manchester Strike.
8. Cousin Marshall.
9. Ireland.
10. Homes Abroad.
11. For Each and For All.
12. French Wines and Politics.
13. The Charmed Sea.
14. Berkeley the Banker. Part 1.
15. Berkeley the Banker. Part 2.
16. Messrs. Vanderput and Snoek.
17. The Loom and the Lugger. Part 1.
18. The Loom and the Lugger. Part 2.
19. Sowers, not Reapers.

Shelf.	No.	
517	6	—— Life in the Sick Room. 12mo. 1844.
107	16	—— Retrospect of Western Travel. 3 vols. 12mo. 1838.
130	5	—— Poor Laws and Paupers. 18mo. 1833.
67	4	MARTYN (H.) Journal and Letters. 12mo. 1851.
60	26	—— Memoir of. 12mo. 1824.
188	22	—— Sermons. 12mo. 1822.
*392	3	MARYLAND, Laws of. 1797–98. Folio. n. d.
126	9	MARY SCHWEIDLER, the Amber Witch. 12mo. 1845.
539	28	—— the Amber Witch. 16mo. 1844.
530	26	MASON (L.) Musical Letters from Abroad. 12mo. 1854.
*607	5	MASSACHUSETTS Agricultural Societies' Transactions. 8 vols. 8vo. 1845–52.

Shelf.	No.	
*338	9	Massachusetts Board of Education. Secretary's Tenth Report. 8vo. 1849.
338	10	——— Board of Education. Secretary's Tenth Report. 8vo. 1849.
338	11	——— Board of Education. Secretary's Tenth Report. 8vo. 1849.
338	12	——— Board of Education. Secretary's Tenth Report. 8vo. 1849.
338	13	——— Board of Education. Secretary's Tenth Report. 8vo. 1849.
338	14	——— Board of Education. Secretary's Tenth Report. 8vo. 1849.
480	11	——— Constitution of, and of the United States. 12mo. 1807.
*479	7	——— Convention of 1779–80, Journal of the. 8vo. 1832.
587	7	——— Convention of 1779–80, Journal of the. 8vo. 1832.
587	8	——— Convention of 1779–80, Journal of the. 8vo. 1832.
587	10	——— Convention of 1779–80, Journal of the. 8vo. 1832.
*480	9	——— Debates of the Convention of 1788, to ratify the Federal Constitution. 12mo. 1808.
13	4	——— Debates of the Convention of 1820. 8vo. 1853.
*474	14	——— Debates of the Convention of 1820. 8vo. 1853.
587	13	——— Debates of the Convention of 1820. 8vo. 1853.
353	9	——— Debates, &c. of the Convention of 1853. 3 vols. 8vo. 1853.
*587	15	——— Elections, Reports of Contested. 8vo. 1834.
587	16	——— Elections, Reports of Contested. 8vo. 1834.
344	9	——— Elections, Reports of Contested. 8vo. 1834.
*587	11	——— Elections, Reports of Controverted. 8vo. 1853.
333	3	——— Elections, Reports of Controverted. 8vo. 1853.
*336	3	——— General Laws, from 1780 to 1822, by A. Stearns, L. Shaw, and T. Metcalf. 2 vols. 8vo. 1823.
*353	6	——— Journal of each Provincial Congress. 1774–75. 8vo. 1838.
353	7	——— Journal of each Provincial Congress. 1774–75. 8vo. 1838.
*336	5	——— Laws and Resolves. 1835–38. 4 vols. 8vo. 1835–38.
		Massachusetts Legislative Documents.
*547	1	Senate. 1836. 8vo.
*547	2	House. 1836. 8vo.
*547	3	Senate. 1837. 8vo.
*547	4	House. 1837. 8vo.
*547	5	Senate. 1838. 8vo.
*547	6	House. 1838. 8vo.
*547	7	Prepared by Secretary. 1838. 8vo.
*547	8	Senate. 1839. 8vo.
*547	9	House. 1839. 8vo.

Shelf.	No.	
		MASSACHUSETTS Legislative Documents, *continued.*
*547	10	Senate. 1840. 8vo.
*557	1	House. 1840. 8vo.
*557	2	Senate. 1841. 8vo.
*557	3	House. 1841. 8vo.
*557	4	Senate. 1842. 8vo.
*557	5	House. 1842. 8vo.
*557	6	Senate. 1843. 8vo.
*557	7	House. 1843. 8vo.
*557	8	Senate. 1844. 8vo.
*557	9	House. 1844. 8vo.
*557	10	Senate. 1845. 8vo.
*557	11	House. 1845. 8vo.
*567	1	Senate. 1846. 8vo.
*567	2	House. 1846. 8vo.
*567	3	Prepared by Secretary. 1846. 8vo.
*567	4	Senate. 1847. 8vo.
*567	5	House. 1847. 8vo.
*567	6	Prepared by Secretary. 1847. 8vo.
*567	7	Senate. 1848. 8vo.
*567	8	House. 1848. 8vo.
*567	9	Prepared by Secretary. 1848. 8vo
*567	10	House. 1849. 8vo.
*577	1	Senate. 1849. 8vo.
*577	2	Secretary. 1849. 8vo.
*577	3	Senate. 1850. 8vo.
*577	4	House. 1850. 8vo.
*577	5	Secretary. 1850. 8vo.
*577	6	Senate. 1851. 8vo.
*577	7	House. 1851. 8vo.
*577	8	Secretary. 1851. 8vo.
*577	9	Senate. 1852. 8vo.
*587	1	House. 1852. 8vo.
*587	2	Secretary. 1852. 8vo.
*587	3	Senate. 1853. 8vo.
*587	4	House. 1853. 8vo.
*587	5	Secretary. 1853. 8vo.
*587	14	Plans to Senate Documents, No. 59. 1853. 8vo.
*211	4	MASSACHUSETTS Perpetual Laws. 1780–89. Folio. 1789.
211	5	—— Perpetual Laws. 1780–89. Folio. 1789.
*353	2	—— Reports of the Commissioners to Revise the Statutes. 4 parts, 8vo. 1834–35.
*353	4	—— Report of the Commissioners to Revise the Statutes: chap. 12, of the Militia. 8vo. 1835.
*353	3	—— Report of the Commissioners, &c., Amendments to. 8vo. 1835.
*353	1	—— Revised Statutes. 8vo. 1836.
*344	1	—— Revised Statutes, Suppl. to. 1836–44. 8vo. 1844.

Shelf. No.

*353 5 MASSACHUSETTS, Report of the Penal Code of. 8vo. 1844.

*480 10 —— Rules and Orders of the House of Representatives. 16mo. 1850.

*493 9 —— Sanitary Commissioners' Report. 8vo. 1850.

493 16 —— Sanitary Commissioners' Report. 8vo. 1850.

MASSACHUSETTS Scientific Reports.

*493 8 Fishes and Reptiles, by D. H. Storer. Birds, by W. B. O. Peabody. 8vo. 1839.

*392 8 Geology, by E. Hitchcock. Final Report. 2 vols. 4to. 1841.

*494 17 Herbaceous Plants and Quadrupeds, by C. Dewey. 8vo. 1840.

*587 12 Insects injurious to Vegetation, by T. W. Harris. 8vo. 1852.

*493 7 Invertebrata of Massachusetts, by A. A. Gould. 8vo. 1841.

*492 15 Trees and Shrubs, by G. B. Emerson. 8vo. 1846.

*356 1 MASSACHUSETTS Special Laws. Vols. 6, 7. 2 vols. 8vo. 1837.

*356 2 —— Special Laws. Vol. 7. 8vo. 1837.

16 15 —— Speeches of the Governors of. 1765–75. 8vo. 1818.

*474 9 —— Speeches of the Governors of. 1765–75. 8vo. 1818.

*211 1 MASSACHUSETTS Bay. Acts and Laws, 1736–50. Folio. 1752.

*336 4 —— Bay. Ancient Charters and Laws, by Dane, Prescott, and Story. 8vo. 1814.

*211 2 —— Bay. Charter granted by William and Mary. Folio. 1742.

*211 3 —— Bay. Charter granted by William and Mary. Folio. 1759.

*272 2 —— Bay. Journal of the House of Representatives. Folio. 1748–49.

*272 3 —— Bay. Journal of the House of Representatives. Folio. 1756–57.

*272 4 —— Bay. Journal of the House of Representatives. Folio. 1762–63.

*272 5 —— Bay. Journal of the House of Representatives. Folio. 1763–64.

*272 6 —— Bay. Journal of the House of Representatives. Folio. 1765–66.

*272 7 —— Bay. Journal of the House of Representatives. Folio. 1769–70.

*272 8 —— Bay. Journal of the House of Representatives. Folio. 1770–71.

*272 9 —— Bay. Journal of the House of Representatives. Folio. 1771–72.

*272 10 —— Bay. Journal of the House of Representatives. Folio. 1772–73.

Shelf.	No.	
*382	1	MASSACHUSETTS Bay. Records of the Governor and Company. 1628–49. Edited by N. B. Shurtleff. 2 vols. folio. 1853.

Vol. 1. Introductory Remarks; Colony Charter; Company's Records, 1628–30; Colony Records, 1630–41; List of Freemen, 1631–41; Miscellaneous Records; Indexes.
2. Colony Records, 1642–49; List of Freemen, 1642–49; Indexes.

Shelf.	No.	
		MASSACHUSETTS Historical Society's Collections.
17	1	First Series. 10 vols. 8vo. 1806–09.
17	2	Second Series. 10 vols. 8vo. 1814–23.
17	3	Third Series. 10 vols. 8vo. 1825–49.
18	1	Fourth Series. Vol. 1. 8vo. 1852.
*467	1	First Series. 10 vols. 8vo. 1806–09.
*467	2	Second Series. 10 vols. 8vo. 1814–23.
*467	3	Third Series. 10 vols. 8vo. 1825–49.
494	3	MASSACHUSETTS Medical Society's Report on Cholera. 8vo. 1832.
178	10	MASSILLON (J. B.) Sermons. 2 vols. 8vo. 1803.
159	9	MASSINGER (P.) Plays. Family edition. 3 vols. 18mo. 1851.

Vol. 1. Life; the Virgin-martyr; the Great Duke of Florence; the Bondman; the Maid of Honor.
2. The Duke of Milan; the City Madam; the Unnatural Combat; the Picture; Selections from the Roman Actor.
3. New Way to Pay Old Debts; the Fatal Dowry; the Emperor of the East; a Very Woman; the Bashful Lover.

Shelf.	No.	
163	8	——— Plays. 8vo. 1840.
*395	4	——— Plays, edited by Gifford. 4 vols. 8vo. 1805.

Vol. 1. Introduction, Essay, &c.; the Virgin-martyr; the Unnatural Combat; the Duke of Milan.
2. The Bondman; the Renegado; the Parliament of Love; the Roman Actor; the Great Duke of Florence.
3. The Maid of Honor; the Picture; the Emperor of the East; the Fatal Dowry; New Way to Pay Old Debts.
4. The City Madam; the Guardian; a Very Woman; the Bashful Lover; the Old Law.

Shelf.	No.	
*453	6	MATHER (C.) Magnalia. 2 vols. 8vo. 1820.
*614	7	MATTEUCCI (C.) Lectures on Living Beings. 12mo. 1848.
*650	19	——— Phénomènes Physiques des Corps Vivants. 12mo. 1847.
408	6	MATTHEW of Westminster. Flowers of History. 2 vols. post 8vo. 1853.
486	25	MATTHIÆ (A.) History of Greek and Roman Literature. 16mo. 1841.
180	22	MATTHIAS (B.) Rules of Order. 18mo. 1851.
171	24	MATTISON (H.) Spirit Rapping Unveiled. 12mo. 1853.
110	9	MAURY (Abbé). Principles of Eloquence. 18mo. n. d.
66	7	MAURY (S. M.) Statesmen of America. 12mo. 1847.
523	7	MAVOR (W.) Miscellanies. 8vo. 1829.
194	9	MAXCY (J.) Literary Remains, with Memoir. 8vo. 1844.

Shelf.	No.	
417	9	Maxwell (W. H.) Victories of Wellington and the British Armies. Post 8vo. 1852.
141	41	——— Border Tales. 16mo. 1852.
171	11	Mayo (H.) Popular Superstitions. 12mo. 1852.
104	14	Meares (J.) Voyages, 1786, 1788, and 1789. 2 vols. 8vo. 1791.
*315	5	Mechanic's Magazine. Vols. 5—10, 13. 7 vols. 8vo. 1826–30.
37	1	Medhurst (W. H.) On China. 12mo. 1838.
*404	4	Medical Association (American). Transactions. 3 vols. 8vo. 1848–50.
*404	5	——— Convention. 8vo. 1847.
530	4	Medwin (T.) Conversations with Lord Byron. 12mo. 1824.
*604	8	Meigs (C. D.) Diseases of the Uterus. 8vo. 1852.
*594	6	——— Treatise on Obstetrics. 8vo. 1854.
133	21	Melville (H.) Omoo. 12mo. 1852.
539	15	——— Omoo. 16mo. 1847.
133	22	——— Pierre. 12mo. 1852.
125	14	——— Redburn. 12mo. 1849.
123	10	——— Typee. 12mo. 1852.
539	21	——— Typee. 16mo. 1846.
123	8	——— White Jacket. 12mo. 1850.
133	20	——— Moby-Dick. 12mo. 1851.
103	9	Melish (J.) Travels in United States. 2 vols. 8vo. 1812.
88	20	Memes (J. S.) Memoirs of Josephine. 18mo. n. d.
560	2	Menageries. 3 vols. 12mo. 1848–50.
560	3	——— Monkeys, Opossums, &c. 12mo. n. d.
*395	9	Mendham (Rev. J.) Index of Prohibited Books. 12mo. 1840.
*429	9	Mendoza (A. H. de). Obras. 4to. 1728.
530	24	Mennais (F. de la). People's Own Book. 18mo. 1839.
80	11	Men of the Time. 12mo. 1852.
516	5	Menzel (W.) German Literature. Translated by C. C. Felton. 3 vols. 12mo. 1840.
398	6	——— History of Germany. 3 vols. post 8vo. 1848–49.
167	1	Mercer (J.) Lyric Poems. 16mo. 1804.
97	3	Meredith (Mrs.) My Home in Tasmania. 12mo. 1853.
539	20	——— Residence in New South Wales. 16mo. 1844.
*394	12	Merrick (M. M.) Catalogue of his Library. 8vo. 1783.
*271	5	Messenger, Weekly. Vols. 3, 4. 2 vols. folio. 1813–15.
315	1	Vols. 5- 9. 5 vols. 8vo. 1815–20.
*271	1	,, 10–12. 3 vols. folio. 1820–23.
*543	2	Metcalf (T.) Reports. Vols. 2–7, 10–13. 10 vols. 8vo. 1842–51.
28	6	Méthode Abrégée pour apprendre la Géographie. 12mo. 1823.
200	6	Methodist Episcopal Church, Doctrines and Discipline. 12mo. 1848.
7	8	Miall (J. G.) Footsteps of our Forefathers. 12mo. 1852.

Shelf. No.

24 1 MICHAUD (J. F.) History of the Crusades. 3 vols. 12mo. 1853.

*403 2 MICHAUX (F. A.) North American Sylva. 3 vols. 8vo. 1850–51.

33 7 MICHELET (J.) History of France. 2 vols. 8vo. 1851.

455 7 ——— History of France. 2 vols. 8vo. 1845.

100 7 ——— Modern History. 18mo. n. d.

38 13 ——— Roman Republic. 12mo. 1847.

39 11 ——— Roman Republic. 12mo. 1847.

175 19 ——— The People. 12mo. 1846.

427 3 MIDDLETON (T.) Works. 5 vols. post 8vo. 1840.

Vol. 1. Account of Middleton and his Works; the Old Law; the Mayor of Queenborough; Blurt, Master-constable; the Phœnix; Michaelmas Term.

2. A Trick to Catch the Old One; the Family of Love; Your Five Gallants; a Mad World; My Masters; the Roaring Girl.

3. The Honest Whore; the Witch; the Widow; a Fair Quarrel; More Dissemblers besides Women.

4. A Chaste Maid in Cheapside; the Spanish Gipsy; the Changeling; a Game at Chess; Any Thing for a Quiet Life; Women Beware Women.

5. No { Wit / Help } like a Woman's; the Inner-Temple Masque; the World Tost at Tennis; Part of the Entertainment to King James; the Triumphs of Truth; Civitatis Amor; the Triumphs of Love and Antiquity; the Sun in Aries; the Triumphs of Integrity; the Triumphs of Health and Prosperity; the Wisdom of Solomon Paraphrased; Micro-Cynicon; on the Death of Burbage; to Webster; on the Duchess of Malfi; the Black Book; Father Hubbard's Tales; Appendix; the Triumphs of Honour and Industry; Index to the Notes.

38 9 MIGNET (F. A.) French Revolution. 12mo. 1846.

46 8 ——— French Revolution. 8vo. 1827.

8 28 MILES (H. A.) Lowell as it Was and as it Is. 18mo. 1845.

172 7 MILL (J. S.) System of Logic. 8vo. 1846.

172 1 ——— Political Economy. 2 vols. 8vo. 1848.

339 8 MILLAR (J.) English Government. 4 vols. 8vo. 1818.

189 2 MILLENNIAL Church (Shakers). 12mo. 1823.

95 8 MILLER (H.) First Impressions of England. 12mo. 1851.

506 3 ——— Footprints of the Creator. 12mo. 1851.

508 14 ——— Geology of the Bass Rock. 16mo. 1851.

506 22 ——— Old Red Sandstone. 12mo. 1851.

506 27 ——— Old Red Sandstone. 12mo. 1851.

46 7 ——— Scenes and Legends of Scotland. 12mo. 1851.

*564 1 MILLER (J.) Practice of Surgery. 8vo. 1853.

46 17 MILLER (J. R.) History of Great Britain. 8vo. 1832.

26 4 MILLER (S.) Eighteenth Century. 2 vols. 8vo. 1803.

85 19 MILLER (T.) Country Life. 12mo. 1847.

47 12 ——— History of the Anglo-Saxons. 12mo. 1852.

85 20 ——— Sketches of London. 12mo. n. d.

538 11 ——— Sketches of London. 12mo. n. d.

Shelf.	No.	
26	7	MILLINGEN (J. G.) History of Duelling. 2 vols. 8vo. 1841.
464	8	MILLOT (Abbé). Elements of History. 5 vols. 8vo. 1796.

Vols. 1, 2. Ancient. | Vols. 3–5. Modern.

Shelf.	No.	
62	7	MILLS (A.) Literature and Literary Men of Great Britain and Ireland. 2 vols. 8vo. 1851.
26	8	MILLS (C.) History of Chivalry. 8vo. 1844.
539	18	MILMAN (E. A.) Wayside Cross. 16mo. 1847.
146	5	MILMAN (H. H.) Fall of Jerusalem. 16mo. 1853.
23	8	——— History of Christianity. 8vo. 1844.
24	13	——— History of Christianity. 2 vols. 8vo. 1840.
464	4	——— History of Christianity. 3 vols. 8vo. 1840.
90	2	——— History of the Jews. 3 vols. 18mo. n. d.
150	16	——— History of the Jews. 3 vols. 18mo. 1830.
24	8	MILNER (J.) & HAWEIS (T.) History of the Church. 4 vols. 12mo. 1847.
158	13	MILNES (R. M.) Poems. 16mo. 1846.
166	2	——— Poems. 16mo. 1846.
*426	8	MILTON (J.) Paradise Lost. 8vo. 1796.
153	13	——— Paradise Lost, with Brydge's Notes. 8vo. 1851.
162	10	——— Poetical Works. 2 vols. 8vo. 1850.
159	5	——— Poetical Works. 18mo. 1847.
149	1	——— Poetical Works. 3 vols. 16mo. 1851.
150	5	——— Poetical Works. 18mo. 1808.
162	3	——— Poetical Works. 2 vols. 8vo. 1836.
162	5	——— Poetical Works. 2 vols. 8vo. 1838.
400	7	MILTON (J.) Prose Works. 5 vols. 8vo. 1848–53.

Vol. 1. Defence of the People of England, in Answer to Salmasius; Second Defence of the People of England; Eikonoklastes.
2. The Tenure of Kings and Magistrates; Areopagitica; on the Ruptures of the Commonwealth; Present Means and brief Delineation of a Free Commonwealth; Way to Establish a Free Commonwealth; on the Articles of Peace between Charles I. and the Irish Rebels; Letters of State during the Administration of the Commonwealth, &c.; Manifesto of the Lord Protector; Notes upon Matthew Griffith's Sermon; of Reformation in England; of Prelatical Episcopacy; the Reason of Church Government urged against Prelaty.
3. Means to Remove Hirelings out of the Church; Animadversions upon the Remonstrant's Defence against Smectymnuus; Apology for Smectymnuus; Doctrine of Divorce; Judgment of Martin Bucer concerning Divorce; Tetrachordon; Colasterion; Declaration for the Election of John the III., King of Poland; Familiar Letters.
4. Treatise on Christian Doctrine, Book 1, of the Knowledge of God.
5. Treatise on Christian Doctrine, Book 2, of the Worship of God; History of Britain; History of Moscovia; Accedence commenced Grammar; Index.

Shelf.	No.	
434	1	——— Works. 8 vols. 8vo. 1851.

Vol. 1. Life by Mitford; Samson Agonistes; Comus; Lycidas; Il Penseroso; L'Allegro; Arcades; Miscellaneous Poems; Sonnets; Psalms.
2. Paradise Lost; Paradise Regained.

Shelf. No.

434 1 MILTON (J.) Works, *continued.*

3. Of Reformation touching Church Discipline in England; of Prelatical Episcopacy; Reason of Church Government Urged against Prelaty; Animadversions upon the Remonstrant's Defence against Smectymnuus; Apology against a Pamphlet called A Modest Confutation of the Animadversions upon the Remonstrant against Smectymnuus; Eikonoklastes.
4. Doctrine and Discipline of Divorce; Tetrachordon; Judgment of Martin Bucer, concerning Divorce; Colasterion; of Education; Areopagitica; Tenure of Kings and Magistrates; on the Articles of Peace between Charles I. and the Irish Rebels and Papists.
5. The History of Britain; Civil Power in Ecclesiastical Causes; Means to Remove Hirelings out of the Church; Notes on a Sermon of Matthew Griffith; Letter concerning the Ruptures of the Commonwealth; True Religion; Heresy; Schism; Toleration; Ready Way to Establish a Free Commonwealth; Letter to General Monk on the Present Means, and brief Delineation of a Free Commonwealth.
6. Pro Populo Anglicano Defensio; Joannis Philippi Angli Responsio; Defensio Secunda pro Populo Anglicano; Authoris pro se Defensio contra Alexandrum Morum; Authoris ad Alexandri Mori Supplementum Responsio; Accedence commenced Grammar.
7. Artis Logicæ Plenior Institutio; Praxis Logicæ Analytica ex Dounamo; Petri Rami Vita; Literæ Senatus Anglicani; Literæ Oliverii Protectoris Nomine Scriptæ; Literæ Richardi Protectoris Nomine Scriptæ; Scriptum Dom. Protectoris; Autoris Epistolarum Familiarum Liber; Prolusiones Oratoriæ.
8. Defence of the People of England in Answer to Salmasius's Defence of the King; Letters of State during the Administration of the Commonwealth; Letters written in the name of the Protectors Oliver and Richard; Manifesto of the Lord Protector; Declaration for the Election of John the Third, King of Poland; History of Muscovia; Index.

194 10 ——— Treatise on Christian Doctrine. 2 vols. 8vo. 1825.

135 17 MILTON (Mistress), Maiden and Married Life of. 16mo. 1852.

500 2 MIND among the Spindles. 18mo. 1845.

3 6 MINER (C.) History of Wyoming. 8vo. 1845.

502 6 MINIFIE (W.) Geometrical Drawing. 8vo. 1851.

*469 36 MINOT (G. R.) History of Massachusetts. 2 vols. in one. 8vo. 1798–1803.

*478 2 ——— History of Insurrection in Massachusetts. 8vo. 1810.

139 8 MINSTREL. 3 vols. 12mo. 1793.

8 22 MIRANDA'S Expedition to South America. 12mo. 1808.

8 23 ——— Expedition to South America. 12mo. 1810.

*18 16 ——— Expedition to South America. 12mo. 1810.

*477 20 MIRICK (B. L.) History of Haverhill. 12mo. 1832.

139 14 MISERRIMUS. 18mo. 1833.

122 20 MITCHELL (D. H.) Battle Summer. 12mo. 1852.

85 12 ——— Fresh Gleanings. 12mo. 1851.

121 15 ——— Lorgnette. Vol. 2. 12mo. n. d.

122 18 ——— Reveries of a Bachelor. 12mo. 1853.

141 35 MITCHELL (N.) The Traduced. 8vo. 1843.

Shelf.	No.	
538	27	MITCHELL (O. M.) Planetary and Stellar Worlds. 12mo. 1853.
507	9	——— Planetary and Stellar Worlds. 12mo. 1851.
128	11	MITFORD (M. R.) Country Stories. 16mo. 1850.
141	49	——— Country Stories. 16mo. 1852.
526	9	——— Literary Life. 12mo. 1852.
112	3	——— Works. 8vo. 1850.
466	1	MITFORD (W.) History of Greece. 8 vols. 8vo. 1838.
505	3	——— Architecture. 8vo. 1824.
76	2	MOFFAT (J. C.) Life of Chalmers. 12mo. 1853.
*594	12	MOHR, REDWOOD, and PROCTER. Pharmacy. 8vo. 1849.
429	4	MOIR (D. M.) Poetical Works. 2 vols. 16mo. 1852.
435	7	MOLINA (Abbe Don J. I.) History of Chili. 2 vols. 8vo. 1809.
13	5	MONETTE (J. W.) Mississippi Valley. 2 vols. 8vo. 1846.
530	16	MONK (M.) Awful Disclosures. 16mo. 1836.
490	3	MONKEYS, History of. 18mo. 1848.
*175	10	MONROE (J.) Conduct of the Executive of the United States. 8vo. 1797.
108	19	——— Tour. 12mo. 1818.
520	6	MONTAGUE (E.) Letters. 3 vols. 12mo. 1825.
540	2	MONTAGUE (M. W.) Works. 5 vols. 12mo. 1803.
*430	2	MONTAIGNE (M. de). Essais de. 7 vols. 12mo. 1745.
524	2	——— Essays. 3 vols. 8vo. 1811.
512	9	——— Works, edited by Hazlitt. 8vo. 1851.
51	18	MONTALEMBERT (Count de). St. Elizabeth of Hungary. 12mo. 1854.
340	5	MONTESQUIEU (Baron de). Spirit of Laws. 2 vols. 12mo. 1773.
173	4	——— Spirit of Laws Reviewed. 8vo. 1811.
105	10	MONTGAILLARD (M. Mie. de). Situation de l'Angleterre en 1811. 8vo. 1811.
163	5	MONTGOMERY (J.) Poetical Works. 8vo. 1853.
98	6	——— Lectures. 18mo. n. d.
517	8	——— Lectures. 12mo. 1833.
40	17	——— and SHELLEY. Literary and Scientific Men of Italy, Spain, and Portugal. 3 vols. 18mo. 1835.
*646	4	MONTGOMERY (W. F.) On Pregnancy. 8vo. 1837.
		MONTHLY Review. 144 vols. 8vo. 1749—1837.
*549	1	From 1749—1758.
*559	1	,, 1758—1767.
*569	1	,, 1767—1775.
*579	1	,, 1776—1784.
*589	1	,, 1785—1792
*599	1	,, 1792—1798.
*609	1	,, 1798—1804.
*619	1	,, 1804—1811.
*629	1	,, 1811—1818.

Shelf.	No.	
		MONTHLY Review, *continued.*
*639	1	From 1818—1824.
*649	1	,, 1825—1831.
*659	1	,, 1831—1837.
*669	1	,, 1837.
*669	2	Index. Vols. 1–70. 2 vols. 8vo. 1786.
*669	3	,, From 1790—1816. 2 vols. 8vo. 1818.
107	2	MOODIE (S.) Roughing it in the Bush. 2 vols. 16mo. 1852.
58	4	MOORE (C. C.) George Castriot. 12mo. 1850.
498	7	MOORE (G.) Body and Mind. 16mo. 1847.
93	5	MOORE (J.) Residence in France. 2 vols. 8vo. 1794.
87	4	——— Society in France and Germany. 2 vols. 18mo. 1803.
93	2	——— Society in France and Germany. 2 vols. 8vo. 1783.
40	16	MOORE (T.) History of Ireland. 4 vols. 18mo. 1846.
56	5	——— Life of Lord Byron. 2 vols. 12mo. 1846.
69	17	——— Life of Lord Fitzgerald. 2 vols. 12mo. 1831.
70	13	——— Life of Lord Fitzgerald. 12mo. 1831.
67	9	——— Life of Sheridan. 2 vols. 12mo. 1853.
162	12	——— Poetical Works. 8vo. 1852.
147	5	——— Poetical Works. 10 vols. 16mo. 1853.

Vol. 1. Odes of Anacreon; Juvenile Poems.
2. Juvenile Poems; Poems relating to America.
3. Corruption and Intolerance; the Sceptic; Two-penny Post Bag; Satirical and Humorous Poems; Irish Melodies.
4. Irish Melodies; National Airs; Sacred Songs.
5. Evenings in Greece; Ballads; Songs; Miscellaneous Poems, &c. &c.
6. Lalla Rookh.
7. Lalla Rookh; Political and Satirical Poems; the Fudge Family in Paris; Fables for the Holy Alliance; Rhymes on the Road; and Miscellaneous Poems.
8. Loves of the Angels; Miscellaneous Poems; Satirical and Humorous Poems.
9. Satirical and Humorous Poems; the Fudges in England; Miscellaneous.
10. The Epicurean; Alciphron; Index.

Shelf.	No.	
188	7	——— Travels of an Irish Gentleman. 12mo. 1847.
131	35	MORE (H.) Cœlebs in Search of a Wife. 2 vols. 12mo. 1809.
516	1	——— Works. 7 vols. 12mo. 1846–47.

Vol. 1. Repository Tales.
2. Cœlebs in Search of a Wife; Essays; Moriana.
3. Christian Morals; Moral Sketches; Reflections on Prayer.
4. Practical Piety; Life and Writings of St. Paul.
5. On the Manners of the Great; Religion of the Fashionable World; Tragedies; Poems.
6. Modern System of Female Education; Sacred Dramas.
7. Hints for Forming the Character of a Princess; Spirit of Prayer; Bible Rhymes.

Shelf.	No.	
117	18	MORE (Margareta). Household of Sir Thomas More. 16mo. 1852.
26	6	MORELL (J. D.) History of Speculative Philosophy. 8vo. 1853.
65	2	MORGAN (Lady S.) Life of Salvator Rosa. 2 vols. 8vo. 1824.

Shelf.	No.	
29	6	Morgan (Lady S.) France. 8vo. 1817.
136	10	Morier (J.) Ayesha. 3 vols. 12mo. 1834.
135	19	——— Hajji Baba. 16mo. 1851.
139	6	——— Hajji Baba. 3 vols. 12mo. 1824.
135	20	——— Hajji Baba in England. 16mo. 1850.
83	11	——— Journey through Persia, Armenia, and Asia Minor. 8vo. 1816.
392	15	——— Journey through Persia, Armenia, and Asia Minor, Plates to. 4to. n. d.
141	50	——— Martin Tontround. 16mo. 1852.
111	2	——— Mirza. 3 vols. 12mo. 1841.
138	4	——— Zohrab the Hostage. 2 vols. 12mo. 1833.
66	8	Morison (J. H.) Life of Jeremiah Smith. 12mo. 1845.
66	9	——— Life of Jeremiah Smith. 12mo. 1845.
67	18	Morley (H.) Palissy the Potter. 2 vols. 16mo. 1853.
538	20	Mormons, or Latter-day Saints. 12mo. 1852.
540	10	——— or Latter-day Saints. 12mo. 1852.
104	18	Morrell (B. jun.) Voyages. 8vo. 1853.
*392	18	Morritt (J. B. S.) Vindication of Homer. 4to. 1798.
*16	7	Morse (J.) American Gazetteer. 8vo. 1797.
15	10	——— Appeal to the Public. 8vo. 1814.
475	5	——— History of American Revolution. 8vo. 1824.
18	15	——— and Parish (E.) History of New England. 12mo. 1804.
*462	11	Mortality, Yearly Bills of. 4to. 1759.
110	6	Moseley (H.) Mechanics. 18mo. 1844.
*344	14	Moses (M.) Commercial Directory. 8vo. 1830.
22	1	Mosheim (J. L.) Ecclesiastical History. 6 vols. 8vo. 1810–11.
22	5	——— Ecclesiastical History, Murdock's edition. 3 vols. 8vo. 1852.
146	3	Motherwell (W.) Minstrelsy. 2 vols. 16mo. 1846.
166	12	——— Posthumous Poems. 16mo. 1850.
123	7	Motley (J. L.) Merry Mount. 12mo. 1849.
650	2	Mount Auburn Cemetery, Notes on. 12mo. 1849.
135	7	Mountford (W.) Euthanasy. 16mo. 1852.
136	15	——— Martyria. 16mo. 1850.
117	8	——— Thorpe. 12mo. 1852.
80	14	Mowatt (A. C.) Autobiography of an Actress. 16mo. 1854.
51	21	——— Autobiography of an Actress. 16mo. 1854.
89	17	Mudie (R.) Observation of Nature. 18mo. n. d.
508	3	——— Man's Physical Structure. 16mo. 1838.
67	7	Muhlenberg (H. A.) Life of Major-General Muhlenberg. 12mo. 1849.
104	16	Mukattem (El). Lands of the Moslem. 8vo. 1851.
492	6	Müller (J.) Principles of Physics. 8vo. 1848.
25	7	Müller (J. von). Universal History. 4 vols. 12mo. 1831.
179	22	Murat (A.) America and the Americans. 12mo. 1849.
190	1	Murdoch (J. E.) Orthophony. 12mo. 1845.

Shelf.	No.	
135	13	MURRAY (C. A.) Prairie Bird. 16mo. 1845.
108	13	——— Travels in North America. 2 vols. 12mo. 1839.
99	9	MURRAY (H.) British America. 2 vols. 18mo. 1848.
89	11	——— British India. 3 vols. 18mo. 1844.
*613	7	——— Encyclopædia of Geography. 3 vols. 8vo. 1846.
469	26	——— Travels in Africa. 2 vols. 8vo. 1818.
83	5	——— Travels in Africa. 2 vols. 8vo. 1818.
474	4	——— Travels in North America. 2 vols. 8vo. 1829.
88	12	——— and others. Discovery and Adventure in Africa. 18mo. 1844.
*654	5	MURRAY (J.) Materia Medica. 8vo. 1808.
63	12	MURRAY (L.) Memoirs of. 8vo. 1826.
47	1	MURRAY (T. B.) Pitcairn Island. 12mo. 1853.
509	5	MUSEUM, British, Marbles of. 18mo. 1848.
538	2	MUSTON (A.) Israel of the Alps. 12mo. 1852.
538	23	——— Israel of the Alps. 12mo. 1853.
170	4	MUTINY at Spithead and the Nore. 18mo. 1842.

N.

509	27	NAPIER (J.) Chemistry applied to Dyeing. 12mo. 1853.
509	25	——— Manual of Electro-Metallurgy. 12mo. 1853.
41	14	NAPIER (W. P. F.) War of the Peninsula. 4 vols. 8vo. 1842.
88	21	NAPOLEON BUONAPARTE. Court and Camp. 18mo. 1848.
170	2	——— History of. 2 vols. 18mo. 1835.
540	11	NARRATIVE of Loss of the Amazon. 16mo. 1852.
*646	17	NASMYTH (A.) On the Teeth. 8vo. 1849.
*212	17	NATIONAL Government Journal, 1823–24. 4to.
23	3	NEAL (D.) History of the Puritans. 5 vols. 8vo. 1816–17.
538	24	NEALE (F. A.) Residence at Siam. 12mo. 1852.
70	2	NEANDER (A.) Emperor Julian. 12mo. 1850.
399	3	——— History of the Church. 8 vols. post 8vo. 1850–52.
22	2	——— History of the Church. 4 vols. 8vo. 1852.
399	4	——— History of the Planting of the Church. 2 vols. post 8vo. 1851.
397	8	——— Life of Christ. Post 8vo. 1851.
400	8	——— Memorials of Christian Life. Post 8vo. 1852.
121	6	NEELE (H.) Romance of History. 3 vols. 8vo. 1828.
60	21	NEFF (F.) Letters and Biography. 12mo. 1843.
*614	8	NELIGAN (J. M.) Diseases of the Skin. 12mo. 1852.
*574	2	——— Medicines, their Uses and Administration. 8vo. 1851.
456	3	NELSON (Lord). Despatches and Letters. 7 vols. 8vo. 1845–46
*432	11	NERO CÆSAR, an Historicall Worke. Folio. 1624.

Shelf.	No.	
104	1	NETHERLANDS, Austrian, and Holland, Tour through. 8vo. 1787.
*633	4	NEUMAN & BARRETTI. Spanish and English Dictionary. Vol. 1. 8vo. 1850.
*633	4	——— English and Spanish Dictionary. Vol. 2. 8vo. 1850.
486	21	NEVILE (T.) Imitations of Horace and Juvenal. 2 vols. 12mo. 1769–74.
171	48	NEWCOMBE (H.) Young Ladies' Guide. 12mo. 1853.
*304	2	NEW ENGLAND Magazine, edited by J. T. & E. Buckingham. 5 vols. 8vo. 1831–33.
469	35	——— Present State of. 18mo. 1833.
*325	5	——— Quarterly Magazine. 3 vols. 8vo. 1802.
16	17	NEW HAMPSHIRE, Second Festival. 8vo. 1854.
477	1	NEW IPSWICH, History of. 8vo. 1852.
43	9	NEWBOLD (T. J.) British Settlements in the Straits of Malacca. 2 vols. 8vo. 1839.
184	7	NEWCOME (W.) Observations on our Lord. 8vo. 1810.
79	11	NEWELL (H.) Life and Writings. 18mo. n. d.
187	5	NEWMAN (F. W.) Regal Rome. 12mo. 1852.
180	4	NEWMAN (J. H.) Discourses. 12mo. 1853.
200	9	NEWTON (T.) Dissertations on the Prophecies. 3 vols. 12mo. 1802.
*404	13	NEW YORK Agricultural Transactions. 8vo. 1847.
*504	11	——— Board of Health, Proceedings, 1822. 8vo. 1823.
*339	6	——— City. Messages during the Mayoralty of Gideon Lee. 8vo. n. d.
*472	4	——— Documentary History. 2 vols. 4to. 1850.
478	1	——— Documentary History. 4 vols. 8vo. 1849–51.
*16	19	——— Historical Society's Collections. 8vo. 1811.
*326	3	——— Review and Athenæum. 2 vols. 8vo. 1825–26.
*305	1	——— Review. Vols. 4—10. 7 vols. 8vo. 1839–42.
550	21	NEW ZEALANDERS. 12mo. n. d.
*504	20	NICHOL (J. P.) System of the World. 8vo. 1846.
505	12	——— System of the World. 12mo. 1848.
40	3	NICHOLAS (H.) Chronology of History. 18mo. 1833.
*473	8	NICHOLAS (N. H.) Siege of Carlaverock. 4to. 1828.
46	4	NICHOLSON (A.) Annals of the Famine in Ireland. 12mo. 1851.
97	6	——— Ireland's Welcome to the Stranger. 12mo. 1847.
509	17	NICOLAY (C. G.) Oregon Territory. 18mo. 1846.
118	12	NIEBUHR (B.) Heroic Tales of Ancient Greece. 16mo. 1844.
34	4	NIEBUHR (B. G.) History of Rome. 3 vols. 8vo. 1851.
48	5	——— Lectures on Roman History. 3 vols. 16mo. 1852.
56	12	——— Life and Letters. 12mo. 1852.
178	8	NIKELSBURGER (J.) Koul Jacob in Defence of the Jewish Religion. 8vo. 1814.
70	10	NILES (J. M.) Life of Commodore Perry. 12mo. 1821.

Shelf.	No.	
*312	1	NILES (W. O.) Weekly Register. 7 vols. 4to. 1836–40.
538	10	NINEVEH, the Buried City of the East. 12mo. n. d.
66	14	NOBLE (L. L.) Course of Empire, Voyage of Life, &c. of T. Coles. 12mo. 1853.
178	14	NOBLE (S.) Appeal. 12mo. 1851.
179	5	——— Plenary Inspiration. 12mo. 1839.
189	14	NOEL (B. W.) Christian Baptism. 16mo. 1850.
177	3	——— Church and State. 12mo. 1849.
*339	21	NORFOLK (Va.) Ordinances of. 8vo. 1829.
74	10	NORMAND (M. A. Le). Memoirs of Empress Josephine. 2 vols. 12mo. 1850.
483	2	NORTH (R.) Memoirs of Musick. 4to. 1846.
		NORTH AMERICAN Review. 71 vols. 8vo. 1815—1850.
*307	1	Vols. 1—20. 1815–25.
*308	1	,, 21—37. 1825–33.
*309	1	,, 38—55. 1834–42.
*310	1	,, 56—71. 1843–50.
*344	7	NORTH CAROLINA Revised Statutes. 2 vols. 8vo. 1837.
444	3	NORTHCOTE (J.) Life of Titian. 2 vols. 8vo. 1830.
53	2	——— Memoirs of Sir J. Reynolds. 8vo. 1817.
181	17	NORTHEND (C.) Teacher and Parent. 12mo. 1853.
157	5	NORTHMORE (T.) Washington, or Liberty Restored. 16mo. 1809.
194	12	NORTON (A.) Genuineness of the Gospels. 3 vols. 8vo. 1844–46.
196	1	——— Tracts on Christianity. 8vo. 1852.
*448	13	NORTON (J.) Orthodox Evangelist. 8vo. 1654.
539	17	NORTON (Mrs.) Residence at Sierra Leone. 16mo. 1849.
417	10	NORWAY and its Scenery. Post 8vo. 1853.
*396	1	NOTES and Queries. 1849–53. 8 vols. small 4to. 1850–53.
539	55	NOTES on Noses. 18mo. 1852.
469	8	NOTT (S.) Sixtieth Anniversary Sermon, preached at Franklin. 8vo. 1842.
180	3	NOTT (S. jun.) Sermons. 12mo. 1835.
86	4	NUGENT. Tour through the Netherlands, &c. 4 vols. 12mo. 1778.
510	9	NUGENT (Lord). Lands, Classical and Sacred. 2 vols. 18mo. 1846.
115	7	NUGENT (Lord and Lady). Legends of the Library at Lilies. 2 vols. 12mo. 1847.
139	13	NUN of Arrouca. 16mo. 1822.
*574	5	NUNNELY (T.) On Erysipelas. 8vo. 1844.
*403	5	NUTALL (T.) North American Sylva. 3 vols. 8vo. 1842–49.
103	5	——— Travels in Arkansas Territory. 8vo. 1821.

O.

Shelf.	No.	
78	5	OBERLIN (J. F.) Memoirs of. 16mo. 1845.
2	7	O'CALLAGHAN (E. B.) History of New Netherland. 8vo. 1846.
399	2	OCKLEY (S.) History of the Saracens. Post 8vo. 1848.
173	7	O'CONNOR (A.) State of Ireland. 8vo. 1843.
118	8	ŒHLENSCHLAGER (A. G.) Correggio.—Sappho, by Grillparzer. 12mo. 1846.
395	11	OERSTED (H. C.) Der Geist in der Natur. 8vo. 1850.
395	10	——— Die Naturwissenschaft. 8vo. 1850.
418	16	——— Soul in Nature. Post 8vo. 1852.
154	7	OGILVIE (J.) Poems. 2 vols. 8vo. 1769.
53	13	O'KEEFFE (J.) Recollections. 2 vols. 8vo. 1826.
395	3	OKEN (L.) Physio-philosophy. 8vo. 1847.
408	7	OLD English Chronicles. Post 8vo. 1848.
*168	11	OLDHAM (J.) Works, with Remains. 12mo. 1686.
139	7	OLD NICK. 2 vols. 12mo. 1801.
66	17	OLIN (S.) Life and Letters. 2 vols. 12mo. 1853.
81	13	OLIPHANT (L.) Journey to Katmandu. 16mo. 1852.
97	13	——— Journey to Katmandu. 16mo. 1852.
95	19	——— Russian Shores of the Black Sea. 8vo. 1853.
*664	1	OLIVER (D.) Physiology. 8vo. 1835.
507	7	OLMSTED (D.) Astronomy. 12mo. 1839.
497	26	——— Astronomy. 12mo. 1839.
484	13	——— Astronomy. 8vo. 1850.
504	12	——— Natural Philosophy. 8vo. 1833.
60	9	O'MEARA (B. E.) Memoirs of Napoleon. 12mo. 1820.
76	12	——— Napoleon in Exile. 2 vols. 16mo. 1853.
141	17	OMNIBUS of Modern Romance. 8vo. 1844. Zschokke (H.) Princess of Wolfenbuttel. The Post Captain. Mangin (V.) Camille. Galt (J.) The Fatal Whisper. The Sisters. Bremer (F.) The Curate.
141	18	——— of Modern Romance. 8vo. 1844. Tiller (B.) Frank Heartwell. Crawford (Mrs. H. C.) First and Second Love. Hoffman (C. F. W.) Goldsmith of Paris. ——— Rolandsitten. Pichler (C.) The Wife Hunter. La Motte Fouque (Baroness). The Modern Lothario.
141	19	——— of Modern Romance. 8vo. 1844. Ritchie (L.) The Game of Life. Gore (Mrs.) Marrying for Money. Galt (J.) The Omen. Banim (J.) Loaded Dice. Opie (Mrs.) Murder will Out. James (G. P. R.) Bertrand de la Croix.

Shelf.	No.	
112	2	Opie (A.) Works. 3 vols. 8vo. 1841.

Vol. 1. Madeline; Adeline Mowbray; Simple Tales; Black Velvet Pelisse; the Death-bed; Fashionable Wife, and Unfashionable Husband; the Robber; the Mother and Son; Love and Duty; the Soldier's Return; the Brother and Sister; the Revenge; the Uncle and Nephew; Murder will Out; the Orphan; the Father and Daughter; Happy Faces.

2. Tales of Real Life; Lady Anne and Lady Jane; Austin and his Wife; Mysterious Stranger; Appearance is against Her; Valentine's Eve; New Tales; All is not Gold that Glitters; Proposals of Marriage; Henry Woodville; the Quaker and the Young Man of the World; Tale of Trials; the Ruffian Boy; the Welcome Home.

3. Temper; a Woman's Love; a Wife's Duty; the Two Sons; the Opposite Neighbor; Love, Mystery, and Superstition; After the Ball; False or True; Confessions of an Odd-tempered Man; Illustrations of Lying.

72	4	Ord (G.) Life of A. Wilson. 8vo. 1828.
*664	12	Orfila (M. P.) Poisons. 12mo. 1826.
83	16	Orlich (L. von). Travels in India. 2 vols. 8vo. 1845.
509	11	Orton (J. W.) Miner's Guide. 16mo. 1849.
*529	9	Osborn (F.) Works. 12mo. 1682.
107	4	Osborn (S.) Arctic Journal. 12mo. 1852.
107	18	——— Arctic Journal. 12mo. 1852.
194	1	Osgood (D.) Sermons. 8vo. 1824.
171	32	Osgood (S.) God with Men. 12mo. 1853.
131	14	——— Hearth Stone. 12mo. 1854.
76	9	Osler (E.) Life of Exmouth. 12mo. 1835.
165	19	Ossian's Poems. 12mo. 1841.
166	17	——— Poems. 12mo. n. d.
68	6	Ossoli (M. F.) Memoirs of. 2 vols. 12mo. 1852.
470	14	Otis (H. G.) Letters on Hartford Convention. 8vo. 1824.
131	36	Otis (Mrs. H. G.) Barclays of Boston. 12mo. 1854.
73	13	Otter (W.) Life and Remains of E. D. Clarke. 8vo. 1827.
153	8	Otway (T.) Works. 2 vols. 8vo. 1812.

Vol. 1. Alcibiades; Don Carlos, Prince of Spain; Titus and Berenice; with the Cheats of Scapin; Friendship in Fashion; Soldier's Fortune.

2. Atheist, or the Second Part of the Soldier's Fortune; the Orphan; the History and Fall of Caius Marius; Venice Preserved; Poems and Letters.

592	3	Overman (F.) Manufacture of Iron. 8vo. 1850.
508	16	——— Manufacture of Steel. 16mo. 1851.
492	4	——— Metallurgy. 8vo. 1852.
508	9	——— Mineralogy, Assaying, &c. 16mo. 1851.
508	15	——— Moulders' Guide. 16mo. 1851.
488	6	Ovid. Metamorphoses. (Davidson's Trans.) 8vo. 1759.
488	7	——— Metamorphoses, translated by Clarke. 8vo. 1790.
120	11	——— Metamorphoses, translated by Dryden and others. 2 vols. 18mo. 1852.
410	5	——— Works, translated by Riley. 3 vols. post 8vo. 1851–52.

Shelf.	No.	
*432	1	Owen (R.) Monograph on the Fossil Reptilia. 4to. 1849.
172	6	Owen (Robert). View of Society. 8vo. 1813.
502	1	Owen (R. D.) Hints on Public Architecture. 4to. 1849.
167	12	Oxford Prize Poems. 12mo. 1834.

P.

*554	9	Paget (J.) Surgical Pathology. 8vo. 1854.
85	23	Paget (John). Hungary and Transylvania. 2 vols. 12mo. 1850.
*666	3	Paine (M.) Cholera. 8vo. 1832.
180	5	——— Discourse on the Soul and Instinct. 12mo. 1849.
*502	11	——— Institutes of Medicine. 8vo. 1847.
*498	22	——— Materia Medica and Therapeutics. 12mo. 1848.
*664	2	——— Medical and Physiological Commentaries. 2 vols. 8vo. 1840.
*502	13	——— Medical and Physiological Commentaries. 3 vols. 8vo. 1840.
*442	1	——— Memoir of Robert Troup Paine. 4to. 1852.
*435	1	Paine (R. T. jun.) Works. 8vo. 1812.
63	13	——— Works. 8vo. 1812.
176	16	Paine (T.) Political Works. 8vo. 1844.
508	17	Painter, Gilder, and Varnisher's Companion. 16mo. 1851.
69	12	Painters (Italian). Life of M. Angelo by R. Duppa, and of Raffaello by Q. De Quincy. 12mo. 1846.
507	1	Painting, its Rise and Progress. 12mo. 1846.
408	1	Palestine, Early Travels in. Post 8vo. 1848.
87	9	——— and Lebanon, Three Weeks in. 16mo. 1836.
188	2	Paley (W.) Natural Theology. 2 vols. 12mo. 1836.
199	4	——— Natural Theology. 2 vols. 12mo. 1836.
510	17	——— Natural Theology. 4 vols. 18mo. 1845–51.
98	16	——— Natural Theology. 2 vols. 18mo. n. d.
186	3	——— Philosophy. 8vo. 1806.
195	10	——— Works. 8vo. n. d.
*182	1	——— Works. 5 vols. 8vo. 1810–12.
193	2	Palfrey (J. G.) Lectures on the Evidences of Christianity. 2 vols. 8vo. 1843.
23	10	——— Lectures on Jewish Scriptures. 2 vols. 8vo. 1838–40.
192	4	——— Sermons. 8vo. 1834.
160	23	Palgrave (F.) History of Anglo-Saxons. 18mo. 1837.
*671	4	Pancoast (J.) Operative Surgery. 4to. 1852.
*394	1	Papworth (J. W. & W.) Museums, Libraries, &c. 8vo. 1853.
38	19	Pardoe (J.) City of the Magyar. 3 vols. 12mo. 1840.
56	3	——— Louis XIV. and Court of France. 2 vols. 12mo. 1848.
57	6	——— Reign of Francis I. 2 vols. 12mo. 1849.

Shelf.	No.	
*505	2	PARENT-DUCHATELET (A. J. B.) Prostitution dans la Ville de Paris. 2 vols. 8vo. 1837.
550	19	PARIS and its Historical Scenes. 2 vols. 12mo. n. d.
510	25	PARIS, its Historical Buildings and Revolutions. 18mo. 1849.
392	13	——— Budgets, Comptes, Mont de Piété. 4to. 1841–45.
262	9	——— Dictionnaire des Rues, et de ses Monuments. 4to. 1844.
*586	3	——— Conseil Général de la Seine. 8vo. 1846.
*596	3	——— Journal d'Education Populaire. 8vo. 1842.
*392	11	——— Mont de Piété de. 4to. 1843.
*586	2	——— Monument de Molière. 8vo. 1844.
392	10	——— Rapport sur l'Organization du Commerce de la Boucherie. 4to. 1842.
*596	5	——— Rapport sur les Salles d'Asile. 8vo. 1838–40.
*262	1	——— Recettes et Dépenses. 4to. 1836–40.
*262	2	——— Recettes et Dépenses. 2 vols. 4to. 1838–41.
*262	3	——— Recettes et Dépenses. 4to. 1844–45.
*262	4	——— Recherches Statistiques. 1821. 4to. 1833.
*262	5	——— Recherches Statistiques. 1823. 4to. 1834.
*262	6	——— Recherches Statistiques. 1826. 4to. 1826.
*262	7	——— Recherches Statistiques. 1829. 4to. 1829.
*262	8	——— Recherches Statistiques. 1844. 4to. 1844.
392	5	——— Remercîmens au nom de la Ville de. 4to. 1842.
*281	1	——— Statistique Monumentale. 2 vols. folio. n. d.
*604	17	PARIS (J. A.) Pharmacologia. 8vo. 1843.
408	8	PARIS (M.) English History. 2 vols. 8vo. 1852–53.
99	11	PARK (M.) Life and Travels. 18mo. n. d.
184	10	PARKER (N.) Sermons. 8vo. 1835.
105	9	PARKER (S.) Tour beyond the Rocky Mountains. 12mo. 1838.
171	31	PARKER (T.) Discourse of Religion. 12mo. 1847.
104	5	PARKINSON (R.) Tour in America. 2 vols. 8vo. 1805.
106	1	PARKMAN (F. jun.) California and Oregon. 12mo. 1849.
107	10	——— California and Oregon. 12mo. 1849.
12	8	——— Conspiracy of Pontiac. 8vo. 1851.
12	9	——— Conspiracy of Pontiac. 8vo. 1851.
147	2	PARNELL (T.) Poetical Works. 16mo. 1852.
*422	1	——— Poems. 4to. 1773.
*394	11	PARR (S.) Bibliotheca Parriana. 8vo. 1827.
103	4	PARRY (W. E.) Voyages in 1819–20. 8vo. 1821.
99	13	——— Voyages. 2 vols. 18mo. 1845.
*654	6	PARSONS (U.) Anatomical Preparations. 8vo. 1831.
*664	6	——— Boylston Prize Dissertations. 8vo. 1839.
*666	7	——— Sailors' Physician. 8vo. 1820.
469	7	PARTRIDGE (Captain). Tour of a Detachment of Cadets. 8vo. 1827.
200	14	PASCAL (B.) Provincial Letters. 12mo. 1848.
80	10	PASCAL (J.) Convent Life at Port Royal. 12mo. 1854.

Shelf.	No.	
200	13	Patrick (S.) On Prayer. 16mo. 1841.
*486	23	Patriotic Addresses to the President of the United States. 12mo. 1798.
508	11	Pattison (S. R.) Fossil Botany. 16mo. 1849.
87	6	Paulding (H.) Cruise of the Dolphin. 18mo. 1831.
109	6	Paulding (J. K.) Letters from the South. 2 vols. 12mo. 1817.
98	12	—— Life of Washington. 2 vols. 18mo. n. d.
408	9	Pauli (R.) Life of Alfred the Great. 8vo. 1853.
107	1	Paxton (P.) Yankee in Texas. 16mo. 1853.
57	10	Peabody (W. B. O.) Sermons, with Memoir. 12mo. 1849.
517	2	—— Remains. 12mo. 1850.
70	4	Pearson (H.) Life of C. Buchanan. 12mo. 1818.
195	4	Pearson (J.) On the Creed. 8vo. 1851.
181	7	Pearson (T.) On Infidelity. 8vo. 1854.
180	18	Peck (G.) Appeal from Tradition to Scripture. 12mo. 1852.
181	14	Peirce (B.) Algebra. 12mo. 1850.
181	12	—— Curves, Functions, and Forces. 2 vols. 12mo. 1846–52.
181	13	—— Geometry, Plane and Solid. 12mo. 1851.
181	8	—— Trigonometry, Plane and Spherical. 8vo. 1852.
14	7	Peirce (B.) History of Harvard University. 8vo. 1833.
497	17	Peirce (C. H.) Examinations of Drugs. 12mo. 1853.
134	8	Pen Owen. 3 vols. 12mo. 1822.
190	12	Penn (G.) Christian Survey of the World. 12mo. 1824.
63	4	—— Memorials of Admiral Sir W. Penn. 2 vols. 8vo. 1833.
169	12	Pennecuick (A.) Streams from Helicon. 18mo. 1720.
53	3	Pennington (M.) Memoirs of Elizabeth Carter. 8vo. 1809.
55	10	—— Memoirs of Elizabeth Carter. 8vo. 1809.
*339	22	Pennsylvania, Digest of Road and Election Laws of. 8vo. 1828.
*478	7	—— Historical Review of the Constitution and Government of. 8vo. 1759.
*480	2	—— Historical Review of the Constitution and Government of. 8vo. 1759.
87	7	—— Peregrinations through, by Peregrine Prolix. 18mo 1836.
		Penny Cyclopædia. (Bound as 14.) 27 vols. 8vo. 1833–43
*701	14	Vols. 1–24.

Vols. 1, 2. A—Ath.	Vols. 13, 14. Int—Mass.
3, 4. Ath—Blo.	15, 16. Mass—Org.
5, 6. Blo—Cha.	17, 18. Org—Pri.
7, 8. Cha—Dio.	19, 20. Pri—Sca.
9, 10. Dio—Fue.	21, 22. Sca—Ste.
11, 12. Fue—Int.	23, 24. Ste—Tit.

Shelf.	No.	
*711	14	Vols. 25–27.

Vols. 25, 26. Tit—Wal. \| Vol. 27. Wal—Zyg.

Shelf.	No.	
*711	14	PENNY Cyclopædia, Supplement to. 2 vols. 8vo. 1846–51. Vol. 1. A—Gyr. | Vol. 2. Hab—Zum.
*682	2	——— Magazine. 14 vols. 8vo. 1832–45.
*395	6	PEPYS (S.) Diary and Correspondence. 5 vols. 8vo. 1848.
522	7	PERCY Anecdotes. 8vo. 1850.
134	9	PERCY MALLORY. 3 vols. 12mo. 1824.
524	9	PERCY (T.) Regulations of the Household of H. A. Percy, Duke of Northumberland. 8vo. 1827.
163	10	——— Reliques of Ancient English Poetry. 8vo. 1839.
*544	11	PEREIRA (J.) Materia Medica and Therapeutics. 2 vols. 8vo. 1852.
*315	2	PERIODICAL Literature, Select Journal of. 2 vols. 8vo. 1833.
*315	3	——— Literature, Select Journal of. 2 vols. 8vo. 1834.
57	5	PERKINS (J. H.) Memoir and Writings. 2 vols. 12mo. 1851.
487	15	PERRIN (J.) French Grammar. 12mo. 1804.
119	15	PERSIUS, translated by Drummond. 18mo. n. d.
69	18	PETERS (S.) History of Hugh Peters. 8vo. 1807.
160	5	PETER the Great, Memoirs of. 18mo. 1839.
162	1	PETER (W.) Specimens of Ancient Poets. 8vo. 1847.
*38	2	PETERBOROW (Earl). Conduct in Spain. 12mo. 1707.
*487	16	PETRONIUS ARBITER (T.) Satyr, translated by Burnaby. 12mo. 1694.
538	1	PFEIFFER (I.) Journey to Iceland. 8vo. 1852.
538	25	——— Journey to Iceland. 12mo. 1853.
107	3	——— Journey to Iceland. 12mo. 1852.
538	26	——— Journey round the World. 12mo. 1852.
538	5	——— Visit to Holy Land, Egypt, &c. 8vo. 1853.
*646	13	PHARMACOPŒIA, London. 8vo. 1851.
503	2	——— of the United States. 8vo. 1851.
120	10	PHÆDRUS (J.) Translated by Smart. 18mo. 1852.
*656	12	PHILADELPHIA Medical Journal. 14 vols. 8vo. 1820–27.
*502	15	——— Minutes of the Committee, on Malignant Fever. 8vo. 1848.
*504	5	——— Report of the Trustees of the Gas Works. 8vo. 1838.
*339	19	——— Ordinances of. 1828.
*339	23	——— Statement of Bequests, &c. 8vo. 1832.
*604	19	PHILIP (A. P. W.) Vital Functions. 8vo. 1839.
158	2	PHILIPS (J.) Poems. 18mo. 1776.
*422	14	PHILIPS (K.) Poems, with Tragedies. 8vo. 1669.
55	5	PHILLIPART (J.) Memoirs and Campaigns of Charles John, Prince Royal of Sweden. 8vo. 1815.
5	2	PHILLIPPO (J. M.) Jamaica. 8vo. 1843.
169	6	PHILLIPS (C.) Emerald Isle. 18mo. 1813.
485	2	——— Speeches. 8vo. 1817.
56	11	——— Curran and his Contemporaries. 12mo. 1851.
40	5	PHILLIPS (J.) On Geology. 2 vols. 18mo. 1837–39.
175	20	PHILLIPS (W.) Inventor's Guide. 12mo. 1837.

Shelf.	No.	
175	16	PHILLIPS (W.) On Protection and Free Trade. 12mo. 1850.
173	12	——— Political Economy. 8vo. 1828.
*304	3	PHILOSOPHY, Boston Journal of. 2 vols. 8vo. 1824–25.
*402	8	PHILOSOPHICAL Transactions of the American Philosophical Society. 6 vols. 4to. 1769–1809.
*402	9	——— Transactions, new series. 2 vols. 4to. 1818–25.
404	10	PHRENOLOGY, Annals of. 2 vols. 8vo. 1833–35.
160	8	PHYSICIANS, British, Lives of. 18mo. 1830.
131	37	PICKERING (E.) Cousin Hinton.. 8vo. 1843.
141	16	——— Grandfather. 8vo. 1844.
141	3	——— The Grumbler. 8vo. 1844.
111	9	——— Kate Walsingham. 3 vols. 12mo. 1850.
417	11	PICKERING (C.) Races of Man. Post 8vo. 1850.
*346	1	PICKERING (O.) Reports. Vols. 3, 5–16. 13 vols. 8vo. 1827–38.
*347	1	——— Reports. Vol. 20. 8vo. 1839.
513	5	PICKET (A. & J. W.) Academician. 8vo. 1820.
169	7	PIERCE (W. L.) The Year. 18mo. 1813.
447	4	PIKE (Z. M.) Expedition to the Sources of the Mississippi. 8vo. 1810.
411	6	——— Expedition, &c. Maps to. 4to. n. d.
190	11	PILLANS (J.) Elementary Teaching. 12mo. 1829.
37	13	PILLERSDORF (Baron). Austria in 1848–49. 12mo. 1850.
47	2	PILLET (Maj. Gen.) Views of England. 12mo. 1818.
35	8	PINCKARD (G.) Notes on the West Indies. 2 vols. 8vo. 1816.
410	6	PINDAR. Odes, translated by Turner & Moore. Post 8vo. 1852.
486	24	——— Odes, translated by West. 2 vols. 12mo. 1753.
119	16	——— translated by Wheelwright; and ANACREON, translated by Bourne. 18mo. 1852.
		PINKERTON'S Collection of Voyages. 17 vols. 4to. 1808–14.
*342	2	Vols. 1–10.
*352	1	,, 11–17.

Vols. 1–6. EUROPE.

Vol. 1. Willoughby in Russia and Siberia; Dutch to the North of Europe; Pontanus on North-east Passage; Regnard to Lapland; Maupertius to the Polar Circle; Onthier to the North; Ehrenmalm in W. Nordland; Leems's Danish Lapland; Allison from Archangel; Samoiedia; Seven Seamen at Spitzbergen; Phipps to the North Pole; Le Roy on East Spitzbergen; Backstrom to Spitzbergen; Von Troil's Iceland; Kergueland to the North; Earl of Cumberland to the Azores; Raleigh on an Engagement near the Azores; Tercera, by De Chaste.

2. Gonzales to England and Scotland; Shaw to West of England; Bray & Ferber of Derbyshire; Moritz in England; Skrine & Malkin through Wales; Hassell to the Isle of Wight; Heath's Islands of Scilly; Robertson's Isle of Man.

3. Pennant's Scotland; Garnet's Account of the Drosacks; Martin's Western Islands and St. Kilda; Mackenzie on Hirta and Rona; Brand's Orkneys and Shetland; Young & Hamilton's Ireland.

Shelf. No.

PINKERTON'S Collection of Voyages, *continued.*

Vol. 4. Lister to Paris, 1698; Young in France; Saussure on Mont Blanc; Ramond on Mont Perdu.

5. Spallanzani's Italy; Dolomieu's Earthquakes in Calabria, 1783; Bourgoanne's Spain; Coxe's Switzerland.

6. Riesbeck's Germany; Coxe's Denmark, Norway, and Russia; Fortia's Sweden.

Vols. 7–10. ASIA.

7. Travels of Rabbi Benjamin; Rubruquis; Marco Polo; Two Mahometans; Nieuhoff's China; Bell's Asia; Hamel's Korea; Tibet; Goez from Lahor to China; Missionaries through Tibet; Caron and Kempfer's Japan.

8. Roe's Journal; Bernier & Hamilton's East Indies; Tavernier's Voyages; Low's Discovery of the Banians; Buchanan through Mysore, &c.

9. Delle Valle, Chardin, Francklin, and Forster in Persia; Description of Persia, from Harris's Collection; Independent Tartary; Jenkinson's Bucharia; Balbi & Fitch's Pegu; Symes's Ava; Turpin's Siam; Baron & Richards's Tonquin; Bovis's Cochin China.

10. Niebuhr's Arabia; Blount's Levant; Dandini's Mount Libanus; Maundrell's Aleppo to Jerusalem; Pococke's Travels.

Vol. 11. ASIATIC ISLANDS.

11. Dampier & M. de Guignes's Phillippines; Beeckman's Borneo; Stavorinus's Java, Batavia, Celebes, and Amboyna, &c.; Pigafetta's Voyage round the World; Pigafetta on Navigation; Australasia; Pelsart's Australasia; Tasman's Voyage; Dampier's New Holland; Abstract of Cook's Voyages; Peron's Voyage.

Vols. 12, 13. NORTH AMERICA.

12. Colon's Discovery of West Indies; English Discoveries, from Henry VII. to close of the Reign of Elizabeth; Frobisher's Three Voyages to Discover North-west Passage; Discovery of and Voyages to Virginia; Cartier's Island of New France.

13. Smith's Virginia, New England, and the Summer Isles; Lahontan's Canada; Kalm's North America; Burnaby's Middle Settlements in North America.

Vol. 14. SOUTH AMERICA.

14. Betagh & Bouguer's Peru; Ovalle's Chili; Condamine's South America; Ulloa's Voyage; Nieuhoff's Brazil.

Vols. 15, 16. AFRICA.

15. Lobo & Poncet's Abyssinia; Browne's Dar-fur; Pococke's Egypt; Addison's West Barbary; Windhuss's Mequinez; Shaw's Barbary; Lempriere's Morocco; Allatif's Egypt.

16. Thunberg's Cape of Good Hope; Angelo & Carli's Congo; Merolla's Congo; Battel's Angola; Bonnan's Guinea; Proyart's Loango, Kakongo, &c.; Adamson's Senegal, Goree, and Gambia; Santo's Eastern Ethiopia; Rochon's Madagascar; Glas's Canary Islands; Park's Africa.

Vol. 17. SUPPLEMENT.

17. Retrospect of the Origin and Progress of Discovery in Ancient and Modern Times; Critical Catalogue of Books of Voyages and Travels; General Index.

81 1 PINKERTON'S Collection of Voyages. 6 vols. 4to. 1810–12.

For Contents of vols. 1—3, see the corresponding vols. above, including Brand's Orkneys and Shetland.

Vol. 4. Young & Hamilton's Ireland; Lister's Paris, 1698; Young's France; Saussure's Mont Blanc; Ramond's Mont Perdu.

5. Spallanzani's Italy; Dolomieu's Earthquakes in Calabria, 1783; Bourgoanne's Spain; Coxe's Switzerland.

6. Riesbeck's Germany; Coxe's Denmark, Norway, and Russia; Fortia's Sweden.

Shelf.	No.	
51	5	PINKNEY (W.) Life of Pinkney. 8vo. 1853.
*614	2	PIPER (R. U.) Operative Surgery. 12mo. 1852.
*554	11	PIRRIE (W.) Principles and Practice of Surgery. 8vo. 1852.
89	3	PITCAIRN'S Island, Description of. 18mo. n. d.
14	12	PITKIN (T.) Commerce of the United States. 8vo. 1816.
6	3	——— Commerce of the United States. 8vo. 1835.
4	6	——— History of the United States. 2 vols. 8vo. 1828.
509	12	PLANCHÉ (J. R.) History of British Costume. 18mo. 1847.
550	20	——— History of British Costume. 12mo. 1849.
*494	7	PLANCHES (L. T. des). Lead Diseases. 8vo. 1848.
410	7	PLATO. Works, translated by Cary and others. 5 vols. post 8vo. 1852.
410	8	PLAUTUS. Comedies, translated by Riley. 2 vols. post 8vo. 1852.
430	4	PLAY-HOUSE Companion. 2 vols. 12mo. 1764. Vol. 1. Account of Plays. 2. Account of Authors.
518	4	PLAYS, Four Old. 12mo. 1848.
529	18	PLINY (C. C.) Letters, by Melmoth. 2 vols. 12mo. 1809.
57	2	PLUTARCH. Lives, translated by Langhorne. 4 vols. 12mo. 1851.
72	5	——— Lives, translated by Langhorne. 8vo. 1850.
137	12	PNEUMANEE. 12mo. 1815.
528	12	POE (E. A.) Works. 3 vols. 12mo. 1853. Vol. 1. Notices of Life, by Willis and Lowell; Tales. 2. Poems and Tales. 3. The Literati; Marginalia.
*429	8	POEMS, Dodsley's Collection of. 10 vols. 12mo. 1782–83.
152	6	POETS, British: Jonson to Beattie. Aikin's Selection. 8vo. 1850.
152	7	——— British: Falconer to Scott. 8vo. 1850.
152	8	——— British: Southey to Croly. 8vo. 1850.
150	8	——— British: Specimens of. 2 vols. 18mo. 1809.
16	10	POINSETT (J. R.) Notes on Mexico. 8vo. 1824.
165	12	POLLOK (R.) Course of Time. 12mo. 1851.
100	10	POLO (M.) Travels. 18mo. 1845.
510	8	POMPEII: its Destruction and Re-discovery. 18mo. 1853.
510	11	POOLE (S.) Englishwoman in Egypt. 3 vols. 24mo. 1845–46.
*394	14	POOLE (W. F.) Index to Periodical Literature. 8vo. 1853.
57	9	POORE (B. P.) Louis Philippe. 12mo. 1848.
148	14	POPE (A.) Poetical Works. 3 vols. 16mo. 1851. Vol. 1. Memoir by Dyce; Pastorals; Messiah; Rape of the Lock. 2. Essay on Criticism; Essay on Man; Moral Essays; Odes; Miscellaneous Poems. 3. Satires, Epistles, and Odes of Horace Imitated; Satires of Dr. Donne Versified; Epitaphs; the Dunciad.

Shelf.	No.	
168	6	POPE (A.) Works, from Warburton's edition. 6 vols. 12mo. 1787–88.
		Vol. 1. Juvenile Poems and Translations; Pastorals; Essay on Criticism; Rape of the Lock.
		2. Imitations of English Poets; Essay on Man; Moral Essays; Satires and Epistles of Horace Imitated; Satires of Donne Versified.
		3. The Dunciad; Appendix.
		4. Miscellaneous Pieces; Imitations of Horace; Epistles; Epitaphs.
		5. Letters to and from Wycherley, Walsh, Cromwell, Trumbull, Steele, Addison, &c.
		6. Letters to and from Gay, Swift, &c.; Letters to Warburton.
*428	3	——— Works, with Warburton's Commentary and Notes. 9 vols. 8vo. 1752.
		Vol. 1. Preface; Pastorals; Rape of the Lock.
		2. Translations and Imitations.
		3. Essay on Man; Moral Essays.
		4. Satires and Epistles of Horace Imitated; Satires of Donne Versified.
		5. The Dunciad.
		6. Miscellaneous Pieces in Verse and Prose; Imitations of Horace, &c.; Epitaphs.
		7. Letters: Wycherley, Walsh, Cromwell, Trumbull, Steele, Addison, &c.
		8. Letters: Blount, Digby, Atterbury, Gay, &c.
		9. Letters: Swift, Gay, Warburton.
538	30	——— Poetical Works. 12mo. 1853.
164	8	——— Poetical Works. 2 vols. 12mo. 1851.
168	12	——— Homer's Odyssey. 12mo. 1808.
103	6	PORTER (D.) Journal of a Cruise in the Pacific. 2 vols. 8vo. 1822.
40	8	PORTER (G. R.) On Silk Manufactures. 18mo. 1831.
40	7	——— On Porcelain and Glass. 18mo. 1832.
*646	10	PORTER (W. H.) Larynx and Trachea. 8vo. 1837.
183	13	PORTEUS (B.) Lectures on St. Matthew. 8vo. 1805.
*328	2	PORT FOLIO. 16 vols. 8vo. 1806–13.
485	12	PORT ROYAL Greek Grammar. 8vo. 1808.
485	7	——— Latin Grammar. 2 vols. 8vo. 1816.
339	9	POTHIER (R. J.) Maritime Contracts. 8vo. 1821.
100	3	POTTER (A.) Hand-book for Readers. 18mo. n. d.
110	8	——— Political Economy. 18mo. n. d.
497	21	——— Principles of Science. 12mo. n. d.
185	13	——— School and Schoolmaster. 12mo. 1851.
27	4	POTTER (J.) Archæologia Græca. 2 vols. 8vo. 1740.
40	6	POWELL (B.) History of Natural Philosophy. 18mo. 1834.
68	8	POWELL (T.) Living Authors of America. 12mo. 1850.
69	7	——— Living Authors of England. 12mo. 1849.
69	8	——— Living Authors of England. 12mo. 1849.
44	6	PRADT (D. de). Congress of Vienna. 8vo. 1816.
78	17	PRATT (A.) Dawnings of Genius. 18mo. 1841.
78	16	——— Dawnings of Genius. 18mo. 1850.
509	7	——— Field, Garden, &c. 18mo. 1841.

Shelf.	No.	
510	22	Pratt (A.) Field, Garden, &c. 18mo. 1847.
490	9	——— Flowers; their Associations. 18mo. 1846.
*477	8	Pratt (E.) History of Eastham, Wellfleet, and Orleans. 8vo. 1844.
325	1	Precursor. 2 vols. 8vo. 1836–43.
2	8	Prescott (W. H.) Conquest of Mexico. 3 vols. 8vo. 1843.
2	9	——— Conquest of Peru. 2 vols. 8vo. 1847.
32	8	——— Ferdinand and Isabella. 3 vols. 8vo. 1838.
32	9	——— Ferdinand and Isabella. 3 vols. 8vo. 1838.
522	2	——— Miscellanies. 8vo. 1845.
512	6	——— Miscellanies. 8vo. 1852.
*433	2	Price (J. M.) Tables of Sterling Exchange. 8vo. 1852.
*469	34	Price (R.) Civil Liberty. 12mo. 1776.
469	9	——— Civil Liberty. 8vo. 1776.
*469	11	——— Additional Observations. 8vo. 1777.
183	1	Prichard (J. C.) Egyptian Mythology. 8vo. 1838.
504	16	——— Physical and Animal Life. 8vo. 1829.
*493	3	——— On Insanity. 8vo. 1837.
194	4	Prideaux (H.) Connection between the Old and New Testament. 2 vols. 8vo. 1833.
474	3	Priest (J.) American Antiquities and Discoveries in the West. 8vo. 1833.
26	9	Priestley (J.) Lectures on History. 8vo. 1840.
476	2	Prince (T.) Chronological History of New England. 8vo. 1826.
*480	8	——— Thanksgiving Sermon, July 18, 1745. 12mo. 1746.
80	13	Prior (J.) Life of Burke. 2 vols. 12mo. 1854.
428	11	Prior (M.) Poetical Works. 2 vols. 12mo. 1779.
149	5	——— Poetical Works. 2 vols. 16mo. 1835.
*586	4	Prison Discipline Society Reports. 5 vols. 8vo. 1826–49. Vol. 1. 1826—30. 2. 1831—35. 3. 1836—40. Vol. 4. 1841—45. 5. 1846—49.
514	9	Prize Book of the Latin School. 8vo. 1820–24.
158	12	Procter (B. W.) English Songs. 16mo. 1844.
164	4	——— English Songs, &c. 16mo. 1851.
529	22	——— Essays and Tales. 2 vols. 16mo. 1853.
506	15	Progression, Theory of Human. 12mo. 1851.
*454	4	Proud (R.) History of Pennsylvania. 2 vols. 8vo. 1797.
*445	10	Psalmanazar (G.) Memoirs of. 8vo. 1764.
107	6	Pulszky (F.) White, Red, Black. 2 vols. 12mo. 1853.
35	1	Pulszky (T.) Memoirs of Hungarian Lady. 12mo. 1850.
125	15	——— Tales and Traditions of Hungary. 12mo. 1852.
*448	19	Purbeck. The Turkish Empire. 12mo. 1668.
153	4	Pursuits of Literature. 8vo. 1798.
98	15	Pursuit of Knowledge under Difficulties. 2 vols. 18mo. 1840.
*633	8	Putnam (G. P.) World's Progress. 12mo. 1851.

Shelf.	No.	
*426	5	PUTTENHAM (G.) Arte of English Poesie. 4to. 1811.
45	3	PÜTTER (J. S.) The Germanic Empire. 3 vols. 8vo. 1790.
74	6	PUY (H. W. de). Ethan Allen and Green Mountain Heroes. 12mo. 1853.
190	5	PYCROFT (J.) Course of English Reading. 16mo. 1850.
164	13	PYE (H. J.) Comments on the Commentators of Shakespeare. 8vo. 1807.

Q.

99	10	QUADRUPEDS, Natural History of. 18mo. n. d.
*671	5	QUAIN (J.) Wilson & Pancoast. Anatomical Plates. 4to. 1844.
150	7	QUARLES (F.) Emblems, Divine and Moral. 18mo. 1816.
*		QUARTERLY Review. 90 vols. 8vo. 1809–52.
*316	3	Vols. 1– 3. 8vo. 1809.
*317	1	,, 3–25. 8vo. 1810–21.
*318	1	,, 25–48. 8vo. 1821–32.
*319	1	,, 49–70. 8vo. 1833–42.
*320	1	,, 71–90. 8vo. 1843–52.

Vol. 20. Index to vols. 1—19.
40. Index to vols. 21—39.
60. Index to vols. 41—59.
80. Index to vols. 61—79.

529	16	——— Review, Papers from the. 16mo. 1852.
*304	1	QUARTERLY Review, British. 12 vols. 8vo. 1845–50.
*646	11	QUEKETT (J.) Histology. 8vo. 1852.
*646	12	——— On the Microscope. 8vo. 1852.
*477	7	QUINCY (J.) Municipal History of Boston. 8vo. 1852.
2	3	——— History of Harvard University. 2 vols. 8vo. 1840.

R.

*529	1	RABELAIS (F.) Works. 4 vols. 12mo. 1807.
*646	2	RACIBORSKI (A.) Auscultation and Percussion. 8vo. 1839.
*523	6	RACK (E.) Essays, Letters, and Poems. 8vo. 1781.
115	2	RADCLIFFE (A.) Gaston de Blondeville. 2 vols. post 8vo. 1839.
172	14	RAE (J.) Political Economy. 8vo. 1834.
188	20	RAFFLES (T.) Practical Religion. 12mo. 1820.
*422	8	RAFFLES (T. S.) History of Java. 2 vols. 4to. 1817.
95	6	RAFINESQUE (C. S.) Travels in North America. 12mo. 1836.
*474	5	RALEIGH (Sir W.) Discovery of the Empire of Guiana. 8vo. 1848.
*664	4	RAMADGE (F. H.) Consumption Curable. 8vo. 1839.

16

Shelf.	No.	
490	19	Ramsay (A.) Butler and his Hudibras. 18mo. 1846.
6	9	Ramsay (D.) American Revolution. 2 vols. 8vo. 1789–95.
445	5	——— Life of Washington. 8vo. n. d.
70	19	——— Life of Washington. 12mo. 1840.
*437	3	——— Revolution in South Carolina. 2 vols. 8vo. 1785.
440	3	Ramsay (J.) African Slaves in the British Sugar Colonies. 12mo. 1784.
*413	3	Ramsbotham (F. H.) Process of Parturition. 8vo. 1851.
7	10	Ramsey (A. C.) War in Mexico. 12mo. 1850.
*272	1	Ramusio (G. B.) Navigationi et Viaggi. 3 vols. folio. 1563–83.
51	7	Randolph (T. J.) Memoir, Correspondence, &c. of Jefferson. 4 vols. 8vo. 1829.
37	11	Ranke (L.) Civil Wars in France. 12mo. 1853.
398	10	——— History of the Popes. 3 vols. post 8vo. 1847–51.
23	7	——— Reformation in Germany. 8vo. 1844.
34	9	——— Turkish and Spanish Empires. 8vo. 1845.
51	4	Rantoul (R. jun.) Memoirs, Speeches, and Writings. 8vo. 1854.
*221	2	Rapin (P. de) & Tindal (N.) History of England. 5 vols. folio. 1743–47.
395	12	Rapp (M.) Grammatik. 8vo. 1852.
13	10	Raumer (F. von). America and the Americans. 8vo. 1846.
469	30	——— England in 1835. 3 vols. 12mo. 1836.
469	32	——— England in 1841. 2 vols. 12mo. 1842.
493	5	Ray (I.) Medical Jurisprudence of Insanity. 8vo. 1853.
*446	9	Ray (J.) Travels and Collection of Travels. 2 vols. 8vo 1738.
*671	7	Rayer (P.) Diseases of the Skin. 4to. 1845.
172	13	Raymond (D.) Political Economy. 2 vols. 8vo. 1823.
446	7	Raymond (J. G.) Life of Dermody. 2 vols. 12mo. 1806.
474	4	Raynal (G. T. F.) History of the Indies. 8 vols. 8vo. 1788.
67	12	Rayner (B. L.) Life of Thomas Jefferson. 12mo. 1834.
339	10	Read (C.) American Pleader's Assistant. 8vo. 1806.
152	9	Read (H. F.) Dramatic Poems. 8vo. 1848.
490	21	Reading Abbey, Legend of. 18mo. 1845.
418	1	Redding (C.) History and Description of Modern Wines. Post 8vo. 1851.
494	14	Redfield (J. W.) Comparative Physiognomy. 8vo. 1852.
485	21	Redfield (W. C.) Storms of the Atlantic Coast. 8vo. n. d.
72	3	Reed (J.) Life and Correspondence. 2 vols. 8vo. 1847.
190	7	Reed (S.) Growth of the Mind. 12mo. 1838.
190	19	——— Growth of the Mind. 18mo. 1841.
*326	2	Register, American. Vol. 1, 8vo. 1817.
186	11	Reid (T.) Intellectual and Active Powers. 2 vols. 8vo. 1793.
502	8	Reid (W.) Law of Storms. 8vo. 1838.

Shelf.	No.	
*474	8	REMEMBRANCER. 8vo. 1775.
*7	1	——— American. 3 vols. 8vo. 1795–96.
*476	1	——— American. 17 vols. 8vo. 1775–82.
38	16	RENGGER (J. R.) & LONGCHAMP (M.) Paraguay und die Regierung von Dr. Francia. 8vo. 1827.
16	5	——— Reign of De Francia in Paraguay. 8vo. 1827.
550	16	RENNIE (J.) Architecture of Birds. 12mo. n. d.
490	7	——— Architecture of Birds. 18mo. 1844.
490	6	——— Bird Miscellanies. 18mo. 1847.
550	17	——— Domestic Habits of Birds. 12mo. n. d.
550	18	——— Faculties of Birds. 12mo. n. d.
490	8	——— Insect Architecture. 2 vols. 18mo. 1845.
90	6	RENWICK (J.) Life of De Witt Clinton. 18mo. n. d.
90	9	——— Lives of Jay and Hamilton. 18mo. n. d.
503	16	——— Mechanics. 8vo. 1832.
508	27	——— Natural Philosophy. 18mo. 1846.
*325	4	REPOSITORY and Review. 4 vols. 8vo. 1812–13.
*391	9	RERESBY (T.) Ingenious Thoughts and Reflections. 4to. 1721.
107	12	REVERE (J. W.) Tour of Duty in California. 12mo. 1849.
138	14	REVERIE, The. 2 vols. 12mo. 1776.
*327	1	REVIEW, American. 7 vols. 8vo. 1845–48.
*325	3	——— American. 4 vols. 8vo. 1811–12.
*326	1	——— American Quarterly. 16 vols. 8vo. 1827–34.
53	10	REYNOLDS (F.) Life and Times. 2 vols. 8vo. 1826.
*392	16	REYNOLDS (J.) Triumphs of God's Revenge. 8vo. 1656.
397	11	REYNOLDS (Sir J.) Works. 2 vols. post 8vo. 1852.
493	11	RHODE ISLAND, Geographical and Agricultural Survey of, by C. T. Jackson. 8vo. 1840.
178	11	RICCI (S. de). Secrets of Female Convents Disclosed. 12mo. 1834.
*394	7	RICH (O.) Bibliotheca Americana Nova. 2 vols. 8vo. 1835–46.
		Vol. 1. 1701—1800. | Vol. 2. 1801—1844.
*394	8	——— Supplement to Bibliotheca, 1701–1800. 8vo. 1841.
*394	9	——— Catalogue of Books relating to America, 1500–1700. 8vo. 1832.
*401	1	RICHARDSON (C.) Dictionary. 2 vols. 4to. 1839.
419	1	RICHARDSON (G. F.) Geology, &c. Post 8vo. 1851.
498	4	RICHARDSON (H. D.) On Dogs. 12mo. 1847.
82	1	RICHARDSON (Jas.) Desert of Sahara. 2 vols. 8vo. 1848.
137	10	RICHARDSON (J.) Ecarté. 2 vols. 12mo. 1829.
106	5	RICHARDSON (Sir J.) Arctic Expedition. 12mo. 1852.
*422	9	——— Fauna Boreali Americana. 2 vols. 4to. 1829–31.
111	15	RICHARDSON (S.) Clarissa Harlowe. 8 vols. 8vo. 1811.
518	14	——— Correspondence. 6 vols. 12mo. 1804.
111	14	——— Pamela. 4 vols. 8vo. 1811.

Shelf.	No.	
111	16	RICHARDSON (S.) Sir Charles Grandison. 7 vols. 8vo. 1811.
118	4	RICHTER (J. P. F.) Flower, Fruit, and Thorn Pieces. 2 vols. 16mo. 1845.
68	11	——— Life of. 12mo. 1850.
171	26	RICHMOND (Legh). Annals of the Poor. 18mo. 1852.
79	10	——— Life of. 16mo. 1848.
*554	7	RICORD (P.) Letters on Syphilis. 8vo. 1852.
*604	14	——— Treatise on Venereal. 8vo. 1853.
475	16	RIEDESEL (Mad. de). Letters and Memoirs. 12mo. 1827.
94	1	RIESBECK (Baron). Travels in Germany. 2 vols. 8vo. 1787.
472	11	RIO (A. del). Description of an Ancient City near Palenque. 4to. 1822.
76	8	RIPA (Father). Memoirs of. 12mo. 1846.
539	23	——— Memoirs of. 12mo. 1844.
*633	10	RIPLEY (G.) & TAYLOR (J. B.) Hand-Book of Literature, &c. 12mo. 1852.
196	3	——— "Latest Form of Infidelity" Examined. 8vo. 1839.
12	10	RIPLEY (R. S.) War with Mexico. 2 vols. 8vo. 1849.
502	2	RITCH (J. W.) American Architect. 4to. n. d.
137	15	RITCHIE (L.) Schinderhannes. 12mo. 1833.
131	25	——— Schinderhannes. 16mo. 1848.
*314	5	ROBERTS (G.) Magazine. 8vo. 1841.
68	10	ROBERTS (W.) Memoirs of Mrs. Hannah More. 2 vols. 12mo. 1851.
*339	7	ROBERTSON (D.) Debates of the Convention of Virginia. 8vo. 1805.
35	7	ROBERTSON (W.) India. 8vo. 1812.
36	3	——— History of America. 2 vols. 8vo. 1812.
41	10	——— History of America. 8vo. 1850.
110	10	——— History of America, Abridged. 18mo. 1848.
41	12	——— History of Scotland. 8vo. 1848.
36	5	——— History of Scotland. 2 vols. 8vo. 1811.
36	4	——— History of Charles V. 3 vols. 8vo. 1812.
41	11	——— History of Charles V. 8vo. 1848.
110	21	——— History of Charles V. Abridged. 18mo. n. d.
*455	1	——— Works. 6 vols. 8vo. 1851.

Vols. 1, 2. Scotland. | Vols. 5, 6. America.
3, 4. Charles V.

Shelf.	No.	
*636	5	ROBIN (C.) Du Microscope et des Injections. 8vo. 1849.
*636	4	——— Végéteaux Parasites. 8vo. 1853.
*413	5	——— Végéteaux Parasites, Atlas to. 8vo. 1853.
128	7	ROBINSON (T. A. L.) Exiles. 12mo. 1853.
486	2	——— Languages, &c. of the Slavic Nations. 12mo. 1850.
486	13	——— Languages, &c. of the Slavic Nations. 12mo. 1850.
139	17	——— Vancenza. 2 vols. 16mo. 1792.
138	9	——— Walsingham. 4 vols. 12mo. 1797.
18	10	ROBINSON (W. D.) Mexican Revolution. 8vo. 1821.

Shelf.	No.	
181	19	ROBISON (J.) Proofs of a Conspiracy. 8vo. 1798.
*339	18	ROCHESTER City, Charter of. 8vo. 1850.
408	10	ROGER DE HOVEDEN. Annals. 2 vols. post 8vo. 1853.
408	11	ROGER of Wendover. Flowers of History. 2 vols. post 8vo. 1849.
178	18	ROGERS (H.) Reason and Faith. 12mo. 1853.
*480	1	ROGERS (R.) Account of North America. 8vo. 1765.
168	3	ROGERS (S.) Poems. 12mo. 1782.
*604	16	ROGET (P. M.) Physiology and Phrenology. 8vo. 1839.
*666	9	ROKITANSKY (C.) Pathological Anatomy, part 1, 8vo. 1845.
34	8	ROLLIN (C.) Ancient History. 2 vols. 8vo. 1852.
81	7	ROMAN and Moor, Traces of the. 12mo. 1853.
49	14	ROME, History of. 2 vols. 18mo. 1834.
83	1	ROMER (Mrs.) Temples and Tombs of Egypt, &c. 2 vols. 8vo. 1847.
445	2	ROMILLY (Sir S.) Memoirs of. 3 vols. 8vo. 1840.
78	9	——— Memoirs of. 2 vols. 12mo. 1841.
189	22	RONGE (J.) Holy Coat of Treves. 16mo. 1845.
*394	2	ROORBACH (O. A.) Bibliotheca Americana. 8vo. 1852.
106	16	ROOS (F. F. de). Travels in United States and Canada. 8vo. 1827.
50	6	ROSCOE (H.) Lives of British Lawyers. 18mo. 1830.
160	22	ROSCOE (T.) Life and Writings of Cervantes Saavedra. 18mo. 1839.
397	3	ROSCOE (W.) Lorenzo de Medici. Post 8vo. 1851.
*442	3	——— Lorenzo de Medici. 4to. 1796.
400	3	——— Leo the Tenth. 2 vols. post 8vo. 1846.
442	8	——— Leo the Tenth. 2 vols. 8vo. 1846.
446	2	——— Life, by his Son. 2 vols. 12mo. 1833.
*483	4	ROSE (H. J.) Inscriptiones Græcæ Vetustissimæ. 8vo. 1825.
434	3	ROSE (W. S.) Letters from the North of Italy. 2 vols. 8vo. 1819.
131	9	ROWCROFT (C.) Australian Crusoes. 16mo. 1853.
150	4	ROWE (E.) Poetical Works. 32mo. n. d.
153	6	ROWLEY (T.) and others. (Chatterton.) Poems. 8vo. 1794.
178	1	ROY (R.) Precepts of Jesus. 8vo. 1828.
127	11	RUFFINI. Lorenzo Benoni. 12mo. 1853.
504	15	RUSH (B.) Diseases of the Mind. 8vo. 1827.
92	14	RUSH (R.) Residence at the Court of London. 8vo. 1833.
92	3	——— Residence at the Court of London. 8vo. 1833.
505	19	RUSKIN (J.) Modern Painters. 2 vols. 12mo. 1852–53.
507	22	——— Seven Lamps of Architecture. 12mo. 1849.
		RUSSELL (B.) Columbian Centinel and Massachusetts Federalist. 33 vols. folio. 1800–32.
*251	1	From 1800—1815.
*261	1	,, 1816—1832.
*271	2	For 1812.
*271	3	,, 1816.

Shelf.	No.	
92	9	RUSSELL (J.) Tour in Germany. 8vo. 1825.
8	6	——— History of the United States. 12mo. 1838.
88	15	RUSSELL (M.) Ancient and Modern Egypt. 18mo. n. d.
98	11	——— History of Barbary States. 18mo. 1846.
98	5	——— Life of Cromwell. 2 vols. 18mo. n. d.
98	4	——— Nubia and Abyssinia. 18mo. n. d.
88	19	——— Palestine. 18mo. n. d.
100	19	——— Polynesia. 18mo. 1848.
538	16	RUSSELL (W.) Extraordinary Men. 12mo. 1853.
43	4	——— History of Modern Europe. 3 vols. 8vo. 1845.
107	8	RUXTON (G. F.) Life in the Far West. 12mo. 1849.
539	36	——— Mexico and the Rocky Mountains. 16mo. 1847.
107	7	——— Mexico and the Rocky Mountains. 12mo. 1848.
*271	13	RYCAUT (P.) History of the Turks, 1678–1699. Folio. n. d.

S.

Shelf.	No.	
*2	5	SABINE (L.) American Loyalists. 8vo. 1847.
*475	17	ST. BOTOLPH'S Church, Boston, England, Description of. 8vo. 1842.
34	2	ST. DOMINGO, History of. 8vo. 1824.
115	3	SAINTINE (X. B. de). Picciola. 12mo. 1853.
141	37	——— Picciola. 12mo. 1843.
135	9	——— Solitary of Juan Fernandez. 16mo. 1851.
519	20	——— Woman's Whims.. 12mo. 1850.
97	21	ST. JOHN (B.) Adventures in the Libyan Desert. 12mo. 1849.
539	34	——— Adventures in the Libyan Desert. 12mo. 1849.
110	16	——— Village Life in Egypt. 2 vols. 12mo. 1853.
539	32	ST. JOHN (C.) Wild Sports of the Highlands. 16mo. 1846.
89	7	ST. JOHN (J. A.) Lives of Celebrated Travellers. 3 vols. 18mo. 1844.
*478	12	ST. JOHN (J. H.) Letters from an American Farmer. 8vo. 1782.
506	24	ST. JOHN (S.) Elements of Geology. 12mo. 1851.
449	2	ST. MARIE (Count). Algeria in 1845. 12mo. 1846.
182	2	SAINT-PIERRE (J. H. B. de). Studies of Nature. 3 vols. 8vo. 1808.
539	37	SAINT-PRIEST (A. de). Fall of the Jesuits in the Eighteenth Century. 16mo. 1845.
495	2	SAINT-URSIN (P. J. M. de). Manuel de Santé. 8vo. 1808.
120	3	SALLUST (C. C.) Translated by Rose. 18mo. n. d.
485	3	——— Bellum Catilinarium et Jugurthinum. 8vo. 1789.
410	9	———, FLORUS, and VELLEIUS PATERCULUS, translated by Watson. Post 8vo. 1852.
498	8	SALVERTE (E.) Philosophy of Magic. 2 vols. 12mo. 1847.
185	9	SALZMANN (C. G.) Gymnastics for Youth. 8vo. 1803.
189	12	——— Elements of Morality. 12mo. 1811.
65	7	SAMPSON (W.) Memoirs of. 8vo. 1817.

Shelf. No.

86 14 SANDERSON (J.) American in Paris. 2 vols. 12mo. 1847.
18 12 SANSOM (J.) Sketches of Lower Canada. 12mo. 1817.
109 8 SANTAREM (V.) Vespucius. 12mo. 1850.
109 11 ——— Vespucius. 12mo. 1850.
107 21 SARGENT (J.) Notes on Cuba. 12mo. 1844.
84 3 ——— Notes on Cuba. 12mo. 1844.
167 3 SARGENT (E.) Songs of the Sea. 12mo. 1849.
76 4 SARGENT (J.) Memoir of Henry Martyn. 12mo. 1836.
77 22 SARRANS (B.) Memoir of Lafayette. 2 vols. 12mo. 1833.
150 9 SATIRIST, British. 24mo. 1826.
500 1 SAUNDERS (J.) Pictures of English Life: Chaucer. 18mo. 1845.
490 25 ——— Canterbury Tales, from Chaucer. 2 vols. 18mo. 1845–47.
187 1 SAUSSURE (Mad. N. de). Progressive Education. 12mo. 1835.
111 10 SAVAGE (M. W.) Bachelor of the Albany. Post 8vo. 1848.
124 15 ——— Bachelor of the Albany. 12mo. 1848.
122 17 ——— Reuben Medlicott. 12mo. 1852.
*603 7 SAVAGE (W.) Dictionary of Printing. 8vo. 1841.
83 4 SAVARY (C.) Letters on Egypt. 2 vols. 8vo. 1799.
530 17 SAWYER (F. W.) Plea for Amusements. 16mo. 1847.
166 9 SAXE (J. G.) Poems. 16mo. 1851.
37 14 SAXTON (L. C.) Fall of Poland. 2 vols. 12mo. 1851.
139 1 SAYINGS and Doings. 2 vols. 12mo. 1824.
139 2 ——— and Doings, second series. 2 vols. 12mo. 1825.
139 3 ——— and Doings, third series. 2 vols. 12mo. 1828.
*445 7 SAYOUS (A.) Mémoires et Correspondance de Mallet du Pan. 2 vols. 8vo. 1851.
*636 11 SCARPA (A.) Diseases of the Eyes. 8vo. 1818.
397 6 SCHILLER (F.) Early Dramas and Romances. Post 8vo. 1849.

The Robbers; Fiesco; Love and Intrigue; Demetrius; the Ghost-Seer; the Sport of Destiny.

399 1 ——— Historical Dramas. Post 8vo. 1850.

Don Carlos; Mary Stuart; Maid of Orleans; Bride of Messina.

407 5 ——— Works: Historical. Post 8vo. 1851.

The Thirty Years' War; Revolt of the Netherlands, to the Confederacy of the Gueux.

407 4 ——— Works: Historical and Dramatic. Post 8vo. 1847.

Revolt of the Netherlands (continued); Trials of Counts Egmont and Horn; Wallenstein and Wilhelm Tell.

516 8 ——— and GOETHE, Correspondence between. 12mo. 1845.
539 30 SCHIMMER (K. A.) Sieges of Vienna. 16mo. 1847.
397 4 SCHLEGEL (A. W.) Dramatic Art and Literature. Post 8vo. 1846.
397 7 SCHLEGEL (F.) Æsthetic and Miscellaneous Works. Post 8vo. 1849.
397 5 ——— Modern History. Post 8vo. 1849.
400 4 ——— Philosophy of History. Post 8vo. 1848.
398 11 ——— Philosophy of Life, &c. Post 8vo. 1847.

Shelf.	No.	
505	21	SCHLEIDEN (M. J.) Poetry of Vegetable World. 12mo. 1853.
463	3	SCHLOSSER (F. C.) History of the Eighteenth Century. 8 vols. 8vo. 1843–52.
37	16	SCHMITZ (L.) History of Greece. 12mo. 1851.
29	12	—— History of Rome. 12mo. 1847.
509	23	SCHŒDLER (F.) Book of Nature. 8vo. 1853.
449	12	SCHOMBURGK (R. H.) Fishes of British Guiana. (Nat. Lib. vols. 39, 40.) 2 vols. 16mo. 1852.
117	5	SCHOOLCRAFT (H. R.) Algic Researches. 2 vols. 12mo. 1839.
15	11	—— Indian Tribes. 8vo. 1851.
18	6	—— Lead Mines of Missouri. 8vo. 1819.
12	13	—— Notes on Iroquois. 8vo. 1847.
15	3	—— The Indian in his Wigwam. 8vo. 1848.
419	2	SCHOUW (J. F.) & KOBELL (F. von). Earth, Plants, Man, and the Mineral Kingdom. Post 8vo. 1852.
105	15	SCHRŒDER (F.) Shores of the Mediterranean. 2 vols. 12mo. 1846.
*404	7	SCIENCE, American Association for the Advancement of. Proceedings at the First, Second, and Third Meetings. 8vo. 1848–50.
*404	2	—— American Association. Proceedings at the Fourth Meeting. 8vo. 1851.
509	22	—— Made Easy. 16mo. 1837.
		SCIENCES Médicales, Dictionnaire des. 58 vols. 8vo. 1812–22.
*624	1	Vols. 1–17.
*634	1	,, 18–37.
*644	1	,, 38–56.
*654	1	,, 57, 58.

Vol. 1. A—Amp.
2. Amu—Ban.
3. Ban—Can.
4. Can—Cha.
5. Cha—Col.
6. Col—Cor.
7. Cor—Cys.
8. Dac—Des.
9. Des.—Dis.
10. Dis—Eau.
11. Eau—Emo.
12. Emp—Epi.
13. Epi—Exc.
14. Exc—Fem.
15. Fem—Fis.
16. Fla—Fra.
17. Fre—Gen.
18. Gen—Gom.
19. Gon—Gyp.
20. Hab—Hem.
21. Hem—Hum.
22. Hum—Hyg.
23. Hyg—Ilé.
24. Ili—Inf.
25. Inf—Iod.
26. Ipé—Jus.
27. Kal—Let.
28. Leu—Lom.
29. Lon—Mah.
Vol. 30. Mai—Mar.
31. Mar—Med.
32. Med—Mes.
33. Met—Moi.
34. Mol—Mus.
35. Mus—Név.
36. Nez—Nys.
37. Obé—Ord.
38. Ore—Ouv.
39. Ova—Pea.
40. Pec—Péro.
41. Per—Phr.
42. Pht—Plad.
43. Plai—Pois.
44. Poit—Poum.
45. Pour—Pru.
46. Pse—Rach.
47. Raci—Reso.
48. Resp—Rhu.
49. Rhy—Sap.
50. Sar—Sem.
51. Sén—Sol.
52. Som—Sth.
53. Sti—Sympa.
54. Symph—Tes.
55. Tet—Tric.
56. Trif—Vap.
57. Var—Vie.
58. Vie—Zyt.

Shelf.	No.	
*654	2	Sciences Médicales, Dictionnaire des. Tables des Matières. 8vo. 1822.
*654	3	——— Médicales, Dictionnaire des. Appendices, par F. V. Murat. 8vo. 1822.
503	15	Scientific Men of Seventeenth Century, Correspondence of. 2 vols. 8vo. 1841.
*402	6	Scotland, Views in. 4to. n. d.
492	7	Scott (R.) Cotton Spinner. 8vo. 1851.
*469	27	Scott (T.) Vox Populi. 4to. 1620.
114	2	Scott (Sir W.) Anne of Geierstein. 12mo. 1852.
113	3	——— Antiquary. 12mo. 1852.
116	6	——— Antiquary. 3 vols. 12mo. 1816.
113	5	——— Black Dwarf; Old Mortality. 12mo. 1852.
113	7	——— Bride of Lammermoor; Legend of Montrose. 12mo. 1852.
113	20	——— Chronicles of the Canongate. 12mo. 1852.
114	3	——— Count Robert of Paris. 12mo. 1852.
88	8	——— Demonology and Witchcraft. 18mo. 1848.
160	21	——— Demonology and Witchcraft. 18mo. 1830.
113	13	——— Fortunes of Nigel. 12mo. 1852.
113	2	——— Guy Mannering. 12mo. 1852.
111	19	——— Guy Mannering. 3 vols. 12mo. 1815.
113	6	——— Heart of Mid-Lothian. 12mo. 1852.
111	20	——— Heart of Mid-Lothian. 4 vols. 12mo. 1818.
40	9	——— History of Scotland. 2 vols. 18mo. 1830.
39	10	——— History of Scotland. 2 vols. 12mo. 1830.
113	8	——— Ivanhoe. 12mo. 1852.
113	11	——— Kenilworth. 12mo. 1852.
111	4	——— Kenilworth. 3 vols. 12mo. 1821.
169	4	——— Lady of the Lake. 32mo. 1812.
159	7	——— Lay of the Last Minstrel, Ballads and Lyrics. 18mo. 1835.
72	8	——— Life of Napoleon. 8vo. 1853.
*446	6	——— Life of Napoleon. 9 vols. 12mo. 1827.
77	6	——— Lives of the Novelists. 2 vols. 12mo. 1825.
169	2	——— Lord of the Isles. 32mo. 1815.
166	3	——— Marmion. 16mo. 1849.
113	9	——— Monastery. 12mo. 1852.
111	21	——— Monastery. 3 vols. 12mo. 1820.
113	14	——— Peveril of the Peak. 12mo. 1852.
118	7	——— Peveril of the Peak. 2 vols. 12mo. 1823.
156	3	——— Poetical Works. 16mo. 1852.
159	1	——— Poetical Works. 6 vols. 18mo. 1819.

Vol. 1. Lay of the Last Minstrel; Ballads, &c.
2. Ballads and Lyrical Pieces.
3. Marmion.
4. Lady of the Lake.
5. Rokeby.
6. Lord of the Isles.

Shelf.	No.	
156	10	Scott (Sir W.) Poetical Works. 2 vols. 16mo. 1850.
113	15	——— Quentin Durward. 12mo. 1853.
136	11	——— Quentin Durward. 3 vols. 12mo. 1823.
116	4	——— Quentin Durward. 2 vols. 12mo. 1823.
113	17	——— Redgauntlet. 12mo. 1852.
113	4	——— Rob Roy. 12mo. 1852.
116	3	——— Rob Roy. 3 vols. 12mo. 1818.
169	3	——— Rokeby. 32mo. 1813.
113	16	——— St. Ronan's Well. 12mo. 1852.
114	1	——— St. Valentine's Day. 12mo. 1852.
114	4	——— Tales of a Grandfather. First series. 12mo. 1852.
114	5	——— Tales of a Grandfather. Second series. 12mo. 1852.
114	6	——— Tales of a Grandfather. Third series. 12mo. 1852.
114	7	——— Tales of a Grandfather. Fourth series. 12mo. 1852.
113	10	——— The Abbot. 12mo. 1852.
113	18	——— The Betrothed; the Talisman. 12mo. 1852.
118	1	——— The Betrothed; the Talisman. 2 vols. 12mo. 1825.
113	12	——— The Pirate. 12mo. 1852.
111	24	——— Waverley. 3 vols. 12mo. 1814.
113	1	——— Waverley. 12mo. 1852.
113	19	——— Woodstock. 12mo. 1852.
		Scott (Sir W.) Prose Works. 28 vols. 16mo. 1848–49.
*438	1	Vols. 1–25.
*439	1	,, 26–28.

Vol. 1. Life of Dryden.
2. Life of Swift.
3. Memoirs of Richardson, Fielding, Smollett, Cumberland, Goldsmith, Johnson, Sterne, Horace Walpole, Clara Reeve, Mrs. Radcliffe, Le Sage, Johnstone, Bage.
4. Mackenzie, Charlotte Smith, Sir R. Sadler, Leyden, Mrs. Anna Seward, De Foe, Charles Duke of Buccleugh, John Lord Somerville, George the Third, Lord Byron, Duke of York.
5. Paul's Letters to his Kinsfolk; Abstract of the Eyrbiggia-Saga.
6. Chivalry, Romance, and the Drama.
7. Essay on Border Antiquities; Provincial Antiquities of Scotland.
8–16. Life of Napoleon.
17. Periodical Criticism, being Reviews of Ellis's Specimens of the Early English Poets; Ellis and Ritson's Metrical Romances; Godwin's Life of Chaucer; Todd's Spenser; Herbert's Poems; Evans's Old Ballads; Molière; Chatterton; Burns; Campbell's Gertrude of Wyoming; Battles of Telavera; Southey's Curse of Kehama; Childe Harold, Canto 4.
18. Criticism continued: Amadis of Gaul; Southey's Chronicle of the Cid; Life of Bunyan; Godwin's Fleetwood; Cumberland's John de Lancaster; Maturin's Fatal Revenge; Women, or Pour et Contre; Miss Austen's Novels; Frankenstein; Hoffmann's Novels; the Omen; Hajji Baba in England.

Shelf. No.

SCOTT (Sir W.) Prose Works, *continued.*

Vol. 19. Criticism continued: Tales of My Landlord; Thornton's Sporting Tour; Two Cookery Books; Froissart; Miseries of Human Life; Carr's Caledonian Sketches; Lady Suffolk's Correspondence; Kirkton's Church History; John Home.
20. Criticism continued: the Culloden Papers; Pepys's Memoirs; Kemble; Kelly; Davy's Salmonia; Ancient History of Scotland.
21. Criticism continued: on Planting Waste Lands; on Landscape Gardening; Tytler's History of Scotland; Pitcairn's Criminal Trials; Letters of Malachi Malagrowther on the Currency.
22–26. Tales of a Grandfather (Scotland).
27, 28. Tales of a Grandfather (France); General Index.

131 1 —— Works. 10 vols. 8vo. 1853.

Vol. 1. Poetical Works; Minstrelsy of the Scottish Border; Sir Tristrem; Lay of the Last Minstrel; Ballads; Marmion; Lady of the Lake; Miscellaneous Poems; Rokeby; Vision of Don Roderick; Lord of the Isles; Occasional Poems; Bridal of Triermain; Harold the Dauntless; the Field of Waterloo; Songs and Miscellanies.
2. Waverley; Guy Mannering; Antiquary; Rob Roy; Black Dwarf; Old Mortality.
3. Heart of Mid-Lothian; Bride of Lammermoor; Legend of Montrose; Ivanhoe; Monastery; Abbot.
4. Kenilworth; Pirate; Fortunes of Nigel; Peveril of the Peak; Quentin Durward.
5. St. Ronan's Well; Redgauntlet; Betrothed; Talisman; Woodstock.
6. Highland Widow; Two Drovers; My Aunt Margaret's Mirror; Tapestried Chamber; the Laird's Jock; Fair Maid of Perth; Anne of Geierstein; Count Robert of Paris; Castle Dangerous; the Surgeon's Daughter; Glossary for the Novels.
7. Tales of a Grandfather; History of Scotland.
8. Lives of Dryden, Swift; the Novelists; Dramatical Works; Paul's Letters to his Kinsfolk; Eyrbiggia-Saga; Chivalry, Romance, and the Drama; Religious Discourses; Demonology and Witchcraft.
9. Life of Napoleon.
10. Life of Scott, by J. G. Lockhart.

—— Waverley Novels. 48 vols. 16mo. 1829–33.

*439 2 Vols. 1–26.
*440 1 ,, 27–48.

Vols. 1, 2. Waverley.
3, 4. Guy Mannering.
5, 6. Antiquary.
7, 8. Rob Roy.
9. Black Dwarf; Old Mortality.
10. Old Mortality.
11. Old Mortality; Heart of Mid-Lothian.
12. Heart of Mid-Lothian.
13. Heart of Mid-Lothian; Bride of Lammermoor.
14. Bride of Lammermoor.
15. Legend of Montrose.
16, 17. Ivanhoe.
18, 19. Monastery.
20, 21. Abbot.
22, 23. Kenilworth.
24, 25. Pirate.
26, 27. Fortunes of Nigel.
28–30. Peveril of the Peak.
31, 32. Quentin Durward.

Shelf. No.

SCOTT (Sir W.) Waverley Novels, *continued.*

Vol. 33, 34. St. Ronan's Well.
35, 36. Redgauntlet.
37. Betrothed.
38. Talisman.
39, 40. Woodstock.
41. Highland Widow, &c.
42, 43. Fair Maid of Perth.
44, 45. Anne of Geierstein.
46. Count Robert of Paris.
47. Count Robert of Paris; Castle Dangerous.
48. Castle Dangerous; Surgeon's Daughter; Glossary.

112 11 ——— Waverley Novels. 6 vols. 8vo. 1842.

Vol. 1. Antiquary; Rob Roy; Black Dwarf; Old Mortality.
2. Heart of Mid-Lothian; Bride of Lammermoor; Kenilworth.
3. Ivanhoe; Guy Mannering; Rob Roy.
4. The Monastery; the Abbot; Legend of Montrose.
5. Redgauntlet; Woodstock; Fair Maid of Perth.
6. The Pirate; the Fortunes of Nigel; Highland Widow; the Two Drovers; Aunt Margaret's Mirror; the Tapestried Chamber; the Laird's Jock.

*411 3 SCRIPTURE Illustrated. 4to. 1803.
*626 11 SCUDAMORE (C.) On Gout. 8vo. 1819.
*636 12 ——— Inhalation of Iodine and Conium. 8vo. 1834.
127 8 SEALSFIELD (C.) Cabin Book. 12mo. 1852.
78 21 SEARLE (J.) Life of E. Elliott. 18mo. 1850.
196 15 SEARLE. Horæ Solitariæ. 2 vols. 8vo. 1804.
486 9 SEARS (B.), EDWARDS (B. B.), & FELTON (C. C.) Classical Studies. 12mo. 1849.
179 13 SEARS (E. H.) Regeneration. 12mo. 1853.
18 5 SEARS (R.) Pictorial History of American Revolution. 8vo. 1846.
141 12 SEATSFIELD (W.) Life in the New World. 8vo. n. d.
141 20 ——— Life in the New World. 8vo. n. d.
550 15 SECRET Societies. 12mo. n. d.
509 14 ——— Societies of the Middle Ages. 18mo. 1848.
6 13 ——— Proceedings and Debates of the Convention at Philadelphia, 1787. 12mo. 1839.
124 1 SEDGWICK (C. M.) Clarence. 12mo. 1849.
124 2 ——— Clarence. 12mo. 1849.
129 3 ——— Home. 18mo. 1852.
85 15 ——— Letters from Abroad. 2 vols. 12mo. 1841.
96 8 ——— Letters from Abroad. 2 vols. 12mo. 1845.
129 19 ——— Live and Let Live. 18mo. n. d.
129 8 ——— Love Token. 18mo. n. d.
129 18 ——— Means and Ends. 18mo. n. d.
124 4 ——— New England Tale. 12mo. 1852.
129 10 ——— Poor Rich Man. 18mo. n. d.
124 6 ——— Redwood. 12mo. 1850.
129 20 ——— Stories for Young Persons. 18mo. 1846.
129 28 ——— Tales and Sketches. 18mo. 1844.

Shelf.	No.	
90	18	SEGUR (P. de) History of Expedition to Russia by Napoleon. 2 vols. 18mo. n. d.
160	26	——— History of Expedition to Russia by Napoleon. 2 vols. 18mo. 1840.
540	3	SEGUR (J. A.) Women. 3 vols. 16mo. 1803.
450	2	SELBY (P. J.) Parrots. (Nat. Lib. vol. 10.) 16mo. n. d.
450	2	——— Pigeons. (Nat. Lib. vol. 9.) 16mo. n. d.
529	13	SELDEN (J.) Table Talk. 16mo. 1847.
121	12	SELF. 3 vols. 12mo. 1845.
494	1	SENATE-HOUSE Examination Papers: The Mathematical Problems of the University of Cambridge, Eng. 8vo. 1837.
12	16	SENECA Indians, Case of, in New York. 8vo. 1840.
200	19	SENECA (L. A.) Morals. 12mo. 1794.
344	6	SERGEANT (T.) Constitutional Law. 8vo. 1822.
509	16	SETTLERS and Convicts. 18mo. 1847.
198	5	SEWALL (E. Q.) Unitarian Advocate. 2 vols. 12mo. 1828.
53	9	SEWARD (A.) Memoirs of Darwin. 8vo. 1804.
56	14	SEWARD (W. H.) Life of J. Q. Adams. 12mo. 1849.
488	3	——— Works. 3 vols. 8vo. 1853.

Vol. 1. Biographical Memoir; Speeches in the Senate of New York; Speeches in the Senate of the United States; Debates in the Senate of the United States; Forensic Arguments.
2. Notes on New York; State Papers; Official Correspondence; Pardon Papers.
3. Orations and Discourses; Occasional Speeches and Addresses; Executive Speeches; Political Writings; General Correspondence; Letters from Europe; Speeches in the Senate of the United States.

Shelf.	No.	
125	19	SEWELL (E. M.) Earl's Daughter. 12mo. 1851.
114	7	——— Experience of Life. 12mo. 1853.
125	7	——— Gertrude. 12mo. 1852.
125	16	——— Laneton Parsonage. 3 vols. 12mo. 1850–51.
125	8	——— Margaret Percival. 2 vols. 12mo. 1850.
109	9	——— Summer Tour. 12mo. 1852.
125	4	——— Walter Lorimer. 12mo. 1853.
23	9	SEWEL (W.) History of the Quakers. 2 vols. 8vo. 1844.
462	5	SEYBERT (A.) Statistical Annals of the United States. 4to. 1818.
37	4	SEYMER. Romance of Ancient History. 2 vols. 12mo. 1834.
99	6	SFORZOSI. History of Italy. 18mo. 1847.
*428	6	SHADWELL (T.) Virtuoso, a Comedy; Epsom Wells. 4to. 1704.
131	11	SHADYSIDE. 12mo. 1853.
*617	1	SHAKSPEARE (W.) Plays. Reed's edition, with a Glossarial Index. 21 vols. 8vo. 1813.

Vol. 1. Advertisements of Reed, Steevens, and Richardson; Rowe's Life of Shakspeare; Anecdotes; Coat of Arms; Will.
2. Farmer on the Learning of Shakspeare, with Colman's Remarks; Ancient Translations from Classic Authors; Lists of Editions, Altered Plays, Detached Pieces of Criticism, Editors, &c.; Malone on the Order of the Plays.
3. Malone, Chalmers, and others, on the English Stage.

Shelf. No.

*617 1 Shakspeare (W.) Plays, *continued.*

Vol. 4. Tempest; Two Gentlemen of Verona; Midsummer Night's Dream.
5. Merry Wives of Windsor; Twelfth Night.
6. Much Ado about Nothing; Measure for Measure.
7. Love's Labour's Lost; Merchant of Venice.
8. As you Like It; All's Well that Ends Well.
9. Taming of the Shrew; Winter's Tale.
10. Macbeth; King John.
11. King Richard II.; King Henry IV., part 1.
12. Henry IV., part 2; Henry V.
13. Henry VI., part 1, and part 2.
14. Henry VI., part 3; Dissertation, &c.; King Richard III.
15. King Henry VIII.; Troilus and Cressida.
16. Coriolanus; Julius Cæsar.
17. Antony and Cleopatra; King Lear.
18. Hamlet; Cymbeline.
19. Timon of Athens; Othello.
20. Romeo and Juliet; Comedy of Errors.
21. Titus Andronicus; Pericles; Dissertations; Addenda; and Glossarial Index.

163 1 ——— Dramatic Works. 7 vols. 8vo. 1836.

Vol. 1. Life of Shakspeare; Tempest; Two Gentlemen of Verona; Merry Wives of Windsor; Twelfth Night; Measure for Measure; Much Ado about Nothing.
2. Midsummer Night's Dream; Love's Labour's Lost; Merchant of Venice; As you Like It; All's Well that Ends Well; Taming of the Shrew.
3. Winter's Tale; Comedy of Errors; Macbeth; King John; King Richard II.; King Henry IV., part 1.
4. King Henry IV., part 2; King Henry V.; King Henry VI., part 1, 2, and 3.
5. King Richard III.; King Henry VIII.; Troilus and Cressida; Timon of Athens; Coriolanus.
6. Julius Cæsar; Antony and Cleopatra; Cymbeline; Titus Andronicus; Pericles.
7. King Lear; Romeo and Juliet; Hamlet; Othello.

152 2 ——— Dramatic and Poetical Works. 8 vols. 8vo. 1851.

Contents of Vols. 1—7, as above.
Vol. 8. Venus and Adonis; Rape of Lucrece; Sonnets; Illustration of the Sonnets; Lover's Complaint; Passionate Pilgrim; Verses among the Additional Poems to Chester's Love's Martyrs; Illustrations of a Lover's Complaint; the Passionate Pilgrim, &c.; Supplementary Notices.

166 1 ——— Works, with Emendations from the Folio of 1632, &c. by J. Payne Collier. 8 vols. 16mo. 1853.

Vol. 1. History of the English Drama and Stage; Life of Shakespeare; the Tempest; the Two Gentlemen of Verona; Merry Wives of Windsor.
2. Measure for Measure; Comedy of Errors; Much Ado about Nothing; Love's Labour's Lost; Midsummer Night's Dream; Merchant of Venice.
3. As you Like It; Taming of the Shrew; All's Well that Ends Well; Twelfth Night; the Winter's Tale.
4. King John; King Richard II.; King Henry IV., parts 1, 2; King Henry V.
5. King Henry VI., parts 1, 2, 3; King Richard III.; King Henry VIII.
6. Troilus and Cressida; Coriolanus; Titus Andronicus; Romeo and Juliet; Timon of Athens.
7. Julius Cæsar; Macbeth; Hamlet; King Lear; Othello.
8. Antony and Cleopatra; Cymbeline; Pericles; Venus and Adonis; Rape of Lucrece; Sonnets; Lover's Complaint; Passionate Pilgrim.

Shelf. No.

152 4 SHAKSPEARE (W.) Dramatic Works, with Life, &c., edited by Wheeler. 8vo. 1834.

149 9 —— Works, copied from the Text of Dr. Reed. 10 vols. 16mo. 1821.

Vol. 1. Author's Life; Dr. Johnson's Preface; the Learning of Shakespeare; Tempest; Two Gentlemen of Verona; Merry Wives of Windsor.
2. Measure for Measure; Comedy of Errors; Merchant of Venice; As you Like It.
3. Misdummer Night's Dream; Much Ado about Nothing; Love's Labour's Lost; Taming of the Shrew.
4. All's Well that Ends Well; Twelfth Night; Winter's Tale; Macbeth.
5. King John; Richard II.; Henry IV., parts 1 and 2.
6. King Henry V.; King Henry VI., parts 1, 2, and 3.
7. Richard III.; Henry VIII.; Coriolanus.
8. Julius Cæsar; Antony and Cleopatra; Timon of Athens; Titus Andronicus.
9. Troilus and Cressida; Cymbeline; King Lear; Romeo and Juliet.
10. Hamlet; Othello; Pericles.

*425 1 —— Comedies, Histories, Tragedies, and Poems; with a Biography, and Studies of his Works, by C. Knight. Pictorial edition. 8 vols. 8vo. 1853.

Vol. 1. COMEDIES: Two Gentlemen of Verona; Comedy of Errors; Love's Labour's Lost; All's Well that Ends Well; Taming of the Shrew; Midsummer Night's Dream; Merchant of Venice.
2. COMEDIES: Much Ado about Nothing; Merry Wives of Windsor; As you Like it; Twelfth Night; Measure for Measure; a Winter's Tale; the Tempest.
3. HISTORIES: King John; King Richard II.; King Henry IV., part 1; King Henry IV., part 2; King Henry V.
4. HISTORIES: King Henry VI., parts 1, 2, 3; King Richard III.; King Henry VIII.
5. TRAGEDIES: Romeo and Juliet; Hamlet; Othello; Timon of Athens; King Lear; Macbeth.
6. TRAGEDIES: Troilus and Cressida; Cymbeline; Coriolanus; Julius Cæsar; Antony and Cleopatra; Titus Andronicus; Pericles.
7. POEMS: Venus and Adonis; Rape of Lucrece; Sonnets; Lover's Complaint; Passionate Pilgrim; Biography.
8. Studies of Shakspere; Shakspere's Critics.

SHAKESPEARE Society's Publications, 32 vols. 8vo. 1841–46.

424 28 Alleyn Payers, illustrative of the Early English Stage. 8vo. 1843.

424 4 Chester Plays. Part 1. 8vo. 1843.

424 3 Coventry Mysteries. 8vo. 1841.

424 10 Diary of Philip Henslowe, 1591 to 1609. 8vo. 1845.

424 24 Extracts from Accounts of the Revels at Court in Elizabeth and James's Reigns. 8vo. 1842.

424 33 Fair Maid of the Exchange, by Heywood; and Fortune by Land and Sea, by Heywood and Rowley. 8vo. 1846.

424 26 First Sketches of the Second and Third Parts of Henry the Sixth. 8vo. 1843.

424 14 First Sketch of the Merry Wives of Windsor. 8vo. 1842.

Shelf.	No.	
		SHAKESPEARE Society's Publications, *continued.*
424	17	Fools and Jesters; with Armin's Nest of Ninnies. 8vo. 1842.
424	27	Ghost of Richard III. 8vo. 1844.
424	22	Gosson's School of Abuse, and Heywood's Apology for Actors. 8vo. 1841.
424	19	Heywood's King Edward the Fourth. 8vo. 1842.
424	8	Illustrations of the Fairy Mythology of Shakespeare. 8vo. 1845.
424	16	Jonson's Conversations with Drummond. 8vo. 1842.
424	32	Marriage of Wit and Wisdom. 8vo. 1846.
424	21	Memoirs of Alleyn, Founder of Dulwich College. 8vo. 1841.
424	12	Memoirs of the Principal Actors in Shakespeare's Plays. 8vo. 1846.
424	20	Nash's Pierce Penniless. 8vo. 1842.
424	25	Northbrooke's Treatise. 8vo. 1843.
424	2	Oberon's Vision Illustrated. 8vo. 1843.
424	18	Old Play of Timon. 8vo. 1842.
424	15	Patient Grissell. 8vo. 1841.
424	9	Reprint of a Contemporary Manuscript of Henry the Fourth. 8vo. 1845.
424	13	Riche's Farewell to Militarie Profession. 8vo. 1846.
424	7	Shakespeare Society's Papers. Vols. 1 and 2. 2 vols. 8vo. 1844–45.
424	6	Sir Thomas More; a Play. 8vo. 1844.
424	29	Taming of a Shrew. 8vo. 1844.
424	30	Tarlton's Jests, and Tarlton's Newes out of Purgatory. 8vo. 1844.
424	23	Thynn's Pride and Lowliness. 8vo. 1841.
424	5	Tracts by Forde the Dramatist. 8vo. 1843.
424	31	True Tragedie of Richard the Third. 8vo. 1844.
*427	2	SHAKESPEARE (W.) Spirit of the Plays of, exhibited in a Series of Outline Plates, by Frank Howard. 5 vols. 8vo. 1833.

Vol. 1. Tempest; Two Gentlemen of Verona; Twelfth Night; Measure for Measure; Much Ado about Nothing; Midsummer Night's Dream.
2. Merchant of Venice; As You Like It; All's Well that Ends Well; Taming of the Shrew; Winter's Tale; Love's Labour's Lost.
3. King John; Richard II.; Henry IV.; Merry Wives; Henry V.; Henry VI.; Richard III.; Henry VIII.
4. Comedy of Errors; Troilus and Cressida; Timon; Coriolanus; Julius Cæsar; Antony and Cleopatra; Cymbeline; Pericles.
5. Macbeth; Lear; Romeo and Juliet; Hamlet; Othello; Titus Andronicus.

149	4	——— Poems. 16mo. 1842.
44	12	SHALER (W.) Sketches of Algiers. 8vo. 1826.
*643	2	SHARP (J. A.) Gazetteer of the British Islands. 2 vols. 8vo. 1852.

Shelf.	No.	
487	13	Sharp (R.) Letters and Essays. 16mo. 1834.
*544	1	Sharpey & Quain's Anatomy, edited by Leidy. 2 vols. 8vo. 1849.
6	5	Shattuck (L.) History of Concord. 8vo. 1835.
477	23	Shaw (C.) Description of Boston. 12mo. 1817.
428	2	Sheffield (J.) Works. 2 vols. 8vo. 1740.
80	12	Sheil (R. L.) Sketches of the Irish Bar. 2 vols. 12mo. 1854.
529	12	Shelley (P. B.) Essays, &c. 2 vols. 16mo. 1852.
163	9	——— Poetical Works. 8vo. 1851.
40	4	Shelley (M. M.) Literary and Scientific Men of France. 2 vols. 18mo. 1838.
150	3	Shenstone (W.) Poetical Works. 32mo. 1804.
524	12	——— Works. 3 vols. 8vo. 1764–69. Vol. 1. Elegies, Odes, Songs, Ballads, &c.; Levities; Moral Pieces. 2. Essays. 3. Letters.
73	7	Shepherd (W.) Life of Poggio Bracciolini. 8vo. 1837.
397	10	Sheridan (R. B.) Dramatic Works. Post 8vo. 1848.
482	1	——— Speeches. 3 vols. 8vo. 1842.
86	20	Sherley (A., R., & T.) Travels. 12mo. 1825.
176	2	Ship Master's Assistant. 8vo. 1795.
140	12	Shipp (J.) Eastern Story Teller. 18mo. 1832.
428	7	Shirrefs (A.) Poems. 8vo. 1790.
97	5	Shoberl (F.) Excursions in Normandy. 2 vols. 12mo. 1841.
480	7	——— Description of Persia. 12mo. 1828.
*480	19	Shurtleff (N. B.) Death by Lightning at Marshfield in 1658–66. 12mo. 1850.
*480	16	——— Genealogical Memoir of the Family of Elder Thomas Leverett. 8vo. 1850.
*480	18	——— Notice of William Shurtleff. 12mo. 1850.
*480	17	——— Passengers of the May-Flower in 1620. Small 4to. 1849.
*395	13	——— Perpetual Calendar for Old and New Style. 8vo. 1848.
*452	6	——— Perpetual Calendar for Old and New Style. 4to. 1851.
*607	6	——— Registration Report of Massachusetts, 1852. 8vo. 1853.
173	8	Sidney (A.) Discourses on Government. 3 vols. 8vo. 1805.
43	1	Sidney (H.) Diary of the Times of Charles Second. 2 vols. 8vo. 1843.
46	9	Sidney (S.) Australia. 8vo. 1852.
514	7	——— Australia. 8vo. 1853.
84	16	Siebold (P. F. von). Manners of the Japanese. 1841.
88	22	——— Manners of the Japanese. 18mo. 1848.
530	2	Sigourney (L. H.) Letters to Mothers. 12mo. 1845.
519	1	——— Letters to Young Ladies. 12mo. 1852.

Shelf.	No.	
529	4	SIGOURNEY (L. H.) Scenes in my Native Land. 12mo. 1845.
165	11	——— Select Poems. 12mo. 1852.
181	10	SILJESTRÖM (P. A.) Education in the United States. 12mo. 1853.
493	13	SILK, Cotton, Linen, and Wool. 8vo. 1845.
95	3	SILLIMAN (B.) Tour between Hartford and Quebec. 12mo. 1824.
105	7	——— Visit to Europe. 2 vols. 12mo. 1853.
74	4	SIMMS (W. G.) Life of Bayard. 12mo. 1847.
67	13	——— Life of Francis Marion. 12mo. n. d.
117	3	——— Marie de Bernière; Maroon; Maize in Milk. 12mo. 1853.
166	19	——— Norman Maurice. 12mo. 1853.
124	20	——— Norman Maurice. 12mo. 1853.
122	8	——— Wigwam and Cabin. 12mo. 1853.
93	4	SIMOND (L.) Tour in Switzerland. 2 vols. 8vo. 1822.
92	8	——— Tour in Switzerland. 2 vols. 8vo. 1823.
104	15	SIMPSON (J. H.) Journal of Reconnaissance from Santa Fé to Navajo. 8vo. 1852.
*604	7	SIMPSON (J. Y.) Anæsthesia in Midwifery and Surgery. 8vo. 1849.
3	5	SIMPSON (T.) Discoveries on the North Coast of America. 8vo. 1843.
121	23	SINCLAIR (C.) Beatrice. 12mo. n. d.
135	1	——— Jane Bouverie. 12mo. 1851.
123	6	——— Lord and Lady Harcourt. 12mo. 1851.
133	23	——— Modern Accomplishments. 12mo. 1849.
135	2	——— Modern Flirtations. 12mo. n. d.
122	15	——— Modern Society. 12mo. 1849.
126	5	——— Scotland and the Scotch. 12mo. 1840.
126	10	——— Shetland and the Shetlanders. 12mo. 1840.
28	16	SINCLAIR (J.) Public Revenue of the British Empire. 8vo. 1785.
82	5	SIRR (H. C.) China and the Chinese. 2 vols. 8vo. 1849.
28	11	SISMONDI (J. C. L. S. de). Crusades against the Albigenses. 12mo. 1843.
407	1	——— Literature of the South of Europe. 2 vols. post 8vo. 1850.
50	8	——— History of Fall of Roman Empire. 2 vols. 18mo. 1834.
50	7	——— Italian Republics. 18mo. 1832.
*554	13	SKEY (F. C.) Operative Surgery. 8vo. 1851.
506	2	SKINNER (J. S.) Dog and the Sportsman. 12mo. 1845.
172	17	SLAVE Trade Treaties, Jamaica Movement to Enforce. 8vo. 1850.
*422	7	SMEATON (J.) On Engineering. 4to. 1837.
497	14	SMELLIE (W.) Natural History. 12mo. 1838.
141	52	SMITH (A.) Comic Tales and Sketches. 16mo. 1852.

Shelf.	No.	
141	44	SMITH (A.) Pictures of Life. 16mo. 1852.
105	5	——— Story of Mont Blanc. 12mo. 1853.
175	8	SMITH (Adam). Wealth of Nations. 3 vols. 8vo. 1817.
176	15	——— Wealth of Nations. 12mo. 1848.
171	2	——— Theory of Moral Sentiments. 8vo. 1817.
419	11	——— Theory of Moral Sentiments. 8vo. 1853.
70	9	SMITH (Alex.) Life of. 12mo. 1819.
450	8	SMITH (C. H.) Natural History of Dogs. (Vols. 18, 19, Nat. Lib.) 2 vols. 16mo. n. d.
450	8	——— Natural History of Horses. (Vol. 20, Nat. Lib.) 16mo. n. d.
450	5	——— Introduction to Mammalia. 16mo. n. d.
506	25	——— Natural History of the Human Species. 12mo. 1851.
497	1	——— Natural History of the Human Species. 12mo. 1851.
109	13	SMITH (E.) Fragments. 12mo. 1810.
156	5	——— Fragments. 12mo. 1811.
84	13	SMITH (G.) Consular Cities of China. 12mo. 1847.
104	2	——— Consular Cities of China. 12mo. 1847.
134	7	SMITH (H.) Brambletye House. 3 vols. 12mo. 1826.
121	34	——— Brambletye House. 3 vols. 12mo. 1826.
117	10	——— Gaieties and Gravities. 16mo. 1852.
111	25	——— Midsummer Medley for 1830. 2 vols. 12mo. 1830.
111	13	——— New Forest. 3 vols. 12mo. 1829.
116	2	——— Reuben Apsley. 2 vols. 12mo. 1827.
134	4	——— Tor Hill. 3 vols. 12mo. 1826.
88	17	SMITH (Horatio). Festivals, Games, &c. 18mo. 1847.
158	20	SMITH (H. & J.) Rejected Addresses. 16mo. 1851.
100	17	SMITH (H. I.) Education. 18mo. 1845.
56	4	SMITH (J.) Memoirs, Letters, and Comic Miscellanies. Edited by Horace Smith. 2 vols. 12mo. 1840.
454	5	SMITH (Capt. J.) Travels. 8vo. 1819.
525	10	SMITH (J. C.) Correspondence and Miscellanies. 12mo. 1847.
73	8	SMITH (Sir J. E.) Memoir. 2 vols. 8vo. 1832.
504	8	——— Introduction to Botany. 8vo. 1814.
671	1	SMITH (J. J.) & WATSON (J. F.) American Historical and Literary Curiosities. 4to. 1852.
419	3	SMITH (J. P.) The Scriptures and Geology. Post 8vo. 1852.
*473	4	SMITH (J. V. C.) Boston News Letter. 8vo. 1826.
510	16	SMITH (S.) Philosophy of Health. 2 vols. 18mo. 1851.
650	14	——— Philosophy of Health. 2 vols. 18mo. 1847.
189	3	SMITH (S. S.) Evidences of Christian Religion. 12mo. 1809.
505	14	——— Essay on Variety of Complexion. 8vo. 1810.
185	10	SMITH (Rev. S.) Moral Philosophy. 12mo. 1850.
184	11	——— Sermons. 2 vols. 8vo. 1809.
517	1	——— Works. 3 vols. 12mo. 1844.

Shelf.	No.	
524	4	SMITH (Rev. S.) Works. 8vo. 1844.
*613	6	SMITH (W.) Dictionary of Greek and Roman Biography, &c. 8vo. 1851.
*573	2	——— Dictionary of Greek and Roman Biography, &c. 3 vols. 8vo. 1849.
*463	9	SMITH (Wm.) History of the Province of New York. 8vo. 1792.
29	8	SMITH (Wm.) History of Greece. 12mo. 1854.
46	15	SMOLLETT (T.) History of England. 8vo. 1832. Hume, Smollett, and Miller, vol. 3.
141	15	——— Sir Launcelot Greaves; Adventures of an Atom. 8vo. 1843.
497	6	SMYTH (T.) Unity of the Human Races. 12mo. 1851.
24	4	——— Discourse on the Westminster Divines. 12mo. 1844.
465	2	SMYTH (W.) Modern History. 2 vols. 8vo. 1840.
34	7	——— Modern History. 8vo. 1851.
*451	1	SNOW (C. H.) History of Boston. 8vo. 1825.
		SOCIETY for the Diffusion of Useful Knowledge. 16 vols. 18mo. 1830–32.
119	12	Architecture of Birds. 18mo. 1831.
119	13	Criminal Trials. 18mo. 1832.
119	2	Historical Parallels. 18mo. 1831.
119	4	Insect Architecture. 18mo. 1830.
119	3	Insect Miscellanies. 18mo. 1832.
119	5	Insect Transformations. 18mo. 1831.
119	7	Menageries. 2 vols. 18mo. 1830.
119	11	New Zealanders. 18mo. 1830.
119	1	Paris and its Scenes. 2 vols. 18mo. 1831.
119	6	Pompeii. 18mo. 1833.
119	10	Pursuit of Knowledge under Difficulties. 2 vols. 18mo. 1831.
119	7	Practical Naturalist. 18mo. 1831.
119	8	Vegetable Substances in the Arts. 18mo. 1830.
119	9	Vegetable Substances for Food. 18mo. 1832.
*446	8	SOLIS (A. de). Conquest of Mexico. 2 vols. 8vo. 1753.
		SOMERS'S Tracts. 13 vols. 4to. 1809–15.
*332	2	Vols. 1– 7.
*342	1	,, 8–13.
496	6	SOMERVILLE (M.) Physical Geography. 12mo. 1850.
508	8	——— Connection of the Physical Sciences. 12mo. 1834.
*436	5	SOMETHING. 8vo. 1809–10.
538	4	SONGS, English. 8vo. n. d.
*440	6	——— English and Scotch. 12mo. 1736.
538	3	——— Scottish. 8vo. n. d.
120	8	SOPHOCLES. Translated by Francklin. 18mo. n. d.
*432	9	——— Translated by Francklin. 2 vols. 4to. 1758–59.
410	10	——— Translated by Buckley. Post 8vo. 1849.
*422	13	SOTHEBY (W.) Constance de Castile. 4to. 1810.

Shelf.	No.	
*463	8	SOUTH CAROLINA and Georgia, Historical Account of. 2 vols. 8vo. 1779.
517	4	SOUTHEY (C.) Chapters on Churchyards. 12mo. 1842.
43	7	SOUTHEY (R.) Chronicle of the Cid. 8vo. 1846.
522	4	——— Common Place Book. 2 vols. 8vo. 1849.
159	6	——— Curse of Kehama. 18mo. 1811.
86	3	——— Expedition of Orsua, and Crimes of Aguirre. 12mo. 1821.
52	5	——— Life and Correspondence. 8vo. 1851.
52	12	——— Life and Correspondence. 8vo. 1851.
160	20	——— Life of Nelson. 18mo. 1840.
88	3	——— Life of Nelson. 18mo. n. d.
78	13	——— Life of Oliver Cromwell. 18mo. 1852.
539	31	——— Life of Oliver Cromwell and Bunyan. 16mo. 1844.
65	11	——— Life of Wesley. 2 vols. 12mo. 1847.
158	19	——— Oliver Newman. 12mo. 1845.
162	7	——— Poetical Works. 8vo. 1850.
162	11	——— Poetical Works. 8vo. 1851.
50	9	——— and BELL (R.) Lives of British Admirals. 5 vols. 18mo. 1833–40.
505	13	SOUTHEY (T.) Colonial Sheep and Wools. 8vo. 1852.
505	20	——— Colonial Sheep and Wools. 8vo. 1851.
44	7	SOUTHEY (Capt. T.) History of the West Indies. 3 vols. 8vo. 1827.
84	15	SOUTHGATE (H.) Armenia, Kurdistan, &c. 2 vols. 12mo. 1840.
177	17	——— Visit to the Syrian Church. 12mo. 1844.
123	4	SOUVENIRS de Ma Vie. 12mo. 1815.
48	3	SPAIN and Portugal, History of. 5 vols. 18mo. 1852.
100	15	SPALDING (W.) Italy and Italian Islands. 3 vols. 18mo. 1848.
25	6	SPALDING (M. J.) Review of D'Aubigné's History of the Reformation. 12mo. 1844.
92	1	SPALLANZANI (L.) Travels in the Two Sicilies. 4 vols. 8vo. 1798.
		SPARKS (J.) American Biography, first series. 10 vols. 16mo. 1848–51.
58	13	Vols. 1– 3.
59	1	,, 4–10.

Vol. 1. Life of John Stark, by Edward Everett; Charles Brockden Brown, by W. H. Prescott; Richard Montgomery, by John Armstrong; Ethan Allen, by Jared Sparks.
2. Life of Alexander Wilson, by W. B. O. Peabody; Capt. John Smith, by George S. Hillard.
3. Life of Benedict Arnold, by Jared Sparks.
4. Life of Anthony Wayne, by John Armstrong; Sir Henry Vane, by C. W. Upham.
5. Life of John Eliot, by Convers Francis.
6. Life of William Pinkney, by Henry Wheaton; William Ellery, by E. T. Channing; Cotton Mather, by W. B. O. Peabody.
7. Life of Sir William Phips, by Francis Bowen; Israel Putnam, by O. W. B. Peabody; Lucretia M. Davidson, by Miss Sedgwick; David Rittenhouse, by James Renwick.

Shelf. No.

SPARKS (J.) American Biography, *continued.*

Vol. 8. Life of Jonathan Edwards, by Samuel Miller; David Brainerd, by W. B. O. Peabody.
9. Life of Baron Steuben, by Francis Bowen; Sebastian Cabot, by Charles Hayward, jun.; William Eaton, by C. C. Felton.
10. Life of Robert Fulton, by James Renwick; Joseph Warren, by A. H. Everett; Henry Hudson, by Henry R. Cleveland; Father Marquette, by Jared Sparks; Index.

58 12 Vols. 1–4, first series. 4 vols. 16mo. 1834–35.

59 2 ——— American Biography, second series. 15 vols. 16mo. 1844–48.

Vol. 1. Life of R. C. de la Salle, by Jared Sparks; Patrick Henry, by A. H. Everett.
2. Life of James Otis, by Francis Bowen; James Oglethorpe, by W. B. O. Peabody.
3. Life of John Sullivan, by O. W. B. Peabody; Jacob Leisler, by C. F. Hoffman; Nathaniel Bacon, by William Ware; John Mason, by George E. Ellis.
4. Life of Roger Williams, by William Gammell; Timothy Dwight, by W. B. Sprague; Count Pulaski, by Jared Sparks.
5. Life of Count Rumford, by James Renwick; Zebulon M. Pike, by Henry Whiting; Samuel Gorton, by John M. Mackie.
6. Life of Ezra Stiles, by James L. Kingsley; John Fitch, by Charles Whittlesey; Anne Hutchinson, by George E. Ellis.
7. Life of John Ribault, by Jared Sparks; Sebastian Rale, by Convers Francis; William Palfrey, by J. G. Palfrey.
8. Life of Charles Lee, by Jared Sparks; Joseph Reed, by Henry Reed.
9. Life of Leonard Calvert, by George W. Burnap; Samuel Ward, by William Gammell; Thomas Posey, by James Hall.
10. Life of Nathaniel Greene, by George W. Greene.
11. Life of Stephen Decatur, by A. S. Mackenzie.
12. Life of Edward Preble, by Lorenzo Sabine; William Penn, by George E. Ellis.
13. Life of Daniel Boone, by John M. Peck; Benjamin Lincoln, by Francis Bowen.
14. Life of John Ledyard, by Jared Sparks.
15. Life of W. R. Davie, by Fordyce M. Hubbard; Samuel Kirkland, by S. K. Lothrop.

13 7 ——— Correspondence of the Revolution. 4 vols. 8vo. 1853.

198 6 ——— Essays and Tracts. 6 vols. 12mo. 1823.

Vol. 1. Turretin on Fundamentals in Religion; Abauzit's Essays; Blackburne on Confessions of Faith; Selections from Benjamin Hoadly's Works.
2. Daniel Whitby's Last Thoughts; Bishop Hare on the Study of the Scriptures; Sir Isaac Newton's History of Two Corruptions of Scripture; Butler's Historical Outline.
3. Selection from Robert Robinson's Works; Cogan's Letters to Wilberforce on the Doctrine of Hereditary and Total Depravity.
4. Selection from William Penn's Works; Innocency of Error, by Dr. Sykes; Selection from the Writings of Dr. Benson, Thomas Emlyn, and Mrs. Barbauld.
5. Tracts, &c. of John Hales; Essays by James Foster.
6. Selections from Jeremy Taylor and John Locke; Speech of Bishop Clayton on Subscription to Articles and Creeds; Isaac Watts's Essay on the Causes of Uncharitableness; John le Clerc on the Choice of our Religious Opinions; Index.

Shelf.	No.	
186	5	SPARKS (J.) Letters on the Episcopal Church. 8vo. 1820.
186	6	——— Letters on the Episcopal Church. 8vo. 1820.
65	9	——— Life of Gouverneur Morris. 3 vols. 8vo. 1832.
63	8	——— Life of Ledyard. 8vo. 1828.
52	6	——— Life of Washington. 8vo. 1853.
52	10	——— Life of Washington. 8vo. 1853.
186	7	——— Unitarian and Trinitarian Doctrines. 8vo. 1823.
188	3	SPARROW (A.) Canons, &c., of the Church of England. 12mo. 1846.
*469	12	SPEECH on the Altering of the Charters of Massachusetts Bay. 8vo. 1774.
*252	1	SPEED (J.) Historie of Great Britaine. Folio. 1632.
93	8	SPENCER (E.) Germany and the Germans. 2 vols. 8vo. 1836.
436	2	——— Germany and the Germans. 2 vols. 8vo. 1836.
84	7	SPENCER (J. A.) Travels in the East. 12mo. 1850.
153	9	SPENSER (E.) Poetical Works. 5 vols. 8vo. 1839.
147	1	——— Poetical Works. 5 vols. 16mo. 1839.
27	10	SPINETO (M.) Egyptian Antiquities. 8vo. 1845.
166	7	SPRAGUE (C.) Writings. 16mo. 1850.
1	5	SPRAGUE (J. T.) Florida War. 8vo. 1848.
199	8	SPRING (G.) First Things. 2 vols. 12mo. 1852.
107	20	SPRINGER (J. S.) Forest Life and Forest Trees. 16mo. 1851.
187	7	SPURZHEIM (J. G.) Education. 12mo. 1836.
493	2	——— Insanity. 8vo. 1833.
493	1	——— Phrenology. 8vo. 1846.
102	5	SQUIER (E. G.) Nicaragua. 2 vols. 8vo. 1852.
5	5	——— Archæological Researches. 8vo. 1851.
111	22	STAEL (A. L. G. de). Corinne. 4 vols. 12mo. 1822.
135	18	——— Corinne. 16mo. 1850.
33	4	——— French Revolution. 2 vols. 8vo. 1818.
530	7	——— Germany. 2 vols. 12mo. 1814.
530	6	——— Influence of Literature upon Society. 2 vols. 12mo. 1813.
520	18	——— Influence of Literature upon Society. 12mo. 1813.
84	1	STANHOPE (L.) Greece in 1823–24. 8vo. 1824.
*394	17	STANLEY (T.) History of Philosophy. 8vo. 1655.
*344	4	STANSBURY (A. J.) Report of the Trial of J. H. Peck. 8vo. 1833.
60	23	STARKE (M.) Directions for Travellers. 2 vols. 12mo. 1825.
67	2	STARLING (E.) Noble Deeds of Woman. 12mo. 1850.
*291	1	STATE Papers, Lord Burghley, 1542–70. Edited by Haynes. Folio. 1740.
*262	12	——— Tracts, Reign of Charles II. Folio. 1693.
*262	13	——— Tracts, Reign of William III. 3 vols. folio. 1705–07.
419	4	STAUNTON (H.) Chess Player's Companion. Post 8vo. 1849.
419	5	——— Chess Player's Hand Book. Post 8vo. 1848.
419	6	——— Chess Tournament. Post 8vo. 1852.
352	2	STAUNTON (G. T.) Penal Code of China. 4to. 1810.

Shelf.	No.	
171	35	STEARNS (E. J.) Notes on Uncle Tom's Cabin. 12mo. 1853.
194	5	STEARNS (S. H.) Life and Discourses. 8vo. 1838.
50	11	STEBBING (H.) History of the Church. 2 vols. 18mo. 1833–34.
23	1	——— History of the Church. 3 vols. 8vo. 1839.
50	12	——— History of the Reformation. 2 vols. 18mo. 1836.
*440	4	STEELE (Sir R.) Dramatic Works. 12mo. 1723.
*470	8	STEELE (R.) Tour through the Atlantic. 8vo. 1810.
539	27	STEFFENS (H.) Adventures on the Road to Paris. 12mo. 1848.
24	12	STEINMETZ (A.) History of the Jesuits. 2 vols. 8vo. 1848.
*173	6	STEPHEN (J.) War in Disguise. 8vo. 1806.
33	8	STEPHEN (Sir J.) Lectures on the History of France. 8vo. 1852.
44	1	STEPHENS (A.) History of the Wars following the French Revolution. 2 vols. 8vo. 1804.
493	17	STEPHENS (H.) Book of the Farm. 2 vols. 8vo. 1851.
102	7	STEPHENS (J. L.) Central America. 2 vols. 8vo. 1850.
85	2	——— Egypt, Arabia, &c. 2 vols. 12mo. 1851.
85	3	——— Greece, Turkey, Russia, &c. 2 vols. 12mo. 1849.
102	6	——— Yucatan. 2 vols. 8vo. 1848.
520	1	STERNE (L.) Works. 6 vols. 12mo. 1813.

Vols. 1, 2. Tristram Shandy.
3. Sentimental Journey; History of a Watchcoat.
4, 5. Sermons.
6. Letters; the Koran.

Shelf.	No.	
173	13	STEUART (J.) Political Economy. 3 vols. 8vo. 1796.
103	11	STEVENS (I. I.) Rio Grande and Mexican Campaigns. 8vo. 1851.
503	14	STEVENS (W.) On the Blood. 8vo. 1832.
84	9	STEWART (C. S.) Sandwich Islands. 12mo. 1839.
97	17	——— South Seas. 2 vols. 12mo. 1833.
464	10	STEWART (D.) Manners of the Highlanders. 2 vols. 8vo. 1822.
72	1	STEWART (Dugald). Life and Writings of William Robertson. 4to. 1801.
498	27	STEWART (J.) Stable Economy. 12mo. 1851.
33	6	STILES (W. H.) Austria in 1848–49. 2 vols. 8vo. 1852.
176	5	STIRLING (P. J.) Gold Discoveries. 8vo. 1853.
66	11	STIRLING (W.) Cloister Life of Charles V. 12mo. 1853.
497	15	STÖCKHARDT (J. A.) Chemical Field Lectures. 12mo. 1853.
497	11	——— Principles of Chemistry. 12mo. 1851.
419	7	——— Principles of Chemistry. Post 8vo. 1852.
514	2	STOCQUELER (J. H.) Life of Duke of Wellington. 2 vols. 8vo. 1852–53.
16	11	STODDARD (A.) Sketches of Louisiana. 8vo. 1812.
166	6	STODDARD (R. H.) Poems. 16mo. 1852.
508	18	STOKES (J.) Cabinet Maker's Companion. 16mo. 1850.

Shelf.	No.	
*544	5	STOKES (W.) Diseases of the Chest. 8vo. 1844.
7	21	STONE (E. M.) History of Beverly. 12mo. 1843.
12	12	STONE (J. W.) Festival of the Sons of New Hampshire. 8vo. 1850.
53	1	STONE (W. L.) Life of Joseph Brant. 2 vols. 8vo. 1846.
100	5	——— Border Wars of the American Revolution. 2 vols. 18mo. n. d.
176	18	STORY (J.) Commentaries on the Constitution. 12mo. 1852.
344	13	——— Commentaries on the Constitution. 3 vols. 8vo. 1833.
72	6	——— Life and Letters. 2 vols. 8vo. 1851.
512	7	——— Miscellaneous Writings. 8vo. 1852.
167	6	——— Power of Solitude. 12mo. 1804.
80	7	STORY (R.) Memoir of Isabella Campbell. 18mo. 1830.
70	6	STOUGHTON (J.) Life and Labors of Doddridge. 12mo. 1853.
*282	8	STOW (J.) Chronicle of England. Folio. 1632.
530	20	STOWE (H. B.) Autographs for Freedom. 12mo. 1853.
125	1	——— Uncle Tom's Cabin. Post 8vo. 1852.
125	2	——— Uncle Tom's Cabin. 2 vols. 12mo. 1852.
64	1	STRICKLAND (A.) Queens of England. 6 vols. 8vo. 1851.

Vol. 1. Matilda of Flanders; Matilda of Scotland; Adelicia of Louvaine; Matilda of Boulogne; Eleanora of Aquitaine; Berengaria of Navarre; Isabella of Angouleme; Eleanor of Provence; Eleanora of Castille; Marguerite of France; Isabella of France; Philippa of Hainault; Anne of Bohemia; Isabella of Valois; Joanna of Navarre; Katherine of Valois; Margaret of Anjou; Elizabeth Woodville; Anne of Warwick.
2. Elizabeth of York; Katharine of Arragon; Anne Boleyn; Jane Seymour; Anne of Cleves; Katharine Howard; Katharine Parr; Mary.
3. Elizabeth; Anne of Denmark.
4. Henrietta Maria; Catharine of Braganza; Mary Beatrice of Modena.
5. Mary Beatrice of Modena; Mary II.; Anne.
6. Anne.

Shelf.	No.	
64	2	——— Queens of England. 6 vols. 8vo. 1849.
57	7	——— Queens of Scotland and English Princesses. 3 vols. 12mo. 1851.

Vol. 1. Margaret Tudor; Magdalene of France; Mary of Lorraine.
2. Mary of Lorraine (continued); Lady Margaret Douglas.
3. Mary Stuart.

Shelf.	No.	
13	3	STRICKLAND (W. P.) History of the American Bible Society. 8vo. 1849.
*486	19	STRONG (C.) Speeches. 12mo. 1808.
494	6	STRUTT (J.) English Sports and Pastimes. 8vo. 1850.
*392	21	——— English Sports and Pastimes. 4to. 1810.
*472	13	——— English Dresses. 2 vols. 4to. 1842.
*655	1	STRYKER (J.) American Register. 5 vols. 8vo. 1848–51.
58	2	STUART (A. W.) Lives of the Mrs. Judsons. 12mo. 1853.
33	2	STUART (G.) History of Scotland. 2 vols. 8vo. 1783–84.
35	3	——— History of Scotland. 2 vols. 8vo. 1782.

Shelf.	No.	
175	11	STUART (G.) Society in Europe. 8vo. 1778.
108	6	STUART (J.) Three Years in North America. 2 vols. 12mo. 1833.
171	18	STUART (M.) Miscellanies. 12mo. 1846.
195	2	——— On the Apocalypse. 2 vols. 8vo. 1845.
195	1	——— On the Book of Daniel. 8vo. 1850.
199	9	——— On the Book of Proverbs. 12mo. 1852.
199	7	——— On the Book of Ecclesiastes. 12mo. 1851.
171	15	——— On the Epistle to the Romans. 8vo. 1836.
200	5	——— On the Interpretation of Prophecy. 12mo. 1842.
178	19	——— On the Old Testament. 12mo. 1849.
623	2	STUART (R.) Dictionary of Architecture. 2 vols. 8vo. 1851.
428	9	SUCKLING (J.) Poems, Letters, and Plays. 12mo. 1766.
454	10	SULLIVAN (J.) History of Maine. 8vo. 1795.
46	6	SULLIVAN (W.) Historical Causes and Effects. 12mo. 1838.
52	4	——— Men of the Revolution. 8vo. 1847.
79	6	SULLY (Duke of). Memoirs. 6 vols. 12mo. 1763–78.
10	6	SUMNER (C.) Orations and Speeches. 2 vols. 12mo. 1850.
138	7	SURR (T. S.) Winter in London. 3 vols. 12mo. 1806.
*422	6	SURREY (Earl of) & WYATT. Works. 2 vols. 4to. 1815.
50	3	SWAINSON (W.) Animals in Menageries. 18mo. 1838.
450	3	——— Birds of Western Africa. (Vols. 11, 12, Nat. Lib.) 2 vols. 16mo. n. d.
40	13	——— Classification of Animals. 18mo. 1835.
50	2	——— Classification of Birds. 2 vols. 18mo. 1836.
50	4	——— Classification of Quadrupeds. 18mo. 1835.
40	12	——— Classification of Shells and Shell-fish. 18mo. 1840.
450	3	——— Flycatchers. (Vol. 13, Nat. Lib.) 16mo. n. d.
50	5	——— Habits and Instincts of Animals. 18mo. n. d.
40	14	——— History of Insects. 18mo. 1840.
50	1	——— Natural History of Fishes, &c. 2 vols. 18mo. 1838.
40	11	——— Study of Natural History. 18mo. 1834.
40	10	——— Taxidermy. 18mo. 1840.
179	6	SWEDENBORG (E.) Angelic Wisdom concerning Providence. 12mo. 1851.
179	8	——— Angelic Wisdom concerning Divine Love. 12mo. 1847.
192	8	——— Apocalypse Revealed. 8vo. 1848.
171	1	——— Apocalypse Explained. 5 vols. 8vo. 1846–47.
194	7	——— Delights of Wisdom concerning Conjugial Love. 8vo. 1852.
194	8	——— Delights of Wisdom concerning Conjugial Love. 8vo. 1852.
178	15	——— Divine Love and Divine Wisdom. 12mo. 1841.
179	7	——— Doctrines of the New Jerusalem. 12mo. 1839.
171	5	——— Heaven and Hell. 12mo. 1851.
171	3	——— Heavenly Arcana. 12 vols. 8vo. 1837–47.
171	4	——— Heavenly Arcana, Index to. 8vo. 1848.

Shelf.	No.	
192	9	SWEDENBORG (E.) True Christian Religion. 8vo. 1851.
194	2	—— True Christian Religion. 8vo. 1849.
181	1	—— Compendium of the Writings of. 8vo. 1853.
498	28	SWEETSER (W.) Digestion. 12mo. 1837.
664	15	—— Mental Hygiene. 12mo. 1843.
*604	2	SWETT (J. A.) Diseases of the Chest. 8vo. 1852.
540	5	SWIFT (J.) Works. 18 vols. 12mo. 1765–66.

Vol. 1. Life of Swift; Tale of a Tub; Battle of the Books.
2. Gulliver's Travels.
3. Miscellanies; Swift and Pope.
4. Miscellanies; Swift and Arbuthnot.
5. Miscellanies; Arbuthnot, Pope, and Gay.
6. Poems.
7. Poems.
8. Examiner.
9. Political Tracts.
10. Political Tracts.
11. Miscellanies.
12. Directions to Servants; Correspondence.
13. Sermons; Craftsman, &c.
14. Correspondence.
15. Change of Ministry, 1710; Political Tracts, &c.
16. Tracts; Correspondence.
17. Correspondence; Poems.
18. Poems; Index.

123	9	—— Works. 12mo. 1852.
540	4	—— Letters. 6 vols. 12mo. 1768–69.
148	9	—— Poetical Works. 3 vols. 16mo. 1833–34.
93	1	SWINBURNE (H.) Travels in Spain. 2 vols. 8vo. 1787.
30	1	SWITZERLAND, History of. 18mo. 1832.
*646	8	SYME (J.) Stricture of the Urethra. 8vo. 1849.
83	7	SYMES (M.) Embassy to Ava. 3 vols. 8vo. 1800.

T.

500	3	TABLE Talk. 2 vols. 18mo. 1847.
482	10	TACITUS (C.) Works, translated by Murphy. 8vo. 1851.
167	18	TALFOURD (T. N.) Ion. 16mo. 1837.
86	21	—— Vacation Rambles and Thoughts. 12mo. 1845.
196	7	TAPPAN (D.) Sermons. 8vo. 1807.
86	12	TAPPAN (H. P.) Step from the New World to the Old. 2 vols. 12mo. 1852.
*462	6	TARLETON (B.) History of American Campaigns. 4to. 1787.
*392	9	TARSIS & ZELIE. Translated by Williams. Folio. 1685.
155	4	TASSO (T.) Godfrey of Bulloigne, translated by Fairfax. 12mo. 1851.
490	16	—— Godfrey of Bulloigne, translated by Fairfax. 2 vols. 18mo. 1853.
153	10	—— Jerusalem Delivered, translated by Hoole. 2 vols. 8vo. 1810.

Shelf.	No.	
156	8	TASSO (T.) Jerusalem Delivered, translated by Wiffen. 16mo. 1851.
524	7	TATLER and Guardian. 8vo. n. d.
*402	1	TAVERNIER (J. B.) Six Voyages through Turkey, Persia, and the East Indies. Folio. 1677.
66	10	TAYLER (C. B.) Memorials of the English Martyrs. 12mo. 1853.
165	4	TAYLOR (B.) Book of Romances. 16mo. 1852.
520	8	TAYLOR (H.) Notes from Life. 16mo. 1853.
167	8	——— Philip Van Artevelde. 12mo. 1835.
181	18	TAYLOR (I.) Home Education. 12mo. 1838.
177	10	——— Loyola and Jesuitism. 12mo. 1851.
200	2	——— Natural History of Enthusiasm. 12mo. 1830.
200	4	——— Physical Theory of Another Life. 12mo. 1836.
190	14	——— Self-Cultivation. 18mo. 1842.
200	3	——— Wesley and Methodism. 12mo. 1852.
106	2	TAYLOR (J. B.) Eldorado. 2 vols. 12mo. 1850.
165	14	——— Rhymes of Travel. 12mo. 1849.
96	17	——— Views Afoot. 12mo. 1852.
96	15	——— Views Afoot. 12mo. 1853.
520	12	TAYLOR (Jane). Contributions of Q. Q. 2 vols. 12mo. 1826.
397	12	TAYLOR (J.) Holy Living and Dying. Post 8vo. 1851.
190	8	——— Holy Living and Dying. 12mo. 1810.
193	1	——— Practical Works. 2 vols. 8vo. 1850.
508	6	TAYLOR (John). Agricultural Essays. 16mo. 1814.
184	20	——— Sermons. 8vo. 1806.
426	1	TAYLOR (W.) German Poetry. 3 vols. 8vo. 1828.
34	6	TAYLOR (W. C.) Ancient and Modern History. 8vo. 1852.
32	7	——— Ancient History. 8vo. 1851.
89	13	——— History of Ireland. 2 vols. 18mo. 1847.
63	9	TAYLOR (Z.) Life of. 8vo. 1846.
171	20	TEGG (T.) Young Man's Book of Knowledge. 12mo. 1834.
509	28	TELEGRAPH, Book of. 12mo. 1851.
66	5	TEIGNMOUTH (Lord). Life of Sir William Jones. 8vo. 1805.
540	12	TEMPLETON (W.) Steam and the Steam Engine. 12mo. 1853.
166	10	TENNYSON (A.) In Memoriam. 16mo. 1851.
166	11	——— Poems. 2 vols. 16mo. 1851.
410	11	TERENCE and PHÆDRUS, translated by Riley and Smart. Post 8vo. 1853.
10	3	THACHER (B. B.) Indian Biography. 18mo. 1832.
89	10	——— Indian Biography. 2 vols. 18mo. 1848.
10	2	——— Indian Traits. 2 vols. 18mo. 1840.
63	7	THACHER (J.) American Medical Biography. 8vo. 1828.
*666	6	——— American Medical Biography. 2 vols. 8vo. 1828.
*666	12	——— Hydrophobia. 8vo. 1812.
*475	7	——— Military Journal. 8vo. 1823.
117	14	THACKERAY (W. M.) Confessions of Fitz Boodle. 16mo. 1852.

Shelf.	No.	
105	2	THACKERAY (W. M.) Cornhill to Cairo. 12mo. 1852.
122	2	——— History of Pendennis. 2 vols. 8vo. 1850.
117	15	——— Luck of Barry Lyndon. 2 vols. 16mo. 1853.
117	12	——— Paris Sketch Book. 2 vols. 16mo. 1852.
122	3	——— Vanity Fair. 8vo. n. d.
117	13	——— Yellowplush Papers. 16mo. 1852.
458	1	THACKERAY (F.) State of Ancient Britain. 8vo. 1843.
483	7	THEOCRITUS, BION, et MOSCHUS. 2 vols. 8vo. 1829.
410	12	——— BION, MOSCHUS, &c. translated by Banks. Post 8vo. 1853.
33	9	THIERS (M. A.) Consulate and Empire of Napoleon. 8vo. 1850.
32	2	——— French Revolution. 2 vols. 8vo. 1852.
47	10	THIERRY (A.) Norman Conquest. 2 vols. post 8vo. 1847.
186	10	THINGS New and Old. 8vo. 1845.
50	13	THIRLWALL (Rev. C.) History of Greece. 8 vols. 18mo. 1835–50.
39	3	——— History of Greece. 8 vols. 18mo. 1847.
43	8	——— History of Greece. 2 vols. 8vo. 1848.
6	12	THOMAS (E. S.) Reminiscences of the last Sixty-five Years. 2 vols. 12mo. 1840.
*432	7	THOMAS (G.) Military Memoirs. 4to. 1803.
*474	2	THOMAS (I.) History of Printing. 2 vols. 8vo. 1810.
*271	10	——— Massachusetts Spy. Folio. 1785–89.
*666	15	THOMAS (R.) Modern Practice of Physic. 8vo. 1813.
176	22	THOME (J. A.) & KIMBALL (J. H.) Emancipation in the West Indies. 12mo. 1838.
449	4	THOMS (W. J.) Collection of Early Prose Romances. 3 vols. 12mo. 1828.
148	11	THOMSON (J.) Poetical Works. 2 vols. 16mo. 1847.
158	14	——— Seasons. 16mo. 1825.
158	11	——— Works. 4 vols. 12mo. 1762.

Vol. 1. Seasons.
2. Liberty; Castle of Indolence; Occasional Poems.
3. Sophonisba; Agamemnon; and Alfred.
4. Edward and Eleonora; Tancred and Sigismunda; and Coriolanus.

Shelf.	No.	
504	19	THOMPSON (B.) Count Rumford. Essays. 2 vols. 8vo. 1800.
175	15	THOMPSON (G.) Prison Life and Reflections. 12mo. 1850.
33	10	THOMPSON (P.) History of Boston, England. 8vo. 1820.
103	8	THOMPSON (W.) Recollections of Mexico. 8vo. 1846.
67	16	THORBURN (G.) Life and Writings. 12mo. 1852.
500	11	THORNE (J.) Rambles by Rivers. 4 vols. 18mo. 1844–49.
173	5	THORNTON (H.) Paper Credit of Great Britain. 8vo. 1807.
171	17	THORPE (B.) Northern Mythology. 3 vols. 12mo. 1851.
487	6	——— Anglo-Saxon Gospel. 12mo. 1848.
7	20	THORPE (T. B.) Army at Monterey. 12mo. 1847.

Shelf.	No.	
418	2	Three Courses and a Dessert. Post 8vo. 1852.
120	12	Thucydides. History of the Peloponnesian War, translated by Smith. 2 vols. 18mo. n. d.
*252	5	——— History of the Peloponnesian War, translated by Hobbes. Folio. 1648.
410	13	——— History of the Peloponnesian War, translated by Dale. Post 8vo. 1851.
28	13	Thury (L. H. de). Catacombes de Paris. 8vo. 1815.
*596	4	——— Notice Statistique sur les Produits de l'Industrie. 8vo. 1819.
487	14	Tibullus. Translated by J. Grainger. 2 vols. 12mo. 1759.
99	3	Ticknor (C.) Philosophy of Living. 18mo. 1846.
26	11	Ticknor (G.) History of Spanish Literature. 3 vols. 8vo. 1849.
94	4	Tiffany (O. jun.) Canton Chinese. 12mo. 1849.
*650	15	Tilt (E. J.) Health of Women. 18mo. 1851.
*462	2	Titsingh (M.) Illustrations of Japan. 4to. 1822.
530	15	Times, London, Essays from. 16mo. 1852.
173	1	Tocqueville (A. de). Democracy in America. 2 vols. 8vo. 1845.
172	5	——— Democracy in America. 8vo. 1851.
*443	3	Todd (H. J.) Life of Cranmer. 8vo. 1831.
72	11	——— Life of Cranmer. 2 vols. 8vo. 1831.
*604	1	Todd (R. B. & Bowman W.) Anatomy and Physiology. 8vo. 1850.
53	7	Tomline (G.) Memoir of William Pitt. 2 vols. 8vo. 1821.
117	7	Tonna (C. E.) Falsehood and Truth. 16mo. 1841.
27	11	Tooke (T.) History of Prices. 2 vols. 8vo. 1838.
*465	5	Tooke (W.) Reign of Catherine Second. 3 vols. 8vo. 1799.
93	6	——— Reign of Catherine Second. 3 vols. 8vo. 1800.
55	8	——— Reign of Catherine Second. 3 vols. 8vo. 1799.
141	51	Töpffer (R.) Great St. Bernard. 16mo. 1852.
141	60	——— Inheritance. 16mo. 1852.
475	14	Town (I.) Detail of Services performed in America in 1776–79. 12mo. 1835.
*469	24	Towns and Townships, General Plan for Laying out. 8vo. 1794.
497	23	Townshend (C. H.) Mesmerism. 12mo. 1843.
165	3	Townshend (T.) Poems. 12mo. 1796.
183	4	Tracy (J.) Great Awakening. 8vo. 1842.
560	4	Trail (Mrs.) Backwoods of Canada. 12mo. n. d.
660	11	Treasury of Knowledge. 3 vols. 12mo. 1850.
173	16	Tremenheere (H. S.) Tour in the United States and Canada. 12mo. 1852.
*671	13	Tremont House, Description of. 4to. 1830.
180	9	Trench (R. C.) On the Lessons in Proverbs. 12mo. 1853.
195	5	——— On the Miracles. 8vo. 1852.
196	2	——— On the Parables. 8vo. 1852.

Shelf.	No.	
487	7	Trench (R. C.) Study of Words. 12mo. 1853.
140	17	Trenck (Baron F.) Life of. 18mo. n. d.
8	3	Trescot (W. H.) Diplomacy of the Revolution. 12mo. 1852.
8	16	Trial of the British Soldiers, held at Boston, 1770. 12mo. 1824.
190	24	Trimmer (S.) Antient History. 18mo. 1820.
190	20	——— Antient History, Questions to. 18mo. 1817.
185	4	——— Christian Education. 8vo. 1812.
190	22	——— Companion to Scripture. 18mo. 1816.
187	20	——— Economy of Charity. 2 vols. 12mo. 1801.
187	18	——— Fabulous Histories. 12mo. 1821.
185	5	——— Guardian of Education. 5 vols. 8vo. 1802–06.
190	27	——— History of England. 2 vols. 18mo. 1820.
190	25	——— History of England, Questions to. 18mo. 1817.
187	19	——— Instructive Tales. 12mo. 1812.
190	28	——— Knowledge of Nature. 18mo. 1819
187	13	——— New Testament Abridged. 12mo. n. d.
190	21	——— Prayers and Meditations. 18mo. 1819.
190	26	——— Roman History. 18mo. 1821.
187	17	——— Scripture History Abridged. 12mo. 1811.
187	16	——— Sermons. 12mo. 1812.
187	22	——— Selections from Sacred History. 6 vols. 12mo. 1817.
187	21	——— Selections from Family Magazine. 12mo. 1818.
187	15	——— Study of the Scriptures. 2 vols. 12mo. 1818.
106	13	Trollope (F.) Domestic Manners of Americans. 8vo. 1832.
128	3	——— Lauringtons. 3 vols. 12mo. 1844.
112	12	——— Life of Michael Armstrong. 2 vols. 8vo. 1840.
134	1	——— Old World and New. 3 vols. 8vo. 1849.
128	4	——— One Fault. 3 vols. 12mo. 1840.
94	11	——— Paris and Parisians in 1835. 8vo. 1836.
92	6	——— Paris and Parisians in 1835. 8vo. 1836.
115	4	——— Young Countess. 3 vols. 12mo. 1848.
134	3	——— Young Love. 3 vols. 12mo. 1844.
*636	1	Trousseau (A.) & Belloc (H.) On the Larynx. 8vo. 1841.
*650	12	Trousseau (M.) & Reveil (M.) Prescriber's Hand-Book. 16mo. 1852.
154	5	Trumbull (J.) Poetical Works. 2 vols. 8vo. 1820.
15	8	——— Autobiography, Reminiscences, and Letters. 8vo. 1841.
107	9	Tschudi (J. J. von). Travels in Peru. 12mo. 1852.
81	8	Tucker (Miss). Abbeokuta: the Yoruba Mission. 12mo. 1853.
194	3	Tucker (A.) Light of Nature. 4 vols. 8vo. 1831.
77	1	Tuckerman (H. T.) Artist Life. 12mo. 1847.
77	2	——— Characteristics of Literature. 2 vols. 12mo. 1849–51.
67	11	——— Memorial of Horatio Greenough. 12mo. 1853.

Shelf.	No.	
81	5	TUCKERMAN (H. T.) Month in England. 12mo. 1853.
540	13	——— Optimist. 12mo. 1852.
166	5	——— Poems. 16mo. 1851.
85	9	——— Sicily. 12mo. 1852.
28	10	TUMULTS, Popular, Sketches of. 12mo. 1837.
518	7	TUDOR (W.) Gebel Tier. 12mo. 1829.
8	19	——— Letters on the Eastern States. 12mo. 1820.
520	9	——— Letters on the Eastern States. 12mo. 1820.
444	8	——— Life of James Otis. 8vo. 1823.
520	13	——— Miscellanies. 12mo. 1821.
537	5	TUPPER (M. F.) Works. 4 vols. 12mo. 1851.
		Vol. 1. Crock of Gold; Twins and Heart.
		2. Author's Mind; Essays; Probabilities.
		3. Ballads and Poems.
		4. Proverbial Philosophy, &c.
*448	2	TURELL (E.) Life of Benjamin Colman. 8vo. 1749.
141	56	TURF Characters. 16mo. 1852.
104	13	TURNBULL (D.) Travels in Cuba and Porto Rico. 8vo. 1840.
505	9	TURNBULL (L.) Electro-Magnetic Telegraph. 8vo. 1853.
105	12	TURNBULL (R.) Genius of Italy. 12mo. 1852.
507	21	TURNER (E.) Elements of Chemistry. 12mo. 1835.
99	1	TURNER (S.) Sacred History. 3 vols. 18mo. n. d.
498	17	TURNER'S Companion. 16mo. 1851.
137	9	TUTHILL (L. C.) The Lawyer. 12mo. 1850.
137	8	——— The Merchant. 12mo. 1850.
39	2	TWEDDELL (G.) Shakespeare and his Times. 18mo. 1852.
*584	10	TWEEDIE (A.) Nervous Diseases. 8vo. 1840.
72	9	TWISS (H.) Life of Lord Eldon. 2 vols. 8vo. 1844.
102	3	TYSON (J. L.) Physician in California. 8vo. 1850.
47	3	TYTLER (A. F.) Elements of History. 12mo. 1825.
150	15	——— Universal History. 6 vols. 18mo. 1839.
99	7	——— Universal History. 6 vols. 18mo. n. d.
131	32	TYTLER (Ann F.) Leila at Home. 16mo. 1853.
131	31	——— Leila in England. 16mo. 1853.
131	30	——— Leila, or the Island. 16mo. 1853.
77	13	TYTLER (P. F.) Life of the Admirable Crichton. 12mo. 1823.
170	16	——— Lives of Scottish Worthies. 3 vols. 18mo. 1831.
89	14	——— North Coast of America. 18mo. 1846.

U.

Shelf.	No.	
*554	5	UNDERWOOD (M.) Diseases of Children. 8vo. 1842.
96	14	UNGEWITTER (F. H.) Europe. 12mo. 1850.
198	7	UNITARIAN Miscellany. 6 vols. 12mo. 1821–24.
		UNITED STATES Documents.
*202	1	Journal of the Senate. 1st Cong., 1st Sess. Folio. 1789.
*202	2	Journal of the Senate. 1st Cong., 2d Sess. Folio. 1790.

Shelf.	No.	
		UNITED STATES Documents, *continued.*
*202	3	Journal of the Senate. 1st Cong., 3d Sess. Folio. 1791.
*202	4	Journal of the Senate. 2d Cong., 1st Sess. Folio. 1791.
*202	5	Journal of the Senate. 2d Cong., 2d Sess. Folio. 1792.
*202	6	Journal of the Senate. 3d Cong., 1st Sess. Folio. 1793.
*202	7	Journal of the Senate. 3d Cong., 2d Sess. Folio. 1794.
*202	8	Journal of the House of Representatives. 1st Cong., 1st Sess. Folio. 1789.
*202	9	Journal of the House. 1st Cong., 2d Sess. Folio. 1790.
*202	10	Journal of the House. 1st Cong., 3d Sess. Folio. 1791.
*202	11	Journal of the House. 2d Cong., 1st Sess. Folio. 1791.
*202	12	Journal of the House. 2d Cong., 2d Sess. Folio. 1792.
*204	3	Journal of the House. 1st—13th Cong. 9 vols. 8vo. 1789–1815.
*205	1	Journal of the House. 3d Cong., 1st Sess. 8vo. 1793–94.
*205	2	Journal of the House. 3d Cong., 2d Sess. 8vo. 1794–95.
*205	3	Journal of the Senate. 4th Cong., 1st Sess. 8vo. 1795–96.
*205	4	Journal of the House. 4th Cong., 1st Sess. 8vo. 1795–96.
*205	5	Journal of the Senate. 4th Cong., 2d Sess. 8vo. 1796–97.
*205	6	Journal of the House. 4th Cong., 2d Sess. 8vo. 1796–97.
*205	7	Journal of the House. 4th Cong., 2d Sess. 8vo. 1796–97.
*205	8	Public Documents. 4th Cong., 2d Sess. 2 vols. 8vo. 1796–97.
*205	9	Journal of the Senate. 5th Cong., 1st Sess. 8vo. 1797.
*205	10	Journal of the House. 5th Cong., 1st Sess. 8vo. 1797.
*205	11	Journal of the Senate. 5th Cong., 2d Sess. 8vo. 1797–98.
*205	12	Journal of the House. 5th Cong., 2d Sess. 8vo. 1797–98.
*205	13	Journal of the Senate. 5th Cong., 3d Sess. 8vo. 1798–99.
*205	14	Journal of the House. 5th Cong., 3d Sess. 8vo. 1798–99.
*205	15	Public Documents. 5th Cong., 3d Sess. 8vo. 1799.
*205	16	Journal of the Senate. 6th Cong., 1st and 2d Sess. 8vo. 1799, 1801.
*205	17	Journal of the House. 6th Cong., 1st Sess. 8vo. 1799, 1800.
*205	18	Public Documents. 6th Cong., 1st Sess. 3 vols. 8vo. 1799, 1800.
*205	19	Journal of the House. 6th Cong., 2d Sess. 8vo. 1800–01.
*205	20	Journal of the Senate. 7th Cong., 1st Sess. 8vo. 1801–02.
*205	21	Journal of the House. 7th Cong., 1st Sess. 8vo. 1801–02.
*206	1	Journal of the Senate. 7th Cong., 2d Sess. 8vo. 1802–03.
*206	2	Journal of the House. 7th Cong., 2d Sess. 8vo. 1802–03.
*206	3	Journal of the Senate. 8th Cong., 1st and 2d Sess. 8vo. 1803–05. Trials of Blount, Pickering, and Chase.
*206	4	Journal of the Senate. 8th Cong., 1st Sess. 8vo. 1803–04.
*206	5	Journal of the House. 8th Cong., 1st Sess. 8vo. 1803–04.
*206	6	Journal of the Senate. 8th Cong., 2d Sess. 8vo. 1804–05.
*206	7	Journal of the House. 8th Cong., 2d Sess. 8vo. 1804–05.
*206	8	Journal of the Senate. 9th Cong., 1st Sess. 8vo. 1805–06.
*206	9	Public Documents. 9th Cong., 1st Sess. 8vo. 1805–06.

Shelf.	No.	
		UNITED STATES Documents, *continued.*
*206	10	Journal of the House. 9th Cong., 2d Sess. 8vo. 1806–07.
*206	11	Public Documents. 9th Cong., 2d Sess. 2 vols. 8vo. 1806–07.
*202	13	Executive Reports. 9th Cong., 2d Sess. Folio. 1806–07.
*202	14	Executive Reports. 10th Cong., 1st Sess. Folio. 1807–08.
*206	12	Journal of the House. 10th Cong., 1st Sess. 8vo. 1807–08.
*206	13	Public Documents. 10th Cong., 1st Sess. 2 vols. 8vo. 1807–08.
*202	15	Executive Reports. 10th Cong., 2d Sess. Folio. 1808–09.
*206	14	Journal of the Senate. 10th Cong., 2d Sess. 8vo. 1808–09.
*206	15	Journal of the House. 10th Cong., 2d Sess. 8vo. 1808–09.
*206	16	Public Documents. 10th Cong., 2d Sess. 2 vols. 8vo. 1808–09.
*202	16	Executive Reports. 11th Cong., 1st Sess. Folio. 1809.
*206	17	Journal of the House. 11th Cong., 1st Sess. 8vo. 1809.
*206	18	Public Documents. 11th Cong., 1st Sess. 8vo. 1809.
*202	17	Executive Reports. 11th Cong., 2d Sess. 2 vols. folio. 1809–10.
*206	19	Journal of the Senate. 11th Cong., 2d Sess. 8vo. 1809–10.
*207	1	Journal of the House. 11th Cong., 2d Sess. 8vo. 1809–10.
*207	2	Public Documents. 11th Cong., 2d Sess. 4 vols. 8vo. 1809–10.
*207	3	Senate Papers. 11th Cong., 2d Sess. 8vo. 1809–10.
*202	18	Executive Papers. 11th Cong., 3d Sess. 2 vols. Folio. 1810–11.
*207	4	Journal of the Senate. 11th Cong., 3d Sess. 8vo. 1810–11.
*207	5	Journal of the House. 11th Cong., 3d Sess. 8vo. 1810–11.
*207	6	Public Documents. 11th Cong., 3d Sess. 3 vols. 8vo. 1810–11.
*202	19	Executive Reports and Documents. 12th Cong., 1st Sess. 3 vols. folio. 1811–12
*207	7	Journal of the Senate. 12th Cong., 1st Sess. 8vo. 1811–12.
*207	8	Journal of the House. 12th Cong., 1st Sess. 2 vols. 8vo. 1811–12.
*207	9	Public Documents. 12th Cong., 1st Sess. 3 vols. 8vo. 1811–12.
*202	20	Executive Reports. 12th Cong., 2d Sess. Folio. 1813.
*207	10	Journal of the Senate. 12th Cong., 2d Sess. 8vo. 1812–13.
*207	11	Journal of the House. 12th Cong., 2d Sess. 8vo. 1812–13.
*208	1	Public Documents. 12th Cong., 2d Sess. 8vo. 1812–13.
*208	2	Journal of the Senate. 13th Cong., 1st Sess. 8vo. 1813.
*208	3	Journal of the House. 13th Cong., 1st Sess. 8vo. 1813.
*208	4	Public Documents. 13th Cong., 1st Sess. 8vo. 1813.
*208	5	Journal of the Senate. 13th Cong., 2d Sess. 8vo. 1813–14.
*208	6	Journal of the House. 13th Cong., 2d Sess. 8vo. 1813–14.
*208	7	Senate Papers. 13th Cong., 2d Sess. 8vo. 1813–14.
*208	8	Public Documents. 13th Cong., 2d Sess. 2 vols. 8vo. 1813–14.

Shelf.	No.	
		UNITED STATES Documents, *continued.*
*208	9	Public Documents. 13th Cong., 3d Sess. 2 vols. 8vo. 1814–15.
*222	1	Reports. 13th Cong., 1st and 2d Sess. Folio. 1813.
*222	2	Reports. 13th Cong., 3d Sess. Folio. 1814.
*208	13	Journal of the Senate. 14th Cong., 1st Sess. 8vo. 1815–16.
*208	10	Journal of the House. 14th Cong., 1st Sess. 8vo. 1815–16.
*208	11	Senate Papers. 14th Cong., 1st Sess. 8vo. 1815–16.
*208	12	House Documents. 14th Cong., 1st Sess. 2 vols. 8vo. 1815–16.
*208	14	House Documents. 14th Cong., 2d Sess. 2 vols. 8vo. 1816–17.
*209	6	Senate Journal. 15th Cong., 1st Sess. 8vo. 1817–18.
*209	7	House Journal. 15th Cong., 1st Sess. 8vo. 1817–18.
*209	8	Senate Papers. 15th Cong., 1st Sess. 2 vols. 8vo. 1817–18.
*209	1	House Documents. 15th Cong., 1st Sess. 8 vols. 8vo. 1817–18.
*209	2	Journal of the Senate. 15th Cong., 2d Sess. 8vo. 1818–19.
*209	3	Journal of the House. 15th Cong., 2d Sess. 8vo. 1818–19.
*209	4	Senate Papers. 15th Cong., 2d Sess. 2 vols. 8vo. 1818–19.
		House Documents. 15th Cong., 2d Sess. 8 vols. 8vo. 1818–19.
*209	5	Vol. 1.
*210	1	,, 2–8.
		Executive Papers. 16th Cong., 1st Sess. 9 vols. 8vo. 1819–20.
*210	2	Vols. 1–8.
*213	1	,, 9.
*213	2	Journal of the Senate. 16th Cong., 1st Sess. 8vo. 1819–20.
*213	3	Journal of the House. 16th Cong., 1st Sess. 8vo. 1819–20.
*213	4	Senate Papers. 16th Cong., 1st Sess. 3 vols. 8vo. 1819–20.
*213	5	Report of Committees. 16th Cong., 1st Sess. 8vo. 1819–20.
*213	6	Executive Papers. 16th Cong., 2d Sess. 9 vols. 8vo. 1820–21.
*214	1	Journal of the Senate. 16th Cong., 2d Sess. 8vo. 1820–21.
*214	2	Journal of the House. 16th Cong., 2d Sess. 8vo. 1820–21.
*214	3	Senate Papers. 16th Cong., 2d Sess. 5 vols. 8vo. 1820–21.
*214	4	Reports of Committees. 16th Cong., 2d Sess. 8vo. 1820–21.
*214	5	Executive Papers. 17th Cong., 1st Sess. 9 vols. 8vo. 1821–22.
*214	6	Journal of the Senate. 17th Cong., 1st Sess. 8vo. 1821–22.
*214	7	Journal of the House. 17th Cong., 1st Sess. 8vo. 1821–22.
*215	1	Senate Papers. 17th Cong., 1st Sess. 4 vols. 8vo. 1821–22.
*215	2	Reports of Committees. 17th Cong., 1st Sess. 2 vols. 8vo. 1821–22.
*215	3	Executive Papers. 17th Cong., 2d Sess. 9 vols. 8vo, 1822–23.
*216	1	Journal of the Senate. 17th Cong., 2d Sess. 8vo. 1822–23.

Shelf.	No.	
		UNITED STATES Documents, *continued.*
*216	2	Journal of the House. 17th Cong., 2d Sess. 8vo. 1822–23.
*216	3	Senate Papers. 17th Cong., 2d Sess. 2 vols. 8vo. 1822–23.
*216	4	Reports of Committees. 17th Cong., 2d Sess. 2 vols. 8vo. 1822–23.
		Executive Papers. 18th Cong., 1st Sess. 13 vols. 8vo. 1823–24.
*216	5	Vols. 1–10.
*217	1	,, 11–13.
*217	2	Journal of the Senate. 18th Cong., 1st Sess. 8vo. 1823–24.
*217	3	Journal of the House. 18th Cong., 1st Sess. 8vo. 1823–24.
*217	4	Senate Papers. 18th Cong., 1st Sess. 3 vols. 8vo. 1823–24.
*217	5	Reports of Committees. 18th Cong., 1st Sess. 2 vols. 8vo. 1823–24.
		Executive Papers. 18th Cong., 2d Sess. 9 vols. 8vo. 1824–25.
*217	6	Vols. 1–6.
*218	1	,, 7–9.
*218	2	Journal of the Senate. 18th Cong., 2d Sess. 8vo. 1824–25.
*218	3	Journal of the House. 18th Cong., 2d Sess. 8vo. 1824–25.
*218	4	Senate Papers. 18th Cong., 2d Sess. 4 vols. 8vo. 1824–25.
*218	5	Reports of Committees. 18th Cong., 2d Sess. 2 vols. 8vo. 1824–25.
		Executive Papers. 19th Cong., 1st Sess. 10 vols. 8vo. 1825–26.
*218	6	Vols. 1– 5.
*219	1	,, 6–10.
*219	2	Journal of the Senate. 19th Cong., 1st Sess. 8vo. 1825–26.
*219	3	Journal of the House. 19th Cong., 1st Sess. 8vo. 1825–26.
*219	5	Reports of Committees. 19th Cong., 1st Sess. 2 vols. 8vo. 1825–26.
*219	4	Senate Papers. 19th Cong., 1st Sess. 5 vols. 8vo. 1825–26.
*220	1	Executive Papers. 19th Cong., 2d Sess. 12 vols. 8vo. 1826–27.
*220	2	Journal of the Senate. 19th Cong., 2d Sess. 8vo. 1826–27.
*220	3	Journal of the House. 19th Cong., 2d Sess. 8vo. 1826–27.
*220	4	Senate Papers. 19th Cong., 2d Sess. 3 vols. 8vo. 1826–27.
		Reports of Committees. 19th Cong., 2d Sess. 3 vols. 8vo. 1826–27.
*220	5	Vol. 1.
*223	1	,, 2, 3.
*222	3	Bills of the Senate. 19th Cong., 2d Sess. Folio. 1826–27.
*222	4	Bills of the House. 19th Cong., 2d Sess. Folio. 1826–27.
*223	2	Executive Papers. 20th Cong., 1st Sess. 7 vols. 8vo. 1827–28.
*223	3	Journal of the Senate. 20th Cong., 1st Sess. 8vo. 1827–28.
*223	4	Journal of the House. 20th Cong., 1st Sess. 8vo. 1827–28.

Shelf.	No.	
		UNITED STATES Documents, *continued.*
		Senate Papers. 20th Cong., 1st Sess. 5 vols. 8vo. 1827–28.
*223	5	Vols. 1–4.
*224	1	,, 5.
*224	2	Reports of Committees. 20th Cong., 1st Sess. 4 vols. 8vo. 1827–28.
*224	3	Executive Papers. 20th Cong., 2d Sess. 6 vols. 8vo. 1828–29.
*224	4	Journal of the Senate. 20th Cong., 2d Sess. 8vo. 1828–29.
*224	5	Journal of the House. 20th Cong., 2d Sess. 8vo. 1828–29.
*224	6	Senate Papers. 20th Cong., 2d Sess. 2 vols. 8vo. 1828–29.
*224	7	Reports of Committees. 20th Cong., 2d Sess. 8vo. 1828–29.
		Executive Papers. 21st Cong., 1st Sess. 4 vols. 8vo. 1829–30.
*224	8	Vol. 1.
*225	1	,, 2–4.
*225	2	Journal of the Senate. 21st Cong., 1st Sess. 8vo. 1829–30.
*225	3	Journal of the House. 21st Cong., 1st Sess. 8vo. 1829–30.
*225	4	Senate Papers. 21st Cong., 1st Sess. 2 vols. 8vo. 1829–30.
*225	5	Reports of Committees. 21st Cong., 1st Sess. 3 vols. 8vo. 1829–30.
*225	6	Executive Papers. 21st Cong., 2d Sess. 4 vols. 8vo. 1830–31.
*226	1	Journal of the Senate. 21st Cong., 2d Sess. 8vo. 1830–31.
*226	2	Journal of the House. 21st Cong., 2d Sess. 8vo. 1830–31.
*226	3	Senate Papers. 21st Cong., 2d Sess. 2 vols. 8vo. 1830–31.
*226	4	Reports of Committees. 21st Cong., 2d Sess. 8vo. 1830–31.
*226	5	Executive Papers. 22d Cong., 1st Sess. 6 vols. 8vo. 1831–32.
*226	6	Journal of the Senate. 22d Cong , 1st Sess. 8vo. 1831–32.
*226	7	Journal of the House. 22d Cong., 1st Sess. 8vo. 1831–32.
*226	8	Senate Papers. 22d Cong., 1st Sess. 3 vols. 8vo. 1831–32.
*227	1	Reports of Committees. 22d Cong., 1st Sess. 5 vols. 8vo. 1831–32.
*227	2	Executive Papers. 22d Cong., 2d Sess. 3 vols. 8vo. 1832–33.
*227	3	Journal of the Senate. 22d Cong., 2d Sess. 8vo. 1832–33.
*227	4	Journal of the House. 22d Cong., 2d Sess. 8vo. 1832–33.
*227	5	Senate Papers. 22d Cong., 2d Sess. 8vo. 1832–33.
*227	6	Reports of Committees. 22d Cong., 2d Sess. 8vo. 1832–33.
*227	7	Documents on Manufactures. 22d Cong., 2d Sess. 2 vols. 8vo. 1832–33.
		Executive Papers. 23d Cong., 1st Sess. 6 vols. 8vo. 1833–34.
*227	8	Vol. 1.
*228	1	,, 2–6.
*228	2	Journal of the Senate. 23d Cong., 1st Sess. 8vo. 1833–34.
*228	3	Journal of the House. 23d Cong., 1st Sess. 8vo. 1833–34.

Shelf.	No.	
		UNITED STATES Documents, *continued.*
		Senate Papers. 23d Cong., 1st Sess. 7 vols. 8vo. 1833–34.
*228	4	Vols. 1–5.
*229	1	,, 6, 7.
*229	2	Senate Papers, Indian Affairs. 23d Cong., 1st Sess. 4 vols. 8vo. 1833–34.
*229	3	Senate Papers, Pensions. 23d Cong., 1st Sess. 3 vols. 8vo. 1833–34.
*229	4	Reports of Committees. 23d Cong., 1st Sess. 5 vols. 8vo. 1833–34.
*230	1	Executive Papers. 23d Cong., 2d Sess. 5 vols. 8vo. 1834–35.
*230	2	Journal of the Senate. 23d Cong., 2d Sess. 8vo. 1834–35.
*230	3	Journal of the House. 23d Cong., 2d Sess. 8vo. 1834–35.
*230	4	Senate Papers. 23d Cong., 2d Sess. 4 vols. 8vo. 1834–35.
*230	5	Reports of Committees. 23d Cong., 2d Sess. 2 vols. 8vo. 1834–35.
		Executive Papers. 24th Cong., 1st Sess. 7 vols. 8vo. 1835–36.
*230	6	Vols. 1–3.
*233	1	,, 4–7.
*233	2	Journal of the Senate. 24th Cong., 1st Sess. 8vo. 1835–36.
*233	3	Journal of the House. 24th Cong., 1st Sess. 8vo. 1835–36.
*233	4	Senate Papers. 24th Cong., 1st Sess. 6 vols. 8vo. 1835–36.
		Reports of Committees. 24th Cong., 1st Sess. 3 vols. 8vo. 1835–36.
*233	5	Vols. 1, 2.
*234	1	,, 3.
*234	2	Executive Papers. 24th Cong., 2d Sess. 4 vols. 8vo. 1836–37.
*234	3	Journal of the Senate. 24th Cong., 2d Sess. 8vo. 1836–37.
*234	4	Journal of the House. 24th Cong., 2d Sess. 8vo. 1836–37.
*234	5	Senate Papers. 24th Cong., 2d Sess. 3 vols. 8vo. 1836–37.
*234	6	Reports of Committees. 24th Cong., 2d Sess. 3 vols. 8vo. 1836–37.
*234	7	Journal of the Two Houses. 25th Cong., 1st Sess. 8vo. 1837.
*234	8	Senate and House of Representative Papers. 25th Cong., 1st Sess. 8vo. 1837.
*235	1	Documents accompanying President's Message. 25th Cong., 2d Sess. 8vo. 1837.
*235	2	Executive Papers. 25th Cong., 2d Sess. (Vols. 1, 4, 5, 7, 9–12. 8 vols. 8vo. 1837–38.
*235	3	Journal of the Senate. 25th Cong., 2d Sess. 8vo. 1837–38.
*236	1	Senate Papers. 25th Cong., 2d Sess. (Vols. 1–3, 6.) 4 vols. 8vo. 1837–38.
*236	2	Reports of Committees. 25th Cong., 2d Sess. 8vo. 1837–38.

Shelf.	No.	
		UNITED STATES Documents, *continued.*
*236	3	Executive Papers. 25th Cong., 3d Sess. 6 vols. 8vo. 1838–39.
*237	1	Journal of the Senate. 25th Cong., 3d Sess. 8vo. 1838–39.
*237	2	Journal of the House. 25th Cong., 3d Sess. 8vo. 1838–39.
*237	3	Senate Papers. 25th Cong., 3d Sess. (Vols. 1, 2, 4, 5.) 4 vols. 8vo. 1838–39.
		Executive Documents. 26th Cong., 2d Sess. 6 vols. 8vo. 1840–41.
*237	4	Vols. 1–4.
*238	1	,, 5, 6.
*238	2	Journal of the Senate. 26th Cong., 2d Sess. 8vo. 1840–41.
*238	3	Journal of the House. 26th Cong., 2d Sess. 8vo. 1840–41.
*238	4	Journal of the House. 26th Cong., 2d Sess. 8vo. 1840–41.
*238	5	Senate Documents. 26th Cong., 2d Sess. 5 vols. 8vo. 1840–41.
*238	6	Reports of Committees. 26th Cong., 2d Sess. 8vo. 1840–41.
*238	7	Executive Papers and Reports of Committees. 27th Cong., 1st Sess. 8vo. 1841.
*238	8	Journal of the Senate. 27th Cong., 1st Sess. 8vo. 1841.
*238	9	Journal of the House. 27th Cong., 1st Sess. 8vo. 1841.
*238	10	Senate Documents. 27th Cong., 1st Sess. 8vo. 1841.
*239	1	Executive Documents. 27th Cong., 2d Sess. 6 vols. 8vo. 1841–42.
*239	2	Journal of the Senate. 27th Cong., 2d Sess. 8vo. 1841–42.
*239	3	Journal of the House. 27th Cong., 2d Sess. 8vo. 1841–42.
		Senate Documents. 27th Cong., 2d Sess. 5 vols. 8vo. 1841–42.
*239	4	Vols. 1–3.
*240	1	,, 4, 5.
*240	2	Reports of Committees. 27th Cong., 2d Sess. 5 vols. 8vo. 1841–42.
		Executive Documents. 27th Cong., 3d Sess. 8 vols. 8vo. 1842–43.
*240	3	Vols. 1–5.
*247	1	,, 6–8.
*247	2	Journal of the Senate. 27th Cong., 3d Sess. 8vo. 1842–43.
*247	3	Journal of the House. 27th Cong., 3d Sess. 8vo. 1842–43.
*247	4	Senate Documents. 27th Cong., 3d Sess. 4 vols. 8vo. 1842–43.
*247	5	Reports of Committees. 27th Cong., 3d Sess. 4 vols. 8vo. 1842–43.
*247	6	Executive Documents. 28th Cong., 1st Sess. 6 vols. 8vo. 1843–44.
*248	1	Executive Documents. 28th Cong., 1st Sess. (Vols. 5, 6.) 2 vols. 8vo. 1843–44.
*248	2	Journal of the Senate. 28th Cong., 1st Sess. 8vo. 1843–44.
*248	3	Journal of the House. 28th Cong., 1st Sess. 8vo. 1843–44.

Shelf.	No.	
		UNITED STATES Documents, *continued.*
*248	4	Journal of the House. 28th Cong., 1st Sess. 8vo. 1843–44.
*248	5	Senate Documents. 28th Cong., 1st Sess. 7 vols. 8vo. 1843–44.
*248	6	Reports of Committees. 28th Cong., 1st Sess. 3 vols. 8vo. 1843–44.
*248	7	Reports of Committees. 28th Cong., 1st Sess. (Vols. 2, 3.) 2 vols. 8vo. 1843–44.
*249	1	Executive Documents. 28th Cong., 2d Sess. 4 vols. 8vo. 1844–45. (Vol. 4 has two parts.)
*249	2	Executive Documents. 28th Cong., 2d Sess. 4 vols. 8vo. 1844–45. (Vol. 4 has two parts.)
*249	3	Journal of the Senate. 28th Cong., 2d Sess. 8vo. 1844–45.
*249	4	Journal of the Senate. 28th Cong., 2d Sess. 8vo. 1844–45.
*249	5	Journal of the House. 28th Cong., 2d Sess. 8vo. 1844–45.
*249	6	Journal of the House. 28th Cong., 2d Sess. 8vo. 1844–45.
		Senate Documents. 28th Cong., 2d Sess. 9 vols. 8vo. 1844–45.
*249	7	Vols. 1, 2.
*250	1	,, 3, 7, 8–11. (Vol. 10 has two parts.)
*250	2	Senate Documents. 28th Cong., 2d Sess. (Vols. 1–3, 7–11.) 9 vols. 8vo. 1844–45. (Vol. 10 has two parts.)
*250	3	Reports of Committees. 28th Cong., 2d Sess. 8vo. 1844–45.
*250	4	Reports of Committees. 28th Cong., 2d Sess. 8vo. 1844–45.
		Executive Documents. 29th Cong., 1st Sess. 8 vols. 8vo. 1845–46.
*250	5	Vols. 1, 2.
*253	1	,, 3–8.
		Executive Documents. 29th Cong., 1st Sess. 8 vols. 8vo. 1845–46.
*253	2	Vols. 1–3.
*254	1	,, 4–8.
		Executive Documents. 29th Cong., 1st Sess. 8 vols. 8vo. 1845–46.
*254	2	Vols. 1–4.
*255	1	,, 5–8.
*255	2	Senate Journal. 29th Cong., 1st Sess. 8vo. 1845–46.
*255	3	Senate Journal. 29th Cong., 1st Sess. 8vo. 1845–46.
*255	4	House Journal. 29th Cong., 1st Sess. 8vo. 1845–46.
*255	5	House Journal. 29th Cong., 1st Sess. 8vo. 1845–46.
		Senate Documents. 29th Cong., 1st Sess. 9 vols. 8vo. 1845–46.
*255	6	Vols. 1–3.
*256	1	,, 4–9.
		Senate Documents. 29th Cong., 1st Sess. 9 vols. 8vo. 1845–46.
*256	2	Vols. 1–6.
*257	1	,, 7–9.

Shelf.	No.	
		UNITED STATES Documents, *continued.*
*257	2	Senate Documents. 29th Cong., 1st Sess. [Vol. 4 deficient.] 8 vols. 8vo. 1845–46.
		Reports of Committees. 29th Cong., 1st Sess. 4 vols. 8vo. 1845–46.
*257	3	Vol. 1.
*258	1	,, 2–4.
*258	2	Reports of Committees. 29th Cong., 1st Sess. 4 vols. 8vo. 1845–46.
*258	3	Reports of Committees. 29th Cong., 1st Sess. 4 vols. 8vo. 1845–46.
*260	5	Estimates of Appropriations for 29th Cong., 1st Sess. 8vo. 1845–46.
*259	1	Executive Documents. 29th Cong., 2d Sess. 4 vols. 8vo. 1846–47.
*259	2	Executive Documents. 29th Cong., 2d Sess. 4 vols. 8vo. 1846–47.
*259	3	Senate Journal. 29th Cong., 2d Sess. 8vo. 1846–47.
*259	4	Senate Journal. 29th Cong., 2d Sess. 8vo. 1846–47.
*259	5	House Journal. 29th Cong., 2d Sess. 8vo. 1846–47.
		Senate Documents. 29th Cong., 2d Sess. 3 vols. 8vo.
*259	6	Vol. 1. [1846–47.
*260	1	,, 2, 3.
*260	2	Senate Documents. 29th Cong., 2d Sess. 3 vols. 8vo. 1846–47.
*260	3	Reports of Committees. 29th Cong., 2d Sess. 8vo. 1846–47.
*260	4	Reports of Committees. 29th Cong., 2d Sess. 8vo. 1846–47.
		Executive Documents. 30th Cong., 1st Sess. 9 vols. 8vo. 1847–48.
*260	6	Vols. 1–4.
*263	1	,, 5–9.
*263	2	Executive Documents. 30th Cong., 1st Sess. Vols. 1, 3, 9. 3 vols. 8vo. 1847–48.
*263	3	Senate Journal. 30th Cong., 1st Sess. 8vo. 1847–48.
*263	4	House Journal. 30th Cong., 1st Sess. 8vo. 1847–48.
		Senate Documents. 30th Cong., 1st Sess. 8 vols. 8vo. 1847–48.
*263	5	Vols. 1–3.
*264	2	,, 4–8.
*264	3	Senate Reports. 30th Cong., 1st Sess. 8vo. 1847–48.
*264	4	Senate Miscellaneous. 30th Cong., 1st Sess. 8vo. 1847–48.
		Report of Committees. 30th Cong., 1st Sess. 4 vols. 8vo. 1847–48.
*264	5	Vols. 1–3.
*265	1	,, 4.

Shelf.	No.	
		UNITED STATES Documents, *continued.*
*265	2	Report of Committees. 30th Cong., 1st Sess. 4 vols. 8vo. 1847–48.
*265	3	House Miscellaneous. 30th Cong., 1st Sess. 8vo. 1847–48.
*265	4	House Miscellaneous. 30th Cong., 1st Sess. 8vo. 1847–48.
		Executive Documents. 30th Cong., 2d Sess. 7 vols. 8vo. 1848–49.
*265	5	Vols. 1–3.
*266	1	,, 4–7.
*266	2	Executive Documents. 30th Cong., 2d Sess. Vols. 1, 2, 3, 5. 4 vols. 8vo. 1848–49.
*266	3	Senate Journal. 30th Cong., 2d Sess. 8vo. 1848–49.
*266	4	House Journal. 30th Cong., 2d Sess. 8vo. 1848–49.
*266	5	House Journal. 30th Cong., 2d Sess. 8vo. 1848–49.
		Senate Documents. 30th Cong., 2d Sess. 4 vols. 8vo.
*266	6	Vols. 2, 3, 4. [1848–49.
*267	1	Duplicate of vol. 2.
*267	2	Senate Miscellaneous. 30th Cong., 2d Sess. 2 vols. 8vo. 1848–49.
*267	3	Senate Reports. 30th Cong., 2d Sess. 8vo. 1848–49.
*267	4	Reports of Committees. 30th Cong., 2d Sess. 2 vols. 8vo. 1848–49.
*267	5	House Miscellaneous. 30th Cong., 2d Sess. 8vo. 1848–49.
*267	6	Senate Special Session. 8vo. 1849.
		Senate Documents. 31st Cong., 1st Sess. 2 vols. 8vo.
*267	7	Vols. 11, 12. [1849–50.
*267	8	,, 11, 12.
		Executive Documents. 31st Cong., 2d Sess. 10 vols. 8vo. 1850–51.
*267	9	Vols. 1–5.
*268	1	Vol. 6 (parts 1, 2); vol. 7 (1, 2); vol. 8.
*268	2	Senate Journal. 31st Cong., 2d Sess. 8vo. 1850–51.
*268	3	House Journal. 31st Cong., 2d Sess. 8vo. 1850–51.
*268	4	Senate Documents. 31st Cong., 2d Sess. 5 vols. 8vo. 1850–51.
*268	5	Senate Reports. 31st Cong., 2d Sess. 8vo. 1850–51.
*268	6	Senate Miscellaneous. 31st Cong., 2d Sess. 8vo. 1850–51.
*268	7	Reports of Committees. 31st Cong., 2d Sess. 8vo. 1850–51.
*268	8	House Miscellaneous. 31st Con., 2d Sess. 8vo. 1850–51.
		Senate Documents. 32d Cong., Special Sess. 1851.
*269	1	Vol. 1.
*269	2	,, 1.
*269	3	,, 3.
*269	4	,, 3.

Shelf.	No.	
		UNITED STATES Documents, *continued.*
		Executive Documents. 32d Cong., 1st Sess. 19 vols. 8vo. 1851–52.
*269	5	Vols. 1, 2 (in 3 parts); vols. 3, 4 (2 parts); vols. 5–9, part 1 of vol. 10.
*270	1	Part 2 of vol. 10; vols. 11–15.
		Senate Documents. 32d Cong., 1st Sess. 16 vols. 8vo. 1851–52.
*270	4	Vols. 1–4; vol. 5, part 2.
*273	1	,, 6–16.
*270	2	Senate Journal. 32d Cong., 1st Sess. 8vo. 1851–52.
*270	3	House Journal. 32d Cong., 1st Sess. 8vo. 1851–52.
*273	2	Senate Reports. 32d Cong., 1st Sess. 2 vols. 8vo. 1851–52.
*274	1	Senate Miscellaneous. 32d Cong., 1st Sess. 8vo. 1851–52.
*274	2	Reports of Committees. 32d Cong., 1st Sess. 8vo. 1851–52.
*274	3	House Miscellaneous. 32d Cong., 1st Sess. 8vo. 1851–52.
*203	8	Index to Executive Documents and Reports to Committees. 8vo. 1832.
*203	7	Index to House Documents, 1831–39. 8vo. 1840.
*212	16	Acts of Congress, 1789. Folio. n. d.
*281	7	American Archives, 1774–76. 6 vols. folio. 1837–46.
*281	8	American Archives. 5th series, 1776. Folio. 1848.
		American State Papers. 21 vols. folio. 1832–34.
*232	5	Claims. Folio. 1834.
*222	9	Commerce and Navigation. Vol. 1. Folio. 1832.
*232	1	Commerce and Navigation. Vol. 2. Folio. 1834.
*222	8	Finance. 3 vols. folio. 1832–34.
*222	6	Foreign Relations. 4 vols. folio. 1832–34.
*222	7	Indian Affairs. 2 vols. folio. 1832–34.
*232	4	Military Affairs. 2 vols. folio. 1832–34.
*232	7	Miscellaneous. 2 vols. folio. 1834.
*232	3	Naval Affairs. Folio. 1834.
*232	6	Post Office. Folio. 1834.
*232	2	Public Lands. 3 vols. folio. 1832–34.
*292	1	Annals of Congress, 1789–97. 12 vols. 8vo. 1834–39.
*394	6	Catalogue of the Library of Congress. 8vo. 1840.
*281	2	Census (sixth). Folio. 1840.
281	3	Census (sixth). Folio. 1840.
281	4	Census (sixth): Compendium. Folio. 1841.
*281	5	Census (sixth): Compendium. Folio. 1841.
*281	6	Census (sixth): Compendium. Folio. 1841.
*282	10	Census (seventh). 4to. 1853.
282	11	Census (seventh). 4to. 1853.
283	8	Census (seventh), Abstract of. 8vo. 1853.
*282	6	Census of Pensioners. 4to. 1841.
*339	13	Collection of Precedents from 1st to 11th Congress. 8vo. 1811.

Shelf.	No.	
		UNITED STATES Documents, *continued.*
*338	1	Contested Elections. 1789–1834. 8vo. 1834.
*338	2	Contested Elections. 1789–1834. 8vo. 1834.
*334	1	Debates of Congress. Old series, 1789–91. 2 vols. 8vo. 1834.
*334	2	Debates of Congress. Vol. 1; vol. 2 (part 2); vol. 2 (part 2); vol. 3. 4 vols. 8vo. 1825–29.
		Debates of Congress. 1824–37. 14 vols. 8vo. 1825–37.
*334	3	Vols. 1–7.
*335	1	,, 8–13 (part 1).
*336	1	,, 13 (part 2); vol. 14.
*203	4	Debates on the British Treaty. 8vo. 1796.
*204	1	Digest of Commercial Regulations of Foreign Countries. 3 vols. 8vo. 1833.
*275	15	Digest of Patents, 1790–1839. 8vo. 1840.
		Diplomatic Correspondence of the American Revolution. Edited by J. Sparks. 12 vols. 8vo. 1829–30.
*468	2	Vols. 1– 9.
*469	25	,, 10–12.
174	2	Diplomatic Correspondence. 12 vols. 8vo. 1829–30.
*204	2	Executive Proceedings of the Senate, 1789–1829. 3 vols. 8vo. 1828–29.
*336	11	Index to Laws. 8vo. 1828.
*344	10	Indian Treaties. Laws relating to Indian Affairs. 8vo. 1826.
*345	1	Laws. Vols. 1–8, 19–25. 15 vols. 8vo. 1815–39.
*337	2	Laws relating to the Public Lands. 8vo. 1828.
338	8	Laws relating to the Public Lands. 8vo. 1828.
*338	3	Laws relating to Public Lands. 2 vols. 8vo. 1838.
338	4	Laws relating to Public Lands. 2 vols. 8vo. 1838.
338	7	Laws relating to Public Lands. 2 vols. 8vo. 1838.
*222	5	Letters from the Secretary of the Treasury. Folio. 1796.
*276	7	Messages of the President, with other Documents. 31st Cong., 1st Sess. 3 vols. 8vo. 1849–50.
*276	8	Messages of the President, with other Documents. 31st Cong., 1st Sess. 3 vols. 8vo. 1849–50.
*277	1	Messages of the President, with other Documents. 31st Cong., 1st Sess. 3 vols. 8vo. 1849–50.
*277	5	Message from the President on California and New Mexico. 8vo. 1850.
*277	2	Message of the President, with other Documents. 31st Cong., 2d Sess. 8vo. 1850–51.
*277	3	Message of the President, with other Documents. 31st Cong., 2d Sess. 8vo. 1850–51.
*277	4	Message of the President, with other Documents. 31st Cong., 2d Sess. 8vo. 1850–51.
*277	6	Message of the President, with other Documents. 32d Cong., 1st Sess. 3 vols. 8vo. 1851.

Shelf.	No.	
		UNITED STATES Documents, *continued.*
*277	7	Message of the President, with other Documents. 32d Cong., 2d Sess. Vol. 2. 1852–53.
*278	1	Message of the President, with other Documents. 33d Cong., 1st Sess. 3 vols. 8vo. 1853–54.
*345	2	Opinions of the Attorney-General. 8vo. 1841.
*275	12	Patent Office Reports for 1847. 8vo. 1848.
*275	13	Patent Office Reports for 1848. 8vo. 1849.
275	14	Patent Office Reports for 1848. 8vo. 1849.
*275	1	Patent Office Reports for 1849–50. Mechanical. 8vo. 1850.
275	2	Patent Office Reports for 1849–50. Mechanical. 8vo. 1850.
*275	3	Patent Office Reports for 1849–50. Agricultural. 8vo. 1850.
*171	8	Patent Office Reports for 1849–50. Arts and Manufactures. 8vo. 1850.
*276	5	Patent Office Reports for 1852–53. Agricultural. 8vo. 1853.
*171	7	Patent Office Reports for 1852–53. Arts and Manufactures. 8vo. 1853.
*276	6	Patent Office Reports for 1852–53. Arts and Manufactures. 8vo. 1853.
*272	13	Plates to Magnetic and Meteorological Observations. 8vo. 1845.
*212	1	Receipts and Expenditures. Folio. 1813–15.
*212	2	Receipts and Expenditures. Folio. 1816–18.
*212	3	Receipts and Expenditures. Folio. 1819–21.
*212	4	Receipts and Expenditures. Folio. 1822.
*212	5	Receipts and Expenditures. Folio. 1823.
*212	6	Receipts and Expenditures. Folio. 1824.
212	7	Receipts and Expenditures. Folio. 1824.
*212	8	Receipts and Expenditures. Folio. 1825.
212	9	Receipts and Expenditures. Folio. 1825.
*212	10	Receipts and Expenditures. Folio. 1826.
212	11	Receipts and Expenditures. Folio. 1826.
*212	12	Receipts and Expenditures. Folio. 1827.
212	13	Receipts and Expenditures. Folio. 1827.
*212	14	Receipts and Expenditures. Folio. 1828.
212	15	Receipts and Expenditures. Folio. 1828.
*274	5	Receipts and Expenditures. 8vo. 1829.
*274	6	Receipts and Expenditures. 8vo. 1830.
*274	7	Receipts and Expenditures. 8vo. 1831.
*274	8	Receipts and Expenditures. 8vo. 1832.
*274	9	Receipts and Expenditures. 8vo. 1833.
*274	10	Receipts and Expenditures. 8vo. 1834.
*274	13	Receipts and Expenditures. 8vo. 1841.
*274	12	Receipts and Expenditures. 8vo. 1843.

Shelf.	No.	
		United States Documents, *continued.*
*274	11	Receipts and Expenditures. 8vo. 1844.
*663	5	Register of Officers and Agents. 8vo. 1839.
*660	6	Register of Officers and Agents. 12mo. 1841.
*663	9	Register of Officers and Agents. 8vo. 1853.
*650	1	Register of Officers and Agents. 12mo. 1834.
*283	5	Report on the Amazon Valley, by Herndon. 8vo. 1853.
*283	6	Report on the Amazon Valley, by Herndon. Maps. 8vo. 1853.
*276	3	Report on the Coast Survey, by the Superintendent. 8vo. 1852.
276	4	Report on the Coast Survey, by the Superintendent. 8vo. 1852.
*283	7	Report on the Colonial and Lake Trade, by Andrews. 8vo. 1853.
*275	9	Report on Commerce and Navigation, 1850. 8vo. 1851.
*275	10	Report on Commerce and Navigation, 1851. 8vo. 1852.
*275	11	Report on Commerce and Navigation, 1852. 8vo. 1853.
*274	4	Report on the Finances, 1790–1836. 3 vols. 8vo. 1837.
*203	6	Report on the Finances, 1790–1828. 2 vols. 8vo. 1828–29.
*275	4	Report on the Finances, 1849–50. 8vo.
*275	5	Report on the Finances, 1851–52. 8vo. 1853.
275	6	Report on the Finances, 1851–52. 8vo. 1853.
275	7	Report on the Finances, 1851–52. 8vo. 1853.
*275	8	Report on the Finances, 1852–53. 8vo.
*283	3	Report on Great Salt Lake, by Stansbury. 8vo. 1853.
*283	4	Report on Great Salt Lake, by Stansbury, Maps to. 8vo. 1853.
*276	1	Report on Lake Superior, The Geology of, by Foster and Whitney. 2 vols. 8vo. 1850–51.
*276	2	Report on Lake Superior, The Geology of, by Foster and Whitney, Maps to. 8vo. 1850–51.
*282	1	Report on Wisconsin, Iowa, and Minnesota, Geological Survey of, by Owen. 4to. 1852.
282	2	Report on Wisconsin, Iowa, and Minnesota, Geological Survey of, by Owen. 4to. 1852.
282	3	Report on Wisconsin, Iowa, and Minnesota, Geological Survey of, by Owen, Illustrations to. 4to. 1852.
*282	4	Report on Wisconsin, Iowa, and Minnesota, Geological Survey of, by Owen, Illustrations to. 4to. 1852.
*468	1	State Papers and Public Documents. 12 vols. 8vo. 1819.
174	1	State Papers and Public Documents. 12 vols. 8vo. 1819.
*502	14	Smithsonian Institution. Fifth Annual Report. 8vo. 1851.
*282	5	Statistics, 1790–1830. Folio. 1835.
*201	3	Statistics, 1840. Folio. 1841.
*201	4	Statistics, 1840. Folio. 1841.
*333	1	Statutes at Large. 8 vols. 8vo. 1848–50.
*433	9	Tariffs. 8vo. 1850.

Shelf.	No.	
16	9	UNITED STATES Anti-Masonic Convention, Proceedings of the. 8vo. 1830.
*325	8	——— Literary Gazette. 1 vol. 4to. 1824, 1825.
*325	2	——— Literary Gazette. 4 vols. 8vo. 1825–27.
108	4	——— Sketches of Life and Manners in. 12mo. 1826.
176	17	——— Republic. 12mo. 1848.
8	21	——— and Great Britain, War between, 1812. 12mo. 1815.
56	2	UPDIKE (W.) Rhode Island Bar. 12mo. 1842.
56	10	UPHAM (T. C.) Life of Madame Guyon, and Fenelon. 2 vols. 12mo. 1851.
185	14	——— Mental Philosophy. 2 vols. 12mo. 1848.
98	19	——— Mental Action. 18mo. 1848.
164	12	UPTON (J.) Observations on Shakespeare. 8vo. 1748.
*603	9	URE (A.) Dictionary of Arts, Manufactures, and Mines. 8vo. 1851.
85	4	URQUHART (D.) Pillars of Hercules. 2 vols. 12mo. 1850.
123	17	USE of Sunshine. 12mo. 1852.

V.

Shelf.	No.	
455	5	VALDENSES, Authentic Details of. 8vo. 1827.
*646	21	VALENTIN (G.) Physiology. 8vo. 1853.
*626	6	VALLEIX (F. L. T.) Guide du Médecin Praticien. 5 vols. 8vo. 1853.
137	6	VALLEY of the Shenandoah. 2 vols. 12mo. 1834.
485	17	VALPY. Greek Grammar. 8vo. 1814.
39	6	VANE (C. W.) War in Germany and France, 1813–14. 16mo. 1831.
38	1	——— Story of the Peninsular War. 12mo. 1848.
513	4	VANS (W.) Exposition of the Claims of. 2 vols. 8vo. 1837.
539	14	VARNHAGEN VON ENSE. Sketches of German Life. 12mo. 1847.
407	2	VASARI (G.) Lives of Painters, &c. 6 vols. post 8vo. 1850–51.
510	15	VEGETABLE Substances used for the Food of Man. 2 vols. 18mo. 1846.
100	6	——— Substances used for the Food of Man. 18mo. 1840.
560	5	——— Substances, Materials of Manufactures. 12mo. n. d.
560	7	——— Substances used in the Arts and Domestic Economy. 12mo. n. d.
*564	4	VELPEAU (A. A. L. M.) Operative Surgery, Mott's edition. 3 vols. 8vo. 1846–47.
*671	6	——— Operative Surgery, plates. 4to. 1846–47.
*626	8	——— Surgical Anatomy. 2 vols. 8vo. 1830.
160	12	VENETIAN History. 2 vols. 18mo. 1831.
89	9	——— History. 2 vols. 18mo. 1846.

Shelf.	No.	
*473	7	VENEZUELA. Mensage del Poder ejecutivo y Contestataciones. 8vo. 1842.
486	3	VERICOUR (L. R. de). Modern French Literature. 12mo. 1848.
339	11	VERPLANCK (G. C.) Doctrine of Contracts. 8vo. n. d.
118	5	VERRI (A.) Roman Nights. 2 vols. 12mo. 1825.
520	11	VESTAL. 12mo. 1830.
509	6	VESTIGES of Creation. 18mo. n. d.
503	12	VIART (M.) Le Cuisinier Royal. 8vo. 1844.
*594	2	VIDAL (A.) On Venereal. 8vo. 1854.
41	4	VIEUSSIEUX (A.) History of Switzerland. 8vo. 1840.
500	14	——— Sayings and Deeds of Bonaparte. 2 vols. 18mo. 1846.
184	18	VILLERS (C.) Reformation by Luther. 8vo. 1807.
*430	9	VILLAMEDIANA (J. de T.) Obras. Small 4to. 1634.
179	17	VINET (A.) Pastoral Theology. 12mo. 1853.
486	22	VIRGILIUS (P. M.) Georgics of, translated by Nevile. 12mo. 1767.
487	21	——— Opera. 12mo. 1715.
484	14	——— Works, translated by Davidson. 2 vols. 8vo. 1811.
410	14	——— Works, translated by Davidson and Buckley. Post 8vo. 1850.
487	22	——— Works, translated by Dryden. 3 vols. 18mo. 1806.
120	6	——— Works, translated by Dryden. 2 vols. 18mo. n. d.
*454	12	VIRGINIA, History and Present State of. 8vo. 1705.
*433	6	——— Historical Society. Early Discoveries, and Voyages to America. 8vo. 1848.
517	5	VOLNEY (C. F.) Les Ruines. 8vo. 1822.
66	3	VOLTAIRE (M. de). Age of Louis XIV. and XV. 3 vols. 8vo. 1779–81.

W.

Shelf.	No.	
27	9	WACHSMUTH (W.) Antiquities of the Greeks. 2 vols. 8vo. 1837.
473	9	WADDINGTON (G.) Visit to Ethiopia. 4to. 1822.
24	15	WAGSTAFF (W. R.) History of the Friends. 8vo. 1845.
172	8	WAKEFIELD (E. G.) England and America. 8vo. 1834.
442	7	WALDEGRAVE (J., Earl of). Memoirs. 4to. 1821.
67	20	WALDO (S. P.) Life of Stephen Decatur. 12mo. 1821.
508	4	WALKER (A.) On Beauty. 12mo. 1843.
507	26	——— On Intermarriage. 12mo. 1843.
498	6	——— On Pathology. 12mo. 1842.
508	23	WALKER (D.) Manly Exercises. 16mo. 1837.
480	3	WALKER (H.) Expedition to Canada. 8vo. 1720.
485	10	WALKER (J.) Elocution. 8vo. 1806.
485	9	——— Rhetorical Grammar. 8vo. 1807.
*660	13	——— Rhyming Dictionary. 12mo. 1819.
66	18	WALKER (Jona.) Trial and Imprisonment of. 12mo. 1845.

Shelf.	No.	
35	6	WALLACE (R. G.) Memoirs of India. 8vo. 1824.
150	6	WALLER (E.) Poetical Works. 18mo. 1784.
85	17	WALLIS (S. T.) Glimpses of Spain. 16mo. 1849.
86	13	——— Spain: her Institutions. 12mo. 1853.
523	3	WALPOLE (H.) Letters to Horace Mann. 4 vols. 8vo. 1843–44.
523	2	——— Letters. 6 vols. 8vo. 1840.
445	4	——— Memoirs of. 2 vols. 8vo. 1851.
16	12	WALSH (R. jun.) Appeal from Great Britain. 8vo. 1819.
171	10	——— On the French Government. 8vo. 1810.
45	5	——— On the French Government. 8vo. 1810.
480	4	WALSH (R.) Notices of Brazil. 12mo. 1831.
*614	3	WALSHE (W. H.) On the Heart and Lungs. 12mo. 1851.
137	16	WALTHAM. 12mo. 1833.
*584	4	WALTON (H. H.) Operative Ophthalmic Surgery. 8vo. 1853.
506	4	WALTON (I.) & COTTON. Complete Angler. 12mo. 1852.
538	29	——— Complete Angler. 12mo. 1853.
496	10	——— Complete Angler. 12mo. 1842.
77	5	WALTON (I.) Lives of Donne, &c. 12mo. 1846.
486	27	WANOSTROCHT (N.) French Grammar. 12mo. 1838.
7	7	WARBURTON (E.) Conquest of Canada. 2 vols. 12mo. 1850.
62	11	——— Horace Walpole. 2 vols. 8vo. 1852.
107	5	——— Hochelaga. 12mo. 1846.
96	10	——— Crescent and Cross. 12mo. 1850.
196	6	WARBURTON (W.) Tracts. 8vo. 1789.
*477	11	WARD (A. H.) History of Shrewsbury. 8vo. 1847.
*479	8	——— Ward Family. 8vo. 1851.
85	10	WARD (F. de W.) India and the Hindoos. 12mo. 1851.
141	21	WARD (R. P.) (Ed.) Chatsworth. 8vo. 1844.
111	18	——— De Vere. 4 vols. 12mo. 1827.
117	7	——— De Vere. 2 vols. 12mo. 1831.
111	3	——— Pictures of the World. 3 vols. 12mo. 1839.
128	1	——— Tremaine. 3 vols. 12mo. 1833.
7	11	WARD (N.) Simple Cobbler of Agawam. 12mo. 1843.
173	17	WARDEN (D. B.) Consular Establishments. 8vo. 1813.
60	25	WARDEN (W.) Letters on Buonaparte. 16mo. 1817.
*646	15	WARDROP (J.) Diseases of the Heart. 8vo. 1851.
180	11	WARE (H.) Inquiry into the Evidences, &c. of Religion. 2 vols. 12mo. 1842.
171	28	WARE (H. jun.) Formation of Christian Character. 18mo. 1831.
199	2	——— Works. 4 vols. 12mo. 1846.
188	8	——— Writings of Priestley, with Memoir. 12mo. 1834.
76	10	WARE (J.) Life of Henry Ware, jun. 2 vols. 12mo. 1849.
136	14	WARE (W.) Aurelian. 2 vols. 12mo. 1849.
84	5	——— European Capitals. 12mo. 1851.
507	2	——— Lectures on Washington Allston. 12mo. 1852.
136	13	——— Zenobia. 2 vols. 12mo. 1850.

Shelf.	No.	
*462	8	WARING (E. S.) History of the Mahrattas. 4to. 1810.
175	17	WARNER (H. W.) Liberties of America. 12mo. 1853.
84	18	WARNER (R.) Tour through England and Scotland. 2 vols. 8vo. 1802.
125	13	WARNER. Dollars and Cents. 2 vols. 12mo. 1852.
125	10	——— Queechy. 2 vols. 12mo. 1853.
121	21	——— Wide, Wide World. 2 vols. 12mo. 1852.
*666	13	WARREN (E.) Boylston Prize Dissertations. 8vo. 1840.
404	8	WARREN (J. C.) Address to the Society of Natural History. 8vo. 1853.
507	27	——— Etherization. 12mo. 1848.
*671	3	——— Mastodon Giganteus of North America. 4to. 1852.
*502	9	——— Tumours. 8vo. 1839.
87	14	WARREN (J. E.) Para, or Adventures on the Amazon. 12mo. 1851.
107	19	——— Para, or Adventures on the Amazon. 12mo. 1851.
4	7	WARREN (M.) History of American Revolution. 3 vols. 8vo. 1805.
129	14	WARREN (S.) Diary of a Physician. 3 vols. 18mo. n. d.
186	22	——— Duties of Solicitors. 16mo. 1849.
129	1	——— Lily and the Bee. 16mo. 1851.
126	16	——— Now and Then. 12mo. 1848.
158	21	WARRENIANA. 16mo. 1851.
115	12	WARS of our Times. 2 vols. 12mo. 1829.
485	15	WARTON (J.) Genius and Writings of Pope. 2 vols. 8vo. 1762–82.
75	7	WARWICK (Earl of). History of. 8vo. 1708.
13	11	WASHBURN (E.) Judicial History of Massachusetts. 8vo. 1840.
*80	3	WASHINGTON (G.) Epistles. 8vo. 1796.
*392	14	——— Fac-similes of Letters. 4to. 1844.
515	5	——— Letters. 8vo. 1796.
6	10	——— Letters to Joseph Reed. 8vo. 1852.
518	2	——— Political Legacies. 8vo. 1800.
*485	18	——— Political Legacies. 8vo. 1800.
5	10	——— Writings, with Life by Sparks. 12 vols. 8vo. 1837.
*479	11	——— Writings, with Life by Sparks. 12 vols. 8vo. 1838.
74	7	WASHINGTON and the Generals of American Revolution. 2 vols. 12mo. 1848.
*336	12	WASHINGTON City, Burch's Digest of Laws. 8vo. 1823.
450	10	WATERHOUSE (G. R.) Pouched Animals. (Vol. 24, Nat. Lib.) 16mo. n. d.
*623	4	WATERSTON (W.) Cyclopædia of Commerce. 8vo. n. d.
184	8	WATERWORTH (J.) Council of Trent. 8vo. 1848.
122	4	WATSON (H. C.) Nights in a Block-house. 8vo. 1853.
188	19	WATSON (R.) Apology for the Bible. 16mo. 1796.
196	5	——— Theological Tracts. 6 vols. 8vo. 1785.
54	8	WATSON (Robert). History of Reign of Philip II. 8vo. 1818.

Shelf.	No.	
66	1	WATSON (R.) History of the Reign of Philip III. 8vo. 1818.
*544	9	WATSON (T.) Practice of Physic. 8vo. 1853.
186	2	WATTS (I.) Logic. 12mo. 1806.
196	13	——— Philosophical Essays. 8vo. 1793.
118	16	WAVERLEY Anecdotes. 2 vols. 12mo. 1833.
530	5	——— Novels, Letters on the. 12mo. 1822.
178	16	WAYLAND (F.) Discourses. 12mo. 1833.
177	11	——— Elements of Moral Science. 12mo. 1851.
51	10	——— Life of Adoniram Judson. 2 vols. 12mo. 1853.
200	11	——— Limitations of Human Responsibility. 16mo. 1838.
176	7	——— Political Economy. 12mo. 1851.
186	15	——— Pursuit of Knowledge. 2 vols. 12mo. n. d.
179	12	——— University Sermons. 12mo. 1850.
87	8	WAYLAND (J.) Life in England. 18mo. 1848.
158	8	WEBB (T.) Collection of Epitaphs. 12mo. 1775.
509	19	WEBB (T. S.) Freemason's Monitor. 12mo. 1818.
504	10	WEBBER (S.) Mathematics. 2 vols. 8vo. 1808.
41	13	WEBER (G.) Outlines of Universal History. 8vo. 1854.
70	20	WEBSTER (D.) Life of. 12mo. 1853.
51	12	——— Memorial of. 8vo. 1853.
*616	1	——— Memorial of. 8vo. 1853.
12	17	——— Obituary Addresses on the Death of. 8vo. 1853.
76	18	——— Obituary Addresses on the Death of. 8vo. 1853.
483	5	——— Speeches and Forensic Arguments. 8vo. 1830.
*383	1	——— Works. 6 vols. 8vo. 1851.
523	1	——— Works. 6 vols. 8vo. 1853.
513	1	——— Works. 6 vols. 8vo. 1853.
513	2	——— Works. 6 vols. 8vo. 1853.
*453	2	——— Works. 6 vols. 8vo. 1853.
186	1	WEBSTER (N.) Letters to a Young Gentleman. 8vo. 1823.
*411	1	——— Dictionary. 4to. 1853.
525	2	WEBSTER (N. jun.) Essays. 8vo. 1790.
485	5	——— On the English Language. 8vo. 1789.
418	3	WELLESLEY (A.) Duke of Wellington, Life of. Post 8vo. 1852.
131	12	WELLMONT (E.) Uncle Sam's Palace. 12mo. 1853.
506	20	WELLS (D. A.) Annual of Scientific Discovery. 12mo. 1850.
505	16	——— Annual of Scientific Discovery. 12mo. 1851.
506	19	——— Annual of Scientific Discovery. 12mo. 1852.
540	6	WERNER (H.) Guardian Spirits. 12mo. 1847.
160	15	WESLEY (J.) Natural Philosophy. 3 vols. 18mo. 1836.
182	4	——— Works. 7 vols. 8vo. 1835.

Vols. 1, 2. Sermons.
3, 4. Journal.
5, 6. Miscellaneous.
7. Letters and Miscellaneous.

594	1	WEST (C.) Diseases of Infancy and Childhood. 8vo. 1854.
186	8	WEST (J.) Letters to a Young Lady. 8vo. 1806.
*614	4	WHAT to Observe in Medical Cases. 12mo. 1853.

Shelf.	No.	
200	8	WHATELY (R.) Christianity Independent. 12mo. 1837.
669	8	——— English Synonymes. 12mo. 1852.
193	5	——— Essays, second series. 8vo. 1845.
186	21	——— Historic Doubts. 16mo. 1853.
190	17	——— Logic. 18mo. 1852.
487	19	——— Rhetoric. 18mo. n. d.
399	8	WHEATLY (C.) Book of Common Prayer. Post 8vo. 1850.
444	7	WHEATON (H.) Life and Writings of Pinkney. 8vo. 1826.
348	1	——— On International Law. 8vo. 1846.
51	19	WHEATON (R.) Memoir of. 16mo. 1854.
497	18	WHEELER (G.) Rural Homes. 12mo. 1851.
419	9	WHEWELL (W.) Astronomy and General Physics. Post 8vo. 1852.
520	16	WHIPPLE (E. P.) Essays and Reviews. 2 vols. 16mo. 1851.
518	6	——— Essays and Reviews. 2 vols. 12mo. 1848.
529	11	——— Lectures. 16mo. 1850.
445	9	WHISTON (W.) Life and Writings. 3 vols. 8vo. 1749–50.
525	9	WHITE (C.) Essays in Literature and Ethics. 12mo. 1853.
508	5	WHITE (G.) Natural History of Selborne. 12mo. 1850.
418	4	——— Natural History of Selborne. Post 8vo. 1851.
100	12	——— Natural History of Selborne. 18mo. 1847.
509	9	——— Natural History of Selborne. 18mo. 1832.
52	7	WHITE (G. S.) Memoir of S. Slater. 8vo. 1836.
153	5	WHITE (H. K.) Complete Works. 8vo. 1831.
158	17	——— Life and Writings. 16mo. 1827.
70	5	——— Memoir and Remains. 12mo. 1825.
155	8	——— Memoir and Remains. 12mo. 1853.
148	13	——— Poetical Works. 16mo. 1840.
200	7	WHITE (J. B.) Evidence against Catholicism. 12mo. 1835.
189	26	WHITECROSS (J.) Doctrines and Duties of Religion. 16mo. n.d.
180	15	WHITEFIELD (G.) Eighteen Sermons. 12mo. 1820.
189	10	——— Eighteen Sermons. 12mo. 1820.
*604	13	WHITEHEAD (J.) On Abortion and Sterility. 8vo. 1848.
*646	5	——— Hereditary Diseases. 8vo. 1851.
472	5	WHITELOCKE (B.) On the Government of England. 2 vols. 4to. 1766.
141	23	WHITMORE (W.) Ella Winston. 8vo. n. d.
135	10	WHITTIER (J. G.) Margaret Smith's Journal. 16mo. 1849.
165	5	——— Old Portraits and Modern Sketches. 16mo. 1850.
164	17	——— Poems. 8vo. 1849.
166	8	——— Songs of Labor, &c. 16mo. 1851.
*15	12	WHITMAN (Z. G.) History of the Ancient and Honourable Artillery Company. 8vo. 1820.
262	11	WHYTT (R.) Works. 4to. 1768.
484	5	WICKHAM (H. L.) & CRAMER (J. A.) Passage of Hannibal over the Alps. 8vo. 1828.
492	8	WIESBACH (J.) Mechanics of Machinery and Engineering. 2 vols. 8vo. 1848–49.

Shelf.	No.	
167	13	WIELAND (C. M.) Oberon, transl. by Sotheby. 12mo. 1810.
171	14	WIGHT (O. W.) Philosophy of Sir Wm. Hamilton. 8vo. 1853.
56	6	WILBERFORCE (R. T.) Life of W. Wilberforce. 5 vols. 12mo. 1838.
189	30	WILBERFORCE (W.) View of Christianity. 16mo. n. d.
540	14	WILDE (R. H.) Love, Madness, &c. of Torquato Tasso. 2 vols. 12mo. 1842.
*584	13	WILDE (W. R.) Diseases of the Ear. 8vo. 1853.
10	5	WILDER (D.) History of Leominster. 12mo. 1853.
186	19	WILDERSPIN (S.) On Education. 16mo. 1840.
102	10	WILKES (C.) United States Exploring Expedition. 5 vols. 8vo. 1851.
538	17	——— United States Exploring Expedition. 2 vols. 12mo. 1852.
102	4	——— Voyage round the World. 8vo. 1851.
68	14	WILKES (J.) Correspondence. 5 vols. 12mo. 1805.
8	14	WILKINSON (E.) Letters of. 12mo. 1839.
*475	9	WILKINSON (J.) Memoirs of my Times. 3 vols. 8vo. 1816.
58	6	WILKINSON (J. J. G.) Emanuel Swedenborg. 12mo. 1849.
506	12	——— The Human Body. 12mo. 1851.
34	3	WILKINSON (Sir J. G.) Manners and Customs of the Ancient Egyptians. 3 vols. 8vo. 1837.
464	5	——— Manners and Customs of the Ancient Egyptians. 3 vols. 8vo. 1837.
464	6	——— Manners and Customs of the Ancient Egyptians. Second Series. 2 vols. 8vo. 1841.
464	7	——— Manners and Customs of the Ancient Egyptians. Plates. 8vo. 1841.
8	4	WILLARD (E.) Last Leaves of American History. 16mo. 1849.
408	12	WILLIAM of Malmesbury's Chronicles of the Kings of England. Post 8vo. 1847.
*544	6	WILLIAMS (C. J. B.) and CLYMER (M.) On the Respiratory Organs. 8vo. 1845.
112	10	WILLIAMS (F.) Shakespeare and his Friends. 8vo. 1847.
514	5	WILLIAMS (F. S.) Our Iron Roads. 8vo. 1852.
158	5	WILLIAMS (H. M.) Poems. 2 vols. 18mo. 1786.
87	5	——— Tour in Switzerland. 2 vols. 12mo. 1798.
88	4	WILLIAMS (J.) Alexander the Great. 18mo. 1843.
160	18	——— Alexander the Great. 18mo. 1829.
283	1	WILLIAMS (J. J.) Survey of Tehuantepec Isthmus. 8vo. 1852.
*283	2	——— Maps to Tehuantepec Isthmus.
65	14	WILLIAMS (Mrs.) Biography of Barton and Olney. 12mo. 1839.
454	7	WILLIAMS (S.) History of Vermont. 2 vols. 8vo. 1809.
*664	3	WILLIAMS (S. W.) American Medical Biography. 8vo. 1845.
62	6	——— American Medical Biography. 8vo. 1845.

Shelf.	No.	
60	24	WILLIAMS (S. W.) Memoir of Rev. J. Williams. 12mo. 1837.
84	17	WILLIAMS (S. Wells). Middle Kingdom. 2 vols. 8vo. 1851.
504	13	WILLIAMS (T.) Academical Stenography. 8vo. 1826.
109	4	WILLIAMS (W.) United States Guide Book. 16mo. 1850.
16	3	WILLIAMSON (H.) History of North Carolina. 2 vols. 8vo. 1812.
454	1	WILLIAMSON (W. D.) History of Maine. 2 vols. 8vo. 1832.
*498	25	WILLICH (A. F. M.) Lectures on Diet and Regimen. 2 vols. 12mo. 1800.
131	34	WILLIS (N. P.) Fun Jottings. 12mo. 1853.
87	15	——— Health Trip to the Tropics. 12mo. 1853.
124	11	——— Hurry-graphs. 12mo. 1851.
124	9	——— Life Here and There. 12mo. 1850.
124	10	——— Pencillings by the Way. 12mo. 1852.
124	7	——— People I have Met. 12mo. 1850.
155	6	——— Poems. 12mo. 1852.
152	5	——— Poems. 8vo. 1850.
124	8	——— Rural Letters. 12mo. 1851.
483	13	WILLISTON (E. B.) Eloquence of the United States. 5 vols. 8vo. 1827.
86	7	WILLMOTT (R. A.) Summer in the Country. 16mo. 1852.
*428	6	WILSON ( ). Belphegor, or the Marriage of the Devil. 4to. 1691.
509	10	WILSON (A.) American Ornithology. 4 vols. 18mo. 1831.
503	1	——— American Ornithology. 8vo. 1853.
*282	9	——— American Ornithology. 9 vols. 4to. 1808–14.
52	14	WILSON (B.) Memoir of William White. 8vo. 1839.
*594	16	WILSON (E.) Dissector. 12mo. 1851.
497	24	——— Treatise on the Skin. 12mo. 1846.
181	21	WILSON (John). Illustrations of Unitarianism. 8vo. 1846.
181	20	——— On Grammatical Punctuation. 12mo. 1850.
650	7	WILSON (Joshua). Biographical Index to House of Commons. 16mo. 1808.
118	15	WILSON (J.) Foresters. 12mo. 1840.
155	10	——— Noctes Ambrosianæ. 4 vols. 12mo. 1843.
127	9	——— Trials of Margaret Lyndsay. 12mo. 1845.
190	29	WILSON (T.) Sacra Privata. 32mo. 1851.
443	4	WILSON (W.) Life and Times of De Foe. 3 vols. 8vo. 1830.
451	2	WIMMER (H.) Die Kirche und Schule in Nord-Amerika. 8vo. 1853.
494	12	WINCKELMANN (J.) History of Ancient Art. 8vo. 1850.
*396	2	——— History of Ancient Art. 8vo. 1850.
172	3	WINES (E. C.) Laws of the Ancient Hebrews. 8vo. 1853.
477	3	WINSOR (J.) History of Duxbury. 8vo. 1849.
*478	10	WINTHROP (J.) Journal of New England Colonies. 8vo. 1790.
*463	6	——— History of New England. 2 vols. 8vo. 1825.
1	3	——— History of New England. 2 vols. 8vo. 1853.
482	5	WINTHROP (R. C.) Addresses and Speeches. 8vo. 1852.

Shelf.	No.	
482	6	WINTHROP (R. C.) Addresses and Speeches. 8vo. 1852.
4	8	WINTERBOTHAM (W.) View of United States, &c. 4 vols. 8vo. 1796.
529	10	WIRT (W.) Letters of the British Spy. 12mo. 1832.
66	6	——— Life of Patrick Henry. 8vo. 1818.
*470	4	WISE (J.) Vindication of the Government of New England Churches. 12mo. 1772.
108	2	WISE (W. A.) Los Gringos. 12mo. 1849.
188	1	WISEMAN (N.) Lectures on the Eucharist. 12mo. 1852.
199	3	——— Lectures on Doctrines of Catholic Church. 12mo. 1851.
200	18	——— Lectures. 2 vols. 16mo. 1852.
58	5	WISNER (B. B.) Memoirs of Mrs. Huntingdon. 12mo. 1833.
171	22	WITHINGTON (W.) Growth of Thought. 12mo. 1851.
509	15	WITTICH (W.) Visit to Coast of Norway. 18mo. 1848.
500	15	——— Curiosities of Physical Geography. 2 vols. 18mo. 1853.
167	14	WOLCOTT (J.) Works of Peter Pindar, Esq. 3 vols. 12mo. 1797.
200	1	WOLF (J.) Missionary Journal. 12mo. 1824.
183	5	WOLFF (J.) Mission to Bokhara. 8vo. 1845.
452	5	WOLLASTON (W.) Religion of Nature. 4 vols. 1726.
*544	10	WOOD (G. B.) Practice of Medicine. 2 vols. 8vo. 1852.
*574	3	——— & BACHE (F.) United States Dispensatory. Ninth Edition. 8vo. 1851.
8	25	WOOD (J.) Suppressed History of John Adams's Administration. 12mo. 1846.
57	1	WOOD (M. A. E.) Letters of Royal Ladies of Great Britain. 3 vols. 12mo. 1846.
*432	2	WOOD (S. V.) Description of Shells of East England. 4to. 1848.
348	4	WOOD (W. S.) & GRAY (W.) Report of the Conspiracy Case, Michigan. 8vo. 1851.
513	3	WOODBURY (L.) Writings. 3 vols. 8vo. 1852.
107	17	WOODS (D. B.) Gold Diggings. 16mo. 1851.
445	1	WOOLRYCH (H. W.) Life of Judge Jeffreys. 8vo. 1827
508	26	WORCESTER (E. S.) Century of Inventions. 16mo. 1825.
*325	7	WORCESTER (Noah). Friend of Peace. 2 vols. 8vo. 1820.
*584	1	WORCESTER (N.) Cutaneous Diseases. 8vo. 1850.
76	16	WORDSWORTH (C.) Memoirs of Wm. Wordsworth. 2 vols. 16mo. 1851.
156	13	WORDSWORTH (W.) Excursion. 12mo. 1850.
162	8	——— Poetical Works. 8vo. 1851.
169	1	——— Poetical Works. 6 vols. 18mo. 1849.
146	1	——— Prelude. 12mo. 1850.
156	12	——— Prelude. 12mo. 1850.
510	3	WORKING Man, Memoirs of. 18mo. 1845.
123	16	WORMELEY (E.) Amabel. 12mo. 1853.

Shelf.	No.	
510	19	WORNUM (R. N.) History of Painting. 18mo. 1847.
449	5	WORSLEY (I.) American Indians, and Ten Tribes of Israel. 12mo. 1828.
500	12	WORTHIES, British. 12 vols. 18mo. 1845–47.
79	7	——— British. 12 vols. 18mo. 1845–47.
107	11	WORTLEY (M. E. S.) Travels in the United States. 12mo. 1851.
167	20	WOTY (W) Poetical Works. 12mo. 1770.
100	13	WRANGELL (F.) Expedition to the Polar Sea. 18mo. 1845.
169	10	WREATH. 18mo. 1824.
136	1	WRIGHT (F.) Few Days in Athens. 12mo. 1850.
103	7	——— Society and Manners in America. 8vo. 1821.
28	12	WRIGHT (T.) Sorcery and Magic. 12mo. 1852.
148	2	WYATT (T.) Poetical Works. 16mo. 1831.
497	12	WYMAN (M.) On Ventilation. 12mo. 1846.
75	6	WYNNE (J.) Literary and Scientific Men of America. 12mo. 1850.
*475	8	WYNNE (J. H.) History of the British Empire in America. 2 vols. 8vo. 1776.

X, Y, Z.

Shelf.	No.	
482	9	XENOPHON. Works, translated by Cooper, Spelman, Smith, Fielding, &c. 8vo. 1852.
120	1	——— Translated by Spelman. 2 vols. 18mo. n. d.
*477	17	YATES (J. V. N.) & MOULTON (J. W.) History of New York. Vol. 1 8vo. 1824.
*669	9	YEAR Book of the American Congregational Union. 8vo. 1854.
*664	14	YEOMAN (T. H.) On Consumption. 12mo. 1850.
453	5	YOUNG (A.) Chronicles of the Pilgrim Fathers. 8vo. 1841.
453	3	——— Chronicles of Massachusetts. 8vo. 1846.
453	4	——— Chronicles of Massachusetts. 8vo. 1846.
148	8	YOUNG (E.) Poetical Works. 2 vols. 16mo. 1852.
152	3	——— Works. 3 vols. 8vo. 1813.
427	5	——— Works. 3 vols. 8vo. 1802. Vol. 1. Last Day; Force of Religion; Love of Fame; Ode to the King; Epistles to Mr. Pope; Paraphrase on Job; Ocean; Sea Piece; Busiris. 2. The Revenge; the Brothers; Night Thoughts. 3. Night Thoughts; Centaur not Fabulous.
*472	3	YORKE (P.) (Lord Hardwicke). Miscellaneous State Papers. 1501–1726. 2 vols. 4to. 1778.
408	13	YULE-Tide Stories. Post 8vo. 1853.
*430	10	ZAMORA (A. de). Comedias. 2 vols. 4to. 1744.
141	59	ZSCHOKKE (J. H. D.) Spectre Guest. 16mo. 1852.
136	6	——— Fool of the Nineteenth Century. 12mo. 1845.

PERIODICALS.

THE following works, either Periodicals or partaking of the character of Periodicals, are received regularly at the Library. The latest portions of them that may have come to hand will be found, arranged here for easy reference, in alphabetical order, as they are on the tables of the Reading Room, beginning at the south-east corner with the letter A, and ending with the letter Z at the north-west corner.

The letters affixed to the titles signify respectively, *m.* monthly, *d.* daily, *w.* weekly, *a.* annually, *q.* quarterly, *un.* uncertain, &c.

Shelf.	No.			
*723	1	African Repository. Washington. . . .	8vo.	*m.*
*701	3	Allgemeine Zeitung. Augsburg. . . .	4to.	*d.*
*701	1	American Agriculturist. New York. . . .	4to.	*w.*
*670	1	American Almanac. Boston.	8vo.	*a.*
*723	2	American Journal of Dental Science. Philadelphia.	8vo.	*q.*
*723	3	American Journal of Insanity. Utica. . .	8vo.	*q.*
*723	10	American Journal of Medical Sciences (Hays's). Philadelphia.	8vo.	*q.*
*723	9	American Journal of Science and Arts. New Haven.	8vo.	*once in two m.*
*701	2	American Phrenological Journal. New York. .	4to.	*m.*
*722	1	American Polytechnic Journal. New York. .	8vo.	*m.*
*723	5	Annals and Magazine of Natural History. London.	8vo.	*m.*
*723	4	Annales de Chimie et de Physique. Paris. .	8vo.	*m.*
*723	7	Annales d'Hygiène Publique et de Médecine Légale. Paris.	8vo.	*q.*
*723	6	Annales Médico-Psychologiques. Paris. . .	8vo.	*q.*
*722	2	Annales des Sciences Naturelles. Paris. . .	8vo.	*m.*
*722	3	Annals of Science. Cleveland.	8vo.	*m.*
*605	1	Annual Register. London.	8vo.	*y.*
*711	4	Archæologia, or Miscellaneous Tracts relating to Antiquity. Published by the Society of Antiquaries of London.	4to.	*un.*
*723	8	Archiv für das Studium der Neueren Sprachen und Literaturen. Braunschweig.	8vo.	*un.*
*741	6	Art Journal. London.	4to.	*m.*
*711	2	Athenæum. London.	4to.	*w.*
*722	4	Banker's Magazine. New York. . . .	8vo.	*m.*
*724	1	Bentley's Miscellany. London. . . .	8vo.	*m.*

Shelf.	No.		
*724	2	Biblical Repertory and Princeton Review. Philadelphia.	8vo. *q.*
*724	3	Bibliotheca Sacra. Andover.	8vo. *q.*
*724	5	Bibliothèque Universelle de Genève. Genève. .	8vo. *m.*
*724	6	Blackwood's Edinburgh Magazine. Edinburgh. .	8vo. *m.*
*711	3	Blätter für Literarische Unterhaltung. Leipzig.	4to. *w.*
*722	6	Boston Medical and Surgical Journal. Boston. .	8vo. *w.*
*724	4	Braithwaite's Retrospect of Medicine and Surgery. London, reprinted. New York. . .	8vo. *semi-ann.*
*640	3	British Almanac and Companion. London. .	8vo. *a.*
*722	5	British and Foreign Medico-Chirurgical Review. London.	8vo. *q.*
*724	7	British Quarterly Review. London. . . .	8vo. *q.*
*725	4	Brownson's Quarterly Review. Boston. . .	8vo. *q.*
*725	5	Bulletin de l'Académie Nationale de Médecine. Paris.	8vo. *bi-m.*
*724	8	Bulletin de la Société Géologique de France. Paris.	8vo. *q.*
*724	9	Bulletin Général de Thérapeutique Médicale et Chirurgicale. Paris.	8vo. *bi-m.*
*722	7	Chambers's Journal of Popular Literature. Edinburgh.	8vo. *w.*
*724	10	Christian Examiner. Boston. . .	8vo. *once in two m.*
*725	1	Christian Observer. London.	8vo. *m.*
*725	2	Christian Review. New York.	8vo. *q.*
*721	1	Civil Engineer and Architect's Journal. London.	4to. *m.*
*725	3	Colburn's New Monthly. London. . . .	8vo. *m.*
*721	2	Comptes Rendus Hebdomadaires des Séances de l'Académie des Sciences. Paris.	4to. *w.*
*722	8	De Bow's Review. New Orleans.	8vo. *m.*
*640	1	Dod's Parliamentary Companion. London. .	12mo. *a.*
*640	2	Dod's Peerage, Baronetage, and Knightage. London.	12mo. *a.*
*733	1	Dublin Quarterly Journal of Medical Science. .	8vo. *q.*
*733	2	Dublin Review. London.	8vo. *q.*
*721	3	Dwight's Journal of Music. Boston. . .	4to. *w.*
*722	9	Eclectic Magazine of Foreign Literature. New York.	8vo. *m.*
*721	5	Economist. London.	4to. *w.*
*733	4	Edinburgh Medical and Surgical Journal. Edinburgh.	8vo. *q.*
*735	4	Edinburgh New Philosophical Journal. Edinburgh.	8vo. *q.*
*733	3	Edinburgh Review. Edinburgh.	8vo. *q.*
*721	4	Eliza Cook's Journal. London.	8vo. *w.*
*733	5	Fraser's Magazine. London.	8vo. *m.*
*721	7	Gazette des Hospitaux. Paris.	4to. *tri-w.*
*733	6	Gentleman's Magazine. London.	8vo. *m.*
*722	10	Godey's Lady's Book. Philadelphia. . .	8vo. *m.*
*732	1	Graham's American Monthly Magazine. Philadelphia.	8vo. *m.*
*413	1	Hansard's Parliamentary Debates. London. .	8vo. *un.*
*732	2	Harper's New Monthly Magazine. New York. .	8vo. *m.*
*735	3	Heidelberger Jahrbücher der Literatur. Heidelberg.	8vo. *w.*
*733	7	Hogg's Instructor. Edinburgh.	8vo. *m.*
*732	3	Horticulturist. Rochester.	8vo. *m.*

Shelf.	No.			
*732	4	Household Words. London.	8vo.	*w.*
*733	8	Hunt's Merchants' Magazine. New York.	8vo.	*m.*
*731	1	Illustrated Magazine of Art. New York.	8vo.	*m.*
*721	6	Illustrirter Kalender, 1854. Leipzig.	8vo.	*a.*
*733	9	Jewish Chronicle. New York.	8vo.	*m.*
*733	10	Journal de Médecine et de Chirurgie. Paris.	8vo.	*m.*
*731	7	Journal des Débats. Paris.	4to.	*d.*
*731	2	Journal des Savants. Paris.	4to.	*m.*
*732	5	Journal of the Franklin Institute of Pennsylvania. Philadelphia.	8vo.	*m.*
*731	8	Journal of the Royal Geographical Society of London.	8vo.	*a.*
*734	2	Journal of the Statistical Society of London.	8vo.	*q.*
*734	1	Kidd's Own Journal. London.	8vo.	*m.*
*734	3	Knickerbocker. New York.	8vo.	*m.*
*731	3	Lancet. London.	4to.	*w.*
*731	4	Literary Gazette. London.	4to.	*w.*
*734	4	Littell's Living Age. Boston.	8vo.	*w.*
*734	5	London, Edinburgh, and Dublin Philosophical Magazine. London.	8vo.	*m.*
*734	6	Massachusetts Teacher. Boston.	8vo.	*m*
*734	7	Mechanics' Magazine. London.	8vo.	*m.*
*734	8	Medical Examiner. Philadelphia.	8vo.	*m.*
*731	5	Medical Times. London.	4to.	*w.*
*412	2	Memoirs of the American Academy.	4to.	*un.*
*735	2	Methodist Quarterly Review. New York.	8vo.	*q.*
*734	9	Mining Magazine. New York.	8vo.	*m.*
*734	10	Missionary Herald. Boston.	8vo.	*m.*
*735	1	Mittermaier's Kritische Zeitschrift für Rechtswissenschaft. Heidelberg.	8vo.	*un.*
*731	9	Moniteur Universel. Paris.	4to.	*d.*
*721	10	Memoires de l'Institut de France. Paris.	4to.	
*732	6	Monthly Religious Magazine. Boston.	8vo.	*m.*
*735	5	Müller's Archiv für Anatomie, Physiologie, und Wissenschaftliche Medicin. Berlin.	8vo.	*un.*
*743	1	Nautical Magazine and Naval Chronicle. London.	8vo.	*m.*
*743	2	New Englander. New Haven.	8vo.	*q.*
*732	8	New England Historical and Genealogical Register. Boston.	8vo.	*q.*
*743	3	New Jerusalem Magazine. New York.	8vo.	*m.*
*743	4	Newton's London Journal. London.	8vo.	*m.*
*743	5	New York Journal of Medicine and the Collateral Sciences. New York.	8vo.	*once in two m.*
*732	7	New York Journal of Pharmacy. New York.	8vo.	*m.*
*744	9	New York Quarterly. New York.	8vo.	*q.*
*743	6	North American Review. Boston.	8vo.	*q.*
*743	7	North British Review. Edinburgh.	8vo.	*q.*
*741	1	Norton's Literary Gazette. New York.	4to.	*bi-m.*
*743	8	Notes and Queries. London.	4to.	*w.*

Shelf.	No.	
*741	7	Philosophical Transactions of the Royal Society. London. . . . . 4to. *un.*
*732	9	Plough, Loom, and the Anvil. New York. . 8vo. *m.*
*741	2	Practical Draughtsman's Book of Industrial Design, &c. New York. . . . . 4to. *m.*
*741	3	Practical Mechanics' Journal. New York. . 4to. *m.*
*745	2	Proceedings of the American Academy of Arts and Sciences. Boston. . . . . 8vo. *un.*
*745	3	Proceedings of the Boston Society of Natural History. Boston. . . . . 8vo. *nn.*
*741	4	Punch. London. . . . . 4to. *w.*
*732	10	Putnam's Monthly Magazine. New York. . 8vo. *m.*
*744	2	Quarterly Homœopathic Journal. Boston. . 8vo. *q.*
*743	9	Quarterly Journal of the Geological Society. London. 8vo. *q.*
*743	10	Quarterly Journal of Microscopical Science. London. 8vo. *q.*
*744	1	Quarterly Review. London. . . . : 8vo. *q.*
*745	1	Ranking's Half-yearly Abstract of the Medical Sciences. London. Reprinted, New York. 8vo. *semi-ann.*
*744	3	Retrospective Review. London. . . . . 8vo. *q.*
*742	1	Revue des deux Mondes. Paris. . . . . 8vo. *bi-m.*
*744	4	Revue Médicale. Paris. . . . . . . 8vo. *bi-m.*
*741	5	Scientific American. New York. . . . . 4to. *w.*
*744	6	Séances et Travaux de l'Académie des Sciences Morales et Politiques. Paris. . . . 8vo. *once in two m.*
*742	3	Sharpe's London Magazine. London. . . 8vo. *m.*
*742	4	Southern Literary Messenger. Richmond. . . 8vo. *m.*
*744	5	Southern Quarterly Review. Charleston. . . 8vo. *q.*
*742	5	Tait's Edinburgh Magazine. Edinburgh. . . 8vo. *m.*
*744	10	Universalist Quarterly. Boston. . . . . 8vo. *q.*
*744	7	Universal Phonographer. New York. . . 12mo. *m.*
*744	8	Westminster Review. London. . . . . 8vo. *q.*
*731	6	Zeitschrift für Musick. Leipzig. . . . . 4to. *w.*

Several of the Transactions of learned Societies contained in the preceding list, having not yet been published for the year 1853, are, of course, not received; but they will be found in their appropriate places, as soon as they come to hand.

A considerable number of books have been received during the printing of this Catalogue, which could not be entered in it; and, from month to month, others will be added. These will appear in interleaved copies of the Catalogue, to be found on the tables of the Library.

ERRATA.

Page 27, after CHAMBAUD (L.) insert CHAMBERS (R.) as author of the Cyclopædia of English Literature.

Pages 46–50, place asterisks before the numbers attached to the ENCYCLOPEDIE METHODIQUE.

Page 81, JUNIUS, 2 vols. 8vo. 1833, should be entered 1850, and numbered 400 1.

Page 100, MESSENGER (WEEKLY), vols. 5–9, should have an asterisk before its number.

Page 122, JEFFERSON'S Works are placed under the name of their editor, Randolph.

www.ingramcontent.com/pod-product-compliance
Lightning Source LLC
LaVergne TN
LVHW011228110826
845150LV00006B/1574

* 9 7 8 1 4 2 5 5 1 4 7 5 4 *